Water-Powered Mills

of

Richland County

Water-Powered Mills

of

Richland County

by
Robert A. Carter and Michael C. Cullen

edited by
Theresa Marie Flaherty

www.TursasPublishing.com

All Rights Reserved. No part of this publication may be reproduced or transmitted in any form or by any means, electronic or technical, including photocopying, recording, or by any information storage or retrieval system, without permission in writing from the publisher, except by a reviewer who may quote brief passages in a review.

Copyright © 2016 by Robert A. Carter and Michael C. Cullen

Water-Powered Mills of Richland County

by

Robert A. Carter and **Michael C. Cullen**

edited by

Theresa Marie Flaherty

ISBN-13: 978-0-9832342-1-0

www.TursasPublishing.com

Cover Design: Timothy Brian McKee.

10 9 8 7 6 5 4 3 2 1

to Dwight Wesley Garber

No man shall take the nether or the upper millstone to pledge; for he taketh a man's life to pledge

- Deuteronomy XXIV:6

Table of Contents

Water-Powered Mills of Richland County

Description	Page
List of Figures	xiii
Introduction	xix

Section 1
Water-Powered Mills on the Clear Fork 1

    The Birthplace of the Clear Fork River 3
        The Logan-Kessler-Barr Mills 3
    The Northern Source of the Clear Fork River 4
        The Woods-Otto Grist Mill 4
        Mathew-Mitchell Grist Mill, Saw Mill and Carding Mill 6
    Mills on the Clear Fork of the Mohican 6
        Mitchell's Mill 6
        The Conger-Williams Mill 7
        Watson's Mills, Lexington 8
        Watson Lewis Graves Carter Grist and Saw Mill 10
        The McClain Mill 11
    Feeder Streams in Troy Township 13
        The Mercer-Griebling Grist and Saw Mills 13
        David Miller Saw and Turning Mill 16
        McConnell Saw Mill (Orweiler Road Saw Mill) 17
        The Noah Watson Tavern, Grist Mill, and Saw Mill 17
        Alex W. McConnell Carding & Fulling Mill 19
        Jacob King Saw Mill 19
    Washington Township 20
        The Strausbaugh Mills 20
        George Marshall Grist Mill, Saw Mill & Distillery 21
        The Stump Mill 23
        The Zent-Fitting-Bowers-Shaler-Garber Mill 24
        The Bellville Planing Mill 26

Table of Contents (Continued)

Description   **Page**

- The Moody Mill ... 27
- LeFever Saw and Carding Mill ... 33
- Honey Creek Mills ... 34
- The Greenwood-Crain Grist & Saw Mills ... 34

Feeder Streams in Perry and Jefferson Townships ... 37
- The Shauck Mills, Perry Township ... 37
- The Eby Grist Mill ... 38
- Corbett's Saw Mill, Grist Mill, and Woolen Factory ... 39
- The Hanawalt Grist Mill ... 40
- Shafer Saw and Oil Mill ... 43

Worthington Township ... 43
- The Myers-Kanaga-Plank Mill ... 43
- The Miller Saw Mill ... 49
- The Rummel Mill ... 49
- The Zimmerman Powder Mill ... 55
- The Winchester Mills ... 56
- The Watts Saw Mill and Woolen Factory ... 60
- The Herring Grist and Saw Mills ... 61
- The Alexander Saw Mill ... 64
- Daniel Teeter Saw Mill ... 65
- Henry Foults Saw Mill ... 65
- Samuel Graber Carding Mill ... 65
- Rocky Point Mill (Van Zile Mill) ... 65
- The Manner Grist Mill ... 68
- The Schrack Grist Mill and Oil Mill ... 70
- The William Thompson Saw Mill ... 74
- John Shield's Saw Mill ... 74
- Daniel Teeter Saw Mill ... 75
- The Richland Axe Handle Factory ... 75
- Samuel Brallier Saw Mill and Carding Machine ... 75
- Thomas McMahan Grist and Saw Mill ... 75
- William Garrett Saw and Grist Mills ... 76
- Nicolas Flaherty Saw Mill ... 77
- Jessie Eyster (Oyster) Grist Mill and Saw Mill ... 77

Table of Contents (Continued)

Description **Page**

    Edward Lipset Saw Mill and Oil Mill. 77

Section 2
Water-Powered Mills on the Black Fork 79

Springfield Township 81
    The Joseph Runyon Saw Mill 81
    E.P. & E. Sturges Grist Mill 82
    Nathan Tompkin's Saw Mill 83
    Jacob George Saw Mill 83

Richland County 84

Jackson Township 85
    The Leppo Saw Mill 85
    Joseph Cotterman Grist Mill and Saw Mills 85
    The Abbott Grist Mill 85
    James Kerr Grist Mill 86
    The Briner Saw Mill 86

Sharon Township 86
    John Kerr Grist Mill and Saw Mill 86
    The Coltman Mills 88
    Gamble's Mill 88
    The Briner-Craner Saw Mill 90
    The Wilson Saw Mill 90
    The Heath Brother's Grist Mill 90
    McClure's Mill Site 93
    The Duncan Mill 94

Plymouth Township 95
    The Cline Grist and Saw Mill 95

Cass Township 96
    The Hershiser Saw Mill 96
    The Brodley Saw Mill 96
    The Baker Saw Mill 96
    The Guykendall Grist Mill 97
    The Anderson Grist Mill 97

Blooming Grove Township 98
    The Ganges Grist and Saw Mill 98

Table of Contents (Continued)

Description — **Page**

- The Ayers Grist Mill … 99
- Stoner's Grist and Saw Mill … 100
- The Gibson Carding Machine … 101
- The McGaney & Eunick Carding Machine … 101

Franklin Township … 101
- The Urick (Eurick-Eurich) Grist Mill … 101
- Cline Distillery … 103
- Wurts-Clay Distillery … 104

Weller Township … 104
- The Osbun Grist and Saw Mills … 104
- The Charles-Linn Grist and Saw Mills … 106
- Dickson & Taggart Carding Mill … 108
- The Montgomery Grist Mill … 110
- Israel Dille Grist and Saw Mills … 112
- Williamson Distillery … 113
- The Fleming Grist Mill … 113
- The Kohler Grist Mill … 114
- The John Buler Saw Mill … 115
- The Hershey-Staman Grist Mill … 115
- The Benjamin Staman Grist Mill … 117
- The Staman "Ruffner" Saw Mill … 117
- John Gongawan Distillery … 118
- The Yeaman Grist and Saw Mills … 119
- The Eby Mill … 121
- The Lewis Grist Mill … 121
- The Samuel Lattimore Grist Mill and Saw Mill … 121
- The Archer Saw Mill … 122
- The John Stafford Grist Mill … 122
- The Charles Mill … 122
- John Woodhouse Oil Mill … 127
- The Braden Saw Mill … 128

Monroe Township … 128

Green Township … 129
- Greentown Spring Mills … 130

Table of Contents (Continued)

Description   **Page**

    The George Smith Saw Mill 130
    Nathan DeHaven Saw Mill 133

Honey Creek Mills 134
    Karnahan-Jennings Mill 134
    Weirich Mill 135
    Honey Creek Mill 136
    William Taylor Grist and Saw Mill 136
    Simon Rowland Saw Mill 137

Big Run Mills in Green Township 137
    Thomas Andrews Saw Mill 137
    Joseph Rinehart Saw Mill 137
    Isaac Manor (Meanor, Mennor) Grist Mill, Saw Mill & Carding Machine 137
    The Wolf Grist Mill 138
    The Stringer Grist Mills 142
    The Stringer Mystery 143
    Loudenville Mills 144
    Green Township Distilleries 150
    Mills in Hanover Township 150

Section 3
Water-Powered Mills on the Rocky Fork 151
    Springfield Township 153
        Spring Mills 153
    Madison Township 158
        The Keith Mills 158
        Laird & Bender Carding and Fulling Mill 158
        John Crooks Saw Mill 159
        Jacob Gates Saw Mill 159
        James McCoy Saw Mill 159
        Mendenhall's Improved Patent Grist Mill 160
        The William Tingley Woolen Mill 162
        Carr-Ferson (Tingley) Carding Mill 164
        Tingley and Ferson Carding Mill 165
        Ferson & Baird Fullig Mill 165
        The Newman-Beam-Rogers-Campbell Grist and Saw Mills 166

Table of Contents (Continued)

Description   **Page**

- The Andrew Painter Woolen Mill 167
- The Pollock Carding Mills 170
- Smart Mill and Distillery 171
- The Clark Saw Mill 171

Mansfield North Lake Park Mills 172
- The Jacob Bell Grist Mill 172
- Hedges Paper Mill 177
- Leyman-Robinson-Richland City Mills 177
- John Damp's Grist Mill 178
- Mansfield Woolen Mill 178
- Hedges Oil or Flax Mill 180

Mills South of Mansfield in Washington Township 180
- The Bentley Mill 180
- The Culler Woolen Mill 182
- Daniel Beasore's Saw Mill 185
- The LaRue-Baker Grist Mill 185
- The Ahlefeldt-Rummel Mill . . . . `186

Washington Township 188
- The Stewart-Wickert Grist and Saw Mills 188

The Rocky Fork - Where Did The Water Go? 189
- The Union Woolen Factory 190
- The Balliett Grist and Saw Mills 190

Biography of D.W. Garber 193

Endnotes
- Section 1 - Water-Powered Mills on the Clear Fork of the Mohican River 199
- Section 2 - Water-Powered Mills on the Black Fork of the Mohican River 208
- Section 3 - Water-Powered Mills on the Rocky Fork of the Mohican River 214

Glossary 217

Index 219

List of Figures

Water-Powered Mills of Richland County

| Figure | Description | Page |

Section 1 - Water-Powered Mills on the Clear Fork of the Mohican River

1. Garber's Bungtown Map 3
2. John Garrison 5
3. John K. Williams Residence 7
4. Amariah Watson 8
5. Carter's Millstone 10
6. Millstone with Weighted Cap 11
7. Covered Bridge 11
8. MacLain Mill 12
9. Dam at McLain Mill 13
10. Mercer Griebling Mill 14
11. Waterwheel at Mercer Griebling Mill 14
12. Interior of Mercer Griebling Mill 15
13. Mercer Griebling Mill Leaning 15
14. Millponds at Mercer Griebling Mill 16
15. Noah Watson 17
16. Watson Tavern in 1906 18
17. Watson Tavern in 2000 19
18. Leffel Co. Turbine 20
19. Strausbaugh Home 21
20. Partial Map of Washington Township 22
21. Zent-Fitting-Bowers-Shaler-Garber Mill 24
22. Benton L. Garber 26
23. Moody Mill 27
24. Moody Mill and Alexander Zent Stone Quarry 30
25. Moody Mill Warehouse Addition 30
26. Early Photo of Moody Mill 31
27. Moody Mill 32

List of Figures - *Continued*

Figure	Description	Page
28.	Clara and George O. Neal	33
29.	Greenwood-Crain Grist and Sawmills	35
30.	Sandstone Buhr	36
31.	Sandstone Buhr	36
32.	Granite Buhr	37
33.	Greenwood Mill	37
34.	Shauck Mills	38
35.	Corbett Mill	39
36.	Corbett Mill - Opposite End	40
37.	Hanawalt Mill	41
38.	Hanawalt Mill	41
39.	Hanawalt Grist Mill	42
40.	Millrace for Hanawalt Mill	42
41.	Jacob Myers Sr.	43
42.	Myers-Kanaga-Plank Mill	44
43.	Myers-Kanaga-Plank Mill Dam	45
44.	Myers-Kanaga-Plank Mill Wheel	46
45.	Gate to the Headrace	47
46.	Timber Milldam	47
47.	Elam Plank and Mary	47
48.	Myers-Kanaga-Plank Mill 1900	47
49.	Flood Damage	48
50.	Richland Handle Company	49
51.	Richland Handle Company	49
52.	Rummel Mill	50
53.	Cooper Shop	50
54.	Mill Dam for Rummel Mill	51
55.	Advertisement for Rummel Mill	52
56.	O. B. Rummel and his Wife	52
57.	Second Floor	53
58.	Fourth Floor	53
59.	Post Card of Rummel Mill	54
60.	Rummel Mill	55
61.	Early Photo of Winchester Mill	56
62.	Winchester Mill	57

List of Figures - *Continued*

Figure	Description	Page
63.	Wool Blanket	58
64.	Watts Saw Mill and Woolen Factory	60
65.	Old Watts Mill	60
66.	Herring Mill	61
67.	Millstone for Herring Mill	61
68.	Map of Newville	63
69.	Newville in 1800s or Early 1900s	64
70.	Van Zile Millstone	66
71.	Van Zile Millstone	66
72.	Rocky Point Mill	67
73.	The Manner Mill	69
74.	Marion Manner	70
75.	Toll Dish from Manner Mill	70
76.	Date Carved in Toll Dish	70
77.	Old Charles Schrack Homestead	71
78.	Charles Schrack Grist Mill	72
79.	Remains of Dam at Charles Schrack Mill	73

Section 2 - Water-Powered Mills on the Black Fork of the Mohican River

80.	Remains of Dam for the Runyon Saw Mills	81
81.	Eban P. Sturges	82
82.	Small Stream	83
83.	Map of Boundary Changes to Richland County in 1847	84
84.	Map of Jackson Township	85
85.	Partial 1873 Sharon Township Map	87
86.	Coltman Cemetery	88
87.	Base Stone from Gambles Mills	89
88.	Millstone Flower Pot in Galion, Ohio	89
89.	Dams at Shelby's Seltzer Park	89
90.	School Yard Millstone	90
91.	Roger Heath's Grist Mill	91
92.	Building Next to Black Fork	91
93.	Heath Mill Flooded	92
94.	Flood in Downtown Shelby	93
95.	Shelby Carriage Works	94
96.	Rare Set of Cone Buhrs in Shelby Park	95

List of Figures - *Continued*

Figure	Description	Page
97.	Staley Mill in Champaign County	96
98.	Example of Typical Saw Mills	97
99.	Brick Tavern at the Edge of Ganges	98
100.	Buhr in the Burrer Family Flower Bed	99
101.	Remains of the Mud Sills for Dam	99
102.	Solomon Journeycake	100
103.	Wurts Distillery For Sale	102
104.	Rebuilt Staley Mill Distillery	102
105.	The Staley Mill, Miami County	103
106.	Osbun Grist and Saw Mills	105
107.	Hand Drawn Map by Garber	109
108.	Advertisement for Dickson-Taggery Woolen Mill	110
119.	Illustration of a Side Shoot or Tub Mill Waterwheel	110
110.	Montgomery Mill	111
111.	Olivesburg Mill	112
112.	The Copus Moument	118
113.	The 1812 Ruffner Massacre Monument	118
114.	The Yeaman Mill	119
115.	Mifflin Township Map	120
116.	1847 Charles Mill	123
117.	The Charles Mill	124
118.	The Charles Mill Before Dismantled	125
119.	Surviving Bill for Saw Mill Work	126
120.	Charles Mill Dam on the Black Fork	127
121.	1852 Ad for the John Woodhouse Mill Flax Seed Oil	128
122.	1874 Map of Green Township	129
123.	Sections 9 and 16 of Green Township	133
124.	Robert Karnahan	134
125.	Possible Remains of the Weirich Grist Mill	135
126.	The Rebuilt and Relocated Wolf Mill	138
127.	South Side of the Mill and Foundation	139
128.	Hillside Spring Source of Water for Wolf Mill	140
129.	18-Foot Waterwheel	140
130.	Wolf Mill Frozen Scene	141
131.	Hopper at Wolf Mill	141

List of Figures - *Continued*

Figure	Description	Page
132.	Hopper Holding Grain.	141
133.	Cast Iron Bull Wheel	141
134.	1930 Post Card of Wolf's Mill, Loudenville, Ohio	142
135.	Ad by Miller and Salesman John Stringer	143
136.	Master Wheel of the World	144
137.	Smokestack by Northwestern Elevator and Mill Co.	145
138.	Mill Dam at Taylor Mill.	146
139.	Partial Map of Loudenville	146
140.	An Advertisement from 1884	147
141.	The Old Mill Burned in 1922	148
142.	Most of Flour Shipped in Trucks Daily	149
143.	Con Agra Four Mill Receives Grain by Rail Car	149
144.	54-Inch Stout-Temple Turbine	149

Section 3 - Water-Powered Mills on the Rocky Fork of the Mohican River

145.	The Old Spring Mill About 1910	156
146.	Turn of the Century View of the Two-Acre Millpond.	156
147.	1951 Garber Photograph of Mill	157
148.	Spring Mill Converted to Private Residence	157
149.	Hand Drawn Map by Garber	158
150.	Saw Mill in Nova Scotia	159
151.	Overall Rendering of Water Powered Sawmill	160
152.	Back Movement of the Saw Carriage	160
153.	Operation of the Saw Cut	161
154.	Mendenhall Mill.	161
155.	Tingley Dam and Springs	163
156.	Pool Where Tingley Dam Was Located	163
157.	Hillside Springs Near the Old Reformatory Building.	164
158.	A Monument to the Painter's Graves	168
159.	Liberty Park Lake	169
160.	An Ancient Picker.	170
161.	A Carding Machine and Revolving Drawer.	170
162.	Staley Distillery	171
163.	Dam on Toby Run.	172
164.	The Old Saw Mill	173
165.	Flooding Was a Problem	174

List of Figures - *Continued*

Figure	Description	Page
166.	1853 Map of North End of Mansfield	175
167.	American Miller Magazine	176
168.	1867 Ad in *The Mansfield Herald*	178
169.	Article in *The Mansfield Journal* in 1868	179
170.	1852 Article in the *Shield and Banner*	179
171.	1850 Article in the *Shield and Banner*	179
172.	1853 Article in the *Shield and Banner*	180
173.	1856 Article in the *Shield and Banner*	180
174.	1857 Article in *The Mansfield Herald*	180
175.	Spring at the Bentley Grist and Saw Mills	181
176.	Map of Lucas Area	182
177.	Culler Woolen Mill	183
178.	Jane Kaylor and Her Mother Lillian Manner	183
179.	Mrs. Joan Culler with Shuttle From Culler Woolen Mill	184
180.	Handmade Shuttle for Culler Woolen Mill	184
181.	Ahlefield Mill	186
182.	Undated Photo Taken Near Plymouth	187

Introduction

Sometimes lives unfold in a way that brings certain people together to accomplish something unique. Such is the case with the three of us, Robert Carter, Michael Cullen, and Theresa Flaherty. The common denominator for us is Ohio Historian D. W. Garber (1896-1983) whose work is the foundation for this book of ours.

Garber was born in Butler, Ohio. He served 30 years in the U. S. Navy as a pharmacist, with 7 years served in American Samoa. After his retirement in 1944, he worked for the Veteran's Administration for a time before moving to Bellville, Ohio, where he wrote for the *Mansfield News Journal* from 1956 to 1964. He wrote 176 columns titled, "Tales of Mohican Valley." In 1965 he wrote *Abraham Lincoln's First Endorsement*, based on his own research, followed in 1967 by *The Holmes County Rebellion*. Garber also completed four articles for the *Pacific Historian* about Jedediah Strong Smith, and in 1970, *Waterwheels and Millstones, a History of Mills and Milling in Ohio* was published.

Carter met Garber for the first time during preparations for the 1964 sesquicentennial celebration for Lexington, Ohio. Their mutual interest in local history brought them together, and a warm friendship developed between their families. Cullen is the youngest of Garber's two grandchildren, so Garber was a part of his life from birth. Carter met Cullen through Garber when Cullen visited his grandparents while he was home on leave from the service, but later in life a close personal relationship developed that included their wives. Flaherty met Garber in Stockton, California, in 1970 after the Garbers moved there to be near their recently widowed daughter. Carter and Flaherty met when she accompanied Garber on a research trip to Ohio in 1974, but they did not reconnect until 2001 when Flaherty and her husband traveled through Ohio in their RV. Again, a warm relationship developed between the two couples. Finally, Cullen and Flaherty met for the first time in Florida in 2004 on another Flaherty RV trip.

Although employed fulltime, Carter often accompanied Garber on local researching trips, leaving their wives at home with the Carter children. Carter's interests in and pursuit of local history continue today, and he has continued adding to the body of Garber's work. As a result of Garber's continued prodding and efforts in sharing knowledge acquired over many years, Carter eventually wrote four books that were based on material donated by Garber, *The History of the Sandusky, Mansfield & Newark Railroad, Tom Lyons The Indian That Died Thirteen Times, The History of Lexington, Ohio*, and *The Mansfield Riots of 1900*. All were published after Garber's death, but Garber was definitely the inspiration.

Garber's extensive collection of historical books and material was left to his daughter Connie Cullen. After her death, it was passed on to her son Michael in Florida. He, like his mother, is an avid book collector. Although Cullen never lived in Ohio, he was well aware of his grandfather's friendship with Carter, his interest in mills, and that he had frequently accompanied him on several mill trips. Given the opportunity to examine Garber's lifetime mill collection, consisting of eight 3-ring notebooks, Carter was inspired to document the research done after the completion of Garber's own *Waterwheels and Millstones, a History of Mills and Milling in Ohio*, published in 1970. Cullen signed on to the project. The two agreed to assemble and publish the treasured historical collection rather than leave the somewhat fragile pages lie somewhere on a dusty shelf unused or misused. Part of Garber's mill collection had been donated to the Ohio Historical Society shortly after he moved to California.

On his move to California, Garber hired a young Navy wife, Theresa Flaherty, to do his typing for him, not only for the book, but for much of his extensive correspondence. Both the Garbers missed Carter's young family back in Ohio, and Flaherty's two youngsters helped ease the loss. Garber, a retired Navy Warrant Officer, and Flaherty developed a warm friendship as well with the Navy as a common bond. Over the years he encouraged her to write and provided a huge collection of material for a biography of James Ball Naylor, an early Ohio writer. The material lay dormant for nearly 40 years, but in 2011 Flaherty published *The Final Test – A Biography of James Ball Naylor,* followed by a Tribute Series to Naylor consisting of reprints of some of his published works but with added material, *Vintage Verse, Ralph Marlowe, A Literary Playground - Short Stories*, and the *Misadventures of Marjory*.

Once Carter and Cullen produced the manuscript, Flaherty was enlisted as the editor. Each, touched in a special way by Garber, has contributed to the final product, adding to his legacy.

Section 1

Water-Powered Mills

on the

Clear Fork

of the

Mohican River

Water-Powered Mills of Richland County

Much water runs while the miller sleeps.

- English Proverb

Water-Powered Mills on the Clear Fork of the Mohican River

The Birthplace of the Clear Fork River

The Logan–Kessler–Barr Mills

A hillside spring in the very western part of Troy Township, Morrow County, may well be considered one of two possible origins of the Clear Fork River. The spring fed the Logan water-powered sawmills first, and further down the hillside the same stream powered an early gristmill.

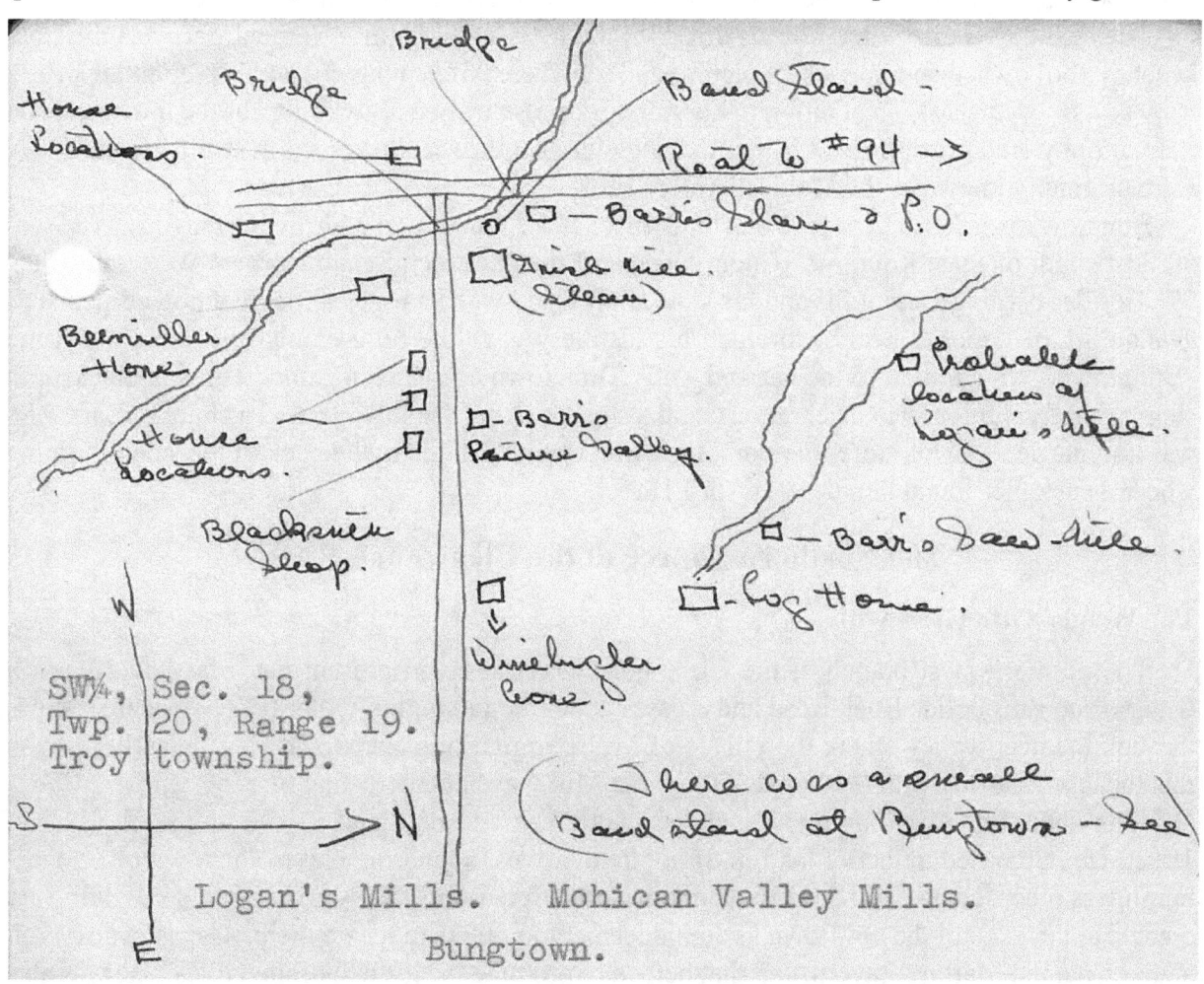

Figure 1. Garber's Bungtown Map.

The sawmill was probably constructed first. At that early date it would have been little more than a log building, possibly on rented land. It would have turned out the lumber and timbers needed for construction of the more complicated gristmill that ground grain for meal and for the distillery on nearby Chestnut Ridge. John Logan, the original mill owner, lived in a log cabin near the mills. The property changed ownership several times in the years that followed.

D. W. Garber interviewed Mrs. Beemiller (no first name noted) and William Long on August 21, 1951. Mrs. Beemiller told Garber that she had sold the farm on which the Logan–Kessler–Barr mills had been located. She took him to the top of a hill overlooking the site of the mill and pointed to the two large springs that were the source of water used to power the mill.

According to Mrs. Beemiller, "the foundation of the old mill is still to be seen, though with difficulty in the tall rushes this time of year."[1]

Mr. Long in his interview at his home in Galion told Garber that "threshing outfits used to fill their water tanks from the spring at the old log house where the Winbiglers lived." The old log house was in all probability used as the miller's home when Logan's Mill was in operation.

The next day Garber interviewed Alfred Winbigler who told him: "Samuel Barr was the store keeper [who] owned and operated a picture gallery where Alf Winbigler had his picture taken as a baby seventy years ago. In addition to his store, Barr also owned a sawmill near the log house and a stream-powered gristmill built by Samuel Kessler near the road intersection at Bungtown. They were originally known as the Mohican Valley Mills"[2]

Bungtown was located west of Steam Corners at the junction of Morrow County roads 45 and 50, just south of State Route 97. County Road 50 runs between Steam Corners West and Route 97. Besides owning these mills and his store, Barr also owned a bar near the junction corner. The availability of liquor at Barr's store and his distillery gave the rural hamlet the unseemly name "Bungtown." In addition to the bar and mills, Bungtown consisted of nine houses, a blacksmith shop, a bandstand for local celebrations, and a stone quarry. The town lacked a church. Barr, who was not married, ran his store for about 25 years. He lived alone in the back of the small building where a customer found him dead in April 1899.[3]

The Northern Source of the Clear Fork River

The Woods–Otto Grist Mill

The northern-most branch of the Clear Fork River starts in present day Marshall's Park in Ontario and runs beside Rock Road and crosses under the Lexington-Ontario Road, where it flows through the deep valley where the village of Millsborough was once located. The early mills in this location, starting with the Woods-Otto Grist Mill, have an interesting history.

John Garrison, a wealthy trader and speculator, came to Richland County during the War of 1812. He purchased a tract of land in Springfield Township and the plat of the town of Edwinsburgh was recorded on April 5, 1816, and lots were offered for sale. A gristmill and sawmill were erected at the edge of the new town as an inducement to others to locate there. Garrison also built a tavern named Martin's Tavern, and that helped to promote the growth of the village. He was also the president of the Richland and Huron Bank of Mansfield. When the bank ran into financial trouble and failed, Garrison had to sell all his holdings at a Sheriff's sale to satisfy his creditors. This sale appeared in *The Ohio Register*, June 5, 1816.

Lots for sale in the town of Edwinsburgh

The subscriber having laid off the above named town will offer lots for sale on the premises, on the 10th day of June. Edwinburgh is situated on an elevated spot of ground six and one half miles west of Mansfield, on the State Road leading west from Mansfield and crosses in the center of town, with a road leading from south to north to Lake Erie. Adjoining the town there is a good saw mill, now in operation. A large spring is in the center of town, sufficient to water the whole town. Liberal encouragement will be given to [word missing] and others who settle and build immediately. The sale will begin at 10 o'clock when the terms will be known by the proprietor. (signed) John Garrison.[4]

In 1819, Garrison petitioned the courts to vacate his town plat. A decree granting his request can be found in the court journal. Colonel Samuel Edsall, also a veteran of the War of 1812, next owned Garrison Mill.[5] The town, later named Millsborough, saw its plat resurrected in 1831 by Joseph Smith and John Martin, and for a while, it was briefly known as Martin's Post Office. Although prospects looked bright, the location was off the main routes and was bypassed by the railroads. Garrison lived to see the decline of Millsborough, and the change in owners of his mills again.[7]

Figure 2. John Garrison.[6]

On February 3, 1950, Garber interviewed Ms. Lola Dickson. She told him that James Dickson, her father-in-law, had torn down the original mill and built the smaller Garrison-Martin-Dickson Mill that continued to operate until 1904 or 1905. Steam was added as there was by then a cider press and a sawmill operating in conjunction with the larger mill.[8] Today few know that when they turn west on Millsborough Road off the Lexington-Ontario Road, they are driving through the site of the former Edwinburgh-Millsborough town and the site of the Garrison mills, which were located in the rise in the road at the west end of the town. The flood of 1913 carried away the mill dam but the headrace was located just above the road and can still be seen today above the north side of the Millsboro West Road.[9]

Mathew-Mitchell Grist Mill, Saw Mill and Carding Mill

The Mathew-Mitchell Mills were located just west of Millsborough on the Millsborough West Road where it crosses the bridge at the bottom of a hill near the intersection of Ruby Road. How long these mills operated is not recorded, but Mathew Mitchell was actively involved in the operation of the Underground Railroad in Springfield Township during the Civil War. Springfield Township was one of the townships best known for its anti-slavery views.[10]

Mills on the Clear Fork of the Mohican

Mitchell's Mill

The Mitchell Grist Mill was located on the Clear Fork in Troy Township, Morrow County, some 500 feet east of State Route 314 and north of Route 97. George Mitchell bought land deep in the Clear Fork Valley in 1815 and built the first water-powered saw- and gristmills in that part of the township. Lands to the west of Route 314 were more flat, and few locations for mills existed. Mitchell, a young millwright, selected an ideal location. By 1824, he had completed his sawmill and was working on the machinery necessary for a gristmill when he died suddenly at age twenty-eight while at Wooster. The conditions in which he lived can only be described as sparse. Squire Mitchell, in the *History of Morrow County and Ohio*, described Mitchell's cabin as follows:

> It was built of logs, without floor or chimney, a large stump stood in the center of the cabin floor (or ground), which was trimmed to a point small enough to fit a two-inch augur hole. A heavy oak slab, with a hole bored in one end, was fitted on the stump, and used as a seat. It would revolve around the stump, as the fire became too hot, or not hot enough for the occupant of this revolving chair. As there was no chimney, the fire was built in one corner of the cabin upon the ground.[11]

After Mitchell's death, his property was advertised in the *Mansfield Gazette* on November 18, 1824:

> Estate of George Mitchell, deceased. The NW ¼, Section 8, Twp. 20, Range 19. The above land is of excellent quality with several never failing springs and well timbered, has a Saw Mill erected thereon and is situated on the Clear Fork of the Mohican about eight miles southwest of Mansfield."[12]

A year later, on November 23, 1825, there appeared another advertisement in the *Mansfield Gazette* announcing that "The subscriber (Thomas Baird) informs the public in general that he carries on the above business at the Fulling Mill, lately occupied by Mr. G. E. Mitchell, in Lexington, Troy Township."[13]

Additional research needs to be done to determine ownership after Thomas Baird. Joseph Mitchell and Francis Mitchell were administrators of George Mitchell's will. We know from the records that Thomas Baird was the owner in 1825, but we do not know how long he owned the mill. Joseph Mitchell acquired the mill and the land between 1825 and 1848. In 1851, he and his wife Nancy transferred the property to their son Jasper who, having no interest or claim to the property, signed a quit claim. The property was sold to James M. Mitchell, who was not a direct descendent but probably a nephew or cousin. According to the records examined, no deeds were recorded from 1848 through 1892.[14]

In an interview on February 3, 1950, Ray J. Baker told Garber that the Baker family had purchased the land from the Mitchell family around 1884 or 1885. Mr. Baker did not remember the mill itself, but he recalled the dam and the layout of the property. He told Garber that the milldam was about four to five feet high and that there was no race. The mill was located on the north side of the dam and took power direct from the dam water.[15]

The Conger–Williams Mill

Located on State Route 97, west of Lexington, between Gass Road and the Clear Fork Sailing Club, the spring-fed pond on the south side of the road was the original millpond and water source for the gristmill, sawmill, and distillery; all of which were referred to by old-timers as the Conger-Williams Mills and distillery. Ichabod Clark originally built the mill and distillery around 1830, and they passed to his son Ezekiel Clark in 1843. Ezekiel ran them until the property was sold to Seymour Beech Conger in 1858. Garber speculated that Conger's brother Everton was also involved in the business, as their father was the minister to the new Presbyterian congregation next door.[16]

Seymour and Everton Conger both enlisted in the Union Army and helped organize companies in southern Richland County during the Civil War. Both men joined the West Virginia Cavalry and both commanded companies in the same regiment and were involved in heavy fighting. Seymour was killed leading a cavalry charge in the battle of Moorefield, West Virginia, on August 4, 1864. Everton commanded the squad of soldiers who cornered and killed John Wilkes Booth, the man who assassinated Abraham Lincoln. The mill and distillery were sold to a man named John Walker and shortly thereafter to John K. Williams.[17]

It was announced in the *Richland Shield & Banner* on March 17, 1883, that "The Conger farm 1 ½ miles west of Lexington will be sold at public auction on Tuesday, March 27th. Also on

Figure 3. This is the artist's portrayal of the John K. Williams residence in 1883. Carter pointed out that the millpond is located in the center where the rowboat is. The Williams' home, to the left and the barn to the right, were both gone by 1947. The building in the center is believed to be part of the original mill.[18]

the farm and same date, horses, cattle, sheep, farm implements and a mill with water power will be sold."[19] In an interview with Garber in Lexington, Ohio, on September 27, 1949, Mr. Morris Graham commented that the mill was 30 x 40 feet and 1 ½ stories high. According to Graham, John Williams, a Yankee who had inherited money, purchased the mill but never did much with it. Williams, according to Graham, was a horse trader who constantly sought get rich-quick schemes, but to no avail. Graham also claimed that an unnamed man succeeded Williams and that this man was suspected of horse stealing.[20] Graham stated that the owner, who succeeded the horse thief, was W. G. Mauer. Mauer was a gentleman who had retired to the area. He purchased the farm and mill property but did little or no work himself, and during his ownership, the mill was relocated and converted to a sheep barn.[21]

Watson's Mills, Lexington

In the fall of 1811, a young, industrious millwright by the name of Amariah Watson tramped through unsettled territory from Fredericktown, to what is now Troy Township, looking for a suitable location to build a mill. The Clear Fork passes through a narrow channel where Lexington is now located and Watson knew he had found the ideal site to build a dam and erect a mill. On January 7, 1812, he purchased all of section 13, (640 acres), the northwest quarter of section 14 and the northwest quarter of section 24, for a total of 960 acres.

The thirty-two year old Watson erected a cabin just south of the present day bridge for his twenty-five year old wife and their three small children; built a dam across the stream and began construction of a water-powered sawmill. Watson's brothers, Noah and Samuel also relocated to the region and partnered with him.[22]

The Watson Mill had not been in operation very long when the War of 1812 broke out. Watson and Calvin Culver were drafted by Captain Newell to serve under Captain Joseph Walker. Given the lack of manpower needed to defend their neighborhood, Watson and Culver petitioned to be excluded from serving. Captain Newell agreed and sent them "seven muskets & ammunition for home defense at home." Watson wrote "Capt. Walker went with his company to Detroit & was there at Hull's surrender and left us in the woods with the Indians."[23]

After the conclusion of the War of 1812, Watson again focused his efforts on growing his businesses. In 1813, Watson opened a post office and by 1814, he had built a larger and more complicated gristmill that had two runs of buhrs (mills stones). One was used to grind the wheat and the other, corn. Watson filed his plat for a town on September 15, 1815, and named the town Lexington, after the Revolutionary War battle in which his father had fought.[24]

Figure 4. Amariah Watson.

Watson prospered and he built three more mills along the Clear Fork north of Lexington. A combination saw and gristmill was built 425 feet south of Cockley Road, west of Lexington-Springmill. A combination oil and flax mill was located halfway between the pump building and the Clear Fork just north of Plymouth Street bridge on the east side. Watson's son, Michael, ran a sawmill near the intersection of Hanley and Lexington-Springmill roads where the stream named Isaacs Run passed the old railroad bridge on the present day bike trail.[25]

After Amariah moved west, his combination grist and sawmill became known as the "Graves-Watson-Lewis Mill," and was run by Watson's son Asahal and sons-in-law Sterling Graves and William Lewis. It was sold to John Carter, who later sold it to his brother Samuel Carter. The millstone was for rough grinding for either animal feed or a distillery as there was no bolting system for the manufacture of flour. The lumber used in the construction of a covered bridge over East Main Street in 1859 came from the sawmill owned by Samuel Carter. Samuel also ran the oil mill but by the 1880s both mills were in ruins, victims to the weather, machinery vibrations, and floods.

Amariah Watson's first wife, Sally Leonard, died in November 1827, leaving him with six children between the ages of four and eighteen. Not long after Sally's death, Watson married Phoebeann Wolf, a widow. It was not a happy marriage and, by 1832, Watson had enough. The grist and sawmills were sold to Samuel Caldwell. Watson's son-in-law, Sterling Graves, took over the oil mill and a distillery. One morning in either 1832 or 1833, Watson, after finishing his breakfast, pushed his chair back from the table and announced that he was going west. He took leave of Phoebeann and moved west with his son Michael to Illinois; leaving behind Riley, Asahal, Theory, Clorisa, and Cynthia. Except for Cynthia, who married William Lewis and stayed in Lexington, all the other children eventually moved west. Watson's sister Elizabeth left her husband in Lexington and with her son went west to be near Amariah. Tax records show that in 1844 Asahal Watson ran a carding and fulling mill.[26]

The grist and sawmills that Amariah Watson owned in Lexington, between the present Senior Center and the cemetery, were sold to Samuel Caldwell. Caldwell was owner of the mills when the flash flood of 1859 washed out the dam at the Carter mill, located above the town. The flood also damaged both the Caldwell dam and his mills. By 1870, ownership had passed to Dr. David "Daddy" Hahn who ran the mills until 1877, when the dam was again washed out in a flood. This winter flood caused Hahn to hire a crew at the cost of four hundred dollars to have the dam rebuilt. One can only imagine the winter conditions that the men faced, working in half-frozen water and winter winds.

Dr. Hahn died shortly thereafter, and the mill passed to his son, Reverend Benjamin J. Hahn, who rented or leased the rebuilt mill to various individuals until the mill was destroyed by fire under mysterious circumstances on August 2, 1894.[27] On September 20, 1949, Garber interviewed Mr. and Mrs. Morris Graham, who remembered that the fire began on the roof, probably the result of falling sparks from a passing train.

As indicated earlier, Garber came from a family that settled in Richland County in the early 1800s. He had a lifelong interest in watermills, especially those located in Richland County and he knew many of the second and third generations of mill owners. He interviewed a number of people in August and September 1949, and his notes are of interest in understanding the last few years of watermills in Lexington.[28] An article quoted from *The Richland Star* on March 6, 1879, set the scene for continued change in mill ownership in Lexington. It was announced that "A. G. Farst is running the Lexington mill night and day, his custom work is increasing rapidly."[29]

James Hiskey, of Lexington, in an interview with Garber on August 19, 1949, stated that the mill was "long referred to as the Hahn Mill," after Dr. David Hahn. Mr. Hiskey described the mill as 2 ½ stories high and that it originally stood 50 or 60 feet north of the bridge in the town on the west side of the stream. The mill was 35 to 40 feet wide and about 40 feet long with two buhrs about 40 inches in diameter. The dam was about 6 feet high and located about 8 or 10 feet above the mill; and the mid-dam brace was about 10 square feet and located in the middle of the dam on the down side and was filled with nigger-heads.[30]

Watson Lewis Graves Carter Grist and Saw Mill

Samuel Carter was great uncle of author Robert Carter. In the summer of 1970, Carter was the Scoutmaster for Troop 131. On a beautiful summer day, Carter and Troop 131 hiked from the Lexington Park along the Clear Fork up to the Clear Fork Dam and along the lake to the Boy Scout Camp at the northern end of the park. Given that there was not much of a trail back in the pioneer days of the 1970s, the boys waded through the water or found their way through the brush and the trees towards their goal of the Scout Camp. One of the boys called back to Mr. Carter, "Look! A stone age wheel." Much to Carter's surprise, lying there in the creek, was a millstone from the old Watson-Lewis-Graves-Carter Mill. Bob immediately knew what it was, and he later returned to this treasured site and obtained permission from the owner to take it. It turned out to be a 36-inch French buhr cap stone that had worn down to the point that it was no longer efficient, and the millwright cut and fashioned a sandstone cap for the top to add additional weight for continued use.[31]

Figure 5. This without a doubt was one of the highlights in Mr. Carter's search for mill memorabilia. Bob and his son Jeff helped haul the millstone out of the stream bed. Years later it was accidentally destroyed when trying to move it. Still the memory is a wonderful one! Who among you who love the history of the old mills would not have loved to stumble upon a treasure like this?

Figure 6. The lands and furrows in the face or grinding surface of the millstone indicated that it had been used for coarse grinding of animal feed or corn mash for a distillery. Garber stated that it was rare to find a millstone that had been backed with a weighted cap. No flour would have been made in the mill which also housed a sawmill.

The McClain Mill

After the Watson Mill–Hahn Mill was destroyed by fire, another smaller mill was built, known as the McLain Mill. Mclain was the miller at the Hahn Mill at the time of the fire. McClain had managed the John Strausbaugh Mill before taking over the operation of Hahn Mill.

A number of the farmers who lived in the creek bottom above the mill felt that their land would be much more valuable if the dam was gone and the bottomland had better drainage. The farmers got together and agreed that they would buy and install a steam engine in the mill if McLain would agree to the removal of the dam.[32] Apparently McLain agreed, and they removed the dam. Among those leaders who pushed for the removal of the dam was Bill Cockley, Mr. Kyner and Dr. Smith. Both Bill Cockley and Mr. Kyner

Figure 7. The covered bridge over the Clear Fork was north of Lexington on Plymouth Street. Built in 1859 some of the timber was cut at Samuel Carter's Saw Mill. His combination grist and sawmill can be seen in the background on the far left. It is doubtful the mill and bridge survived the 1913 flood. The picture is dated 1908. Picture is compliments of Timothy Brian McKee.

also owned land just above the mill and believed that their land values would also increase with the dam's removal. Unfortunately, removal of the dam did not lead to increased property values.

Charles McClain was much liked in the community. Harry Smith, of Lexington, Ohio, in an interview with Garber stated that Charles ran the mill for as long as he could recall. He described the mill as 2 ½ stories, 35 to 40 feet long, and had a bull wheel about 10-12 feet in diameter. It was not as high as the Hahn Mill. Charles often slept in the small mill office where he had a small stove. As a boy, Harry Smith picked up coal that had fallen off the railcars onto the railroad's right of way and sold it to McClain to heat the office. McClain had a clock, called a "Nigger Boy

Figure 8. The smaller McLain Mill was built on the original Watson Mill–Hahn Mill foundation. Originally it was powered by water and later converted to steam. Unable to maintain a profit, McLain eventually closed the mill. It was later torn down, and the material used to build a house on Delaware Street in Lexington.

Clock," that fascinated Smith. The eyes on the face would roll back and forth in tune with the movement of the pendulum.[33]

The McClain Mill had only a six-foot dam to generate power. A Leffell turbine was installed that generated 8 horse power. Of interest, and not often seen in mills, was a hominy pounder that was connected directly to the water power.[34] McClain struggled to keep his mill going but it was a losing proposition. He could not compete with the large steam-powered Cockley Mill that had been built just across the railroad tracks and was producing 500 bushels a day. Cockley resented the farmers continuing to do business with McClain. Eventualy McClain closed his mill and ownership passed to Al Hesket. It was Hesket who tore the mill down and used the lumber to build a house on Delaware Street that still stands – the second house on the west side of the intersection.

Figure 9. Dam and a portion of the McClain Mill. The corner of the original mill is shown at the extreme left. A buggy wash was maintained in the shallows immediately below the dam. The original mill burned and was replaced with the smaller mill pictured above. Graham Morris gave both photographs to Garber in September, 1949.

Feeder Streams in Troy Township

The Mercer-Griebling Grist and Saw Mills

John Garrison, merchant and banker, bought 327 acres of land in the northeast corner of Troy Township sometime after the War of 1812. It is possible, but unconfirmed, that he built or had built for him, a water-powered sawmill sometime around 1820. Garrison was a prominent merchant and banker and quite successful. By 1820, he was President of the Richland and Huron Bank in Mansfield. Sometime around 1830 the bank collapsed, and Garrison lost nearly everything. He was forced to sell most of his assets, including his track of land in Troy Township. Boyd F. Mercer purchased the Troy Township land and by 1831, he had a water-powered sawmill on the Alta South Road, south of Marion Avenue.[35] By 1838, Mercer had another good-sized gristmill in operation. His source of water came from a spring-fed lake north of Alta South Road along the present day bike trail. A portion of the headrace can still be seen in the woods just south of where the road crosses the stream.

Mercer's mill did a comfortable business and provided a good living until 1849, when the railroad came through the valley. Construction of the roadbed disrupted water flow to both mills and also flooded the tailrace to the sawmill. Mercer took the Columbus & Lake Erie Railroad to court and sued for $1000 in damages. He had to replace the waterwheel and wooden gearing inside the mill, and he claimed that the stream to both mills was no longer sufficient to turn the wheel. The case continued until 1855, when the jury awarded him $300 in damages.[36]

Figure 10. The Mercer Griebling Mill in the late 1800s while still operating. Once the mill closed, it began to deteriorate and lean until it collapsed in 1920.

Figure 11. The waterwheel was inside the enclosure on the east end of the mill.

On September 10, 1868, Mercer sold his mills and part of the farmland to Jacob Griebling, a native of Germany, and William Reinhard for $7,725. Reinhard and Griebling continued as partners until February 16, 1881, when Reinhard sold his share to Griebling for $5,523.12. During their partnership, Reinhard operated the mill and Griebling, the farm. With the Reinhard buyout, Jacob Griebling turned the operation of the mill over to his son, John, who added a cider press. A new twenty-foot waterwheel with a four-foot wide face was installed in 1901.

Tragedy struck on August 14, 1905, when a powerful storm struck with such

Figure 12. The interior of the Mercer-Griebling Mill. The millstone on the right is uncovered while the buhr on the left has the hood, hopper rest, and hopper in place. The building was starting to lean when Louis Griebling took this photograph.

force that the dam washed out and lightning set a nearby barn on fire. The mill, 75 years old and starting to lean, never ran again. The cider press, however, continued in operation until 1910.

Louis G. Griebling (1897-1982), George Gust Griebling's son and grandson of Jacob Griebling, provided a great deal of information regarding the Mercer-Griebling Grist Mill in an unpublished family history completed before his death in 1982. Louis also corresponded with Garber between 1949 and 1950. He described the mill as being "approximately 40 x 50 feet and 4 stories high." He wrote: "There were two sets of buhrs, one set for grinding flour and the other for stock feeds." Although the mill ceased operations in 1905, the cider press continued in use until 1910. Griebling wrote about the cider press in his letter to Garber:

The mill pond was directly north of the mill and about 2,000 feet away. A cider press was operated in connection with the mill for a number of years. At first the press was operated with water power but there were times during the cider season when there was insufficient water to operate so a small steam engine was installed to operate the press and also grind feed. The cider press was continued in use and feed ground using the steam press until about 1918.[37]

Figure 13. This picture of the leaning mill was taken a few years before it collapsed on the waterwheel end. Rotted timbers and a foundation around the waterwheel caused the whole mill to go down.

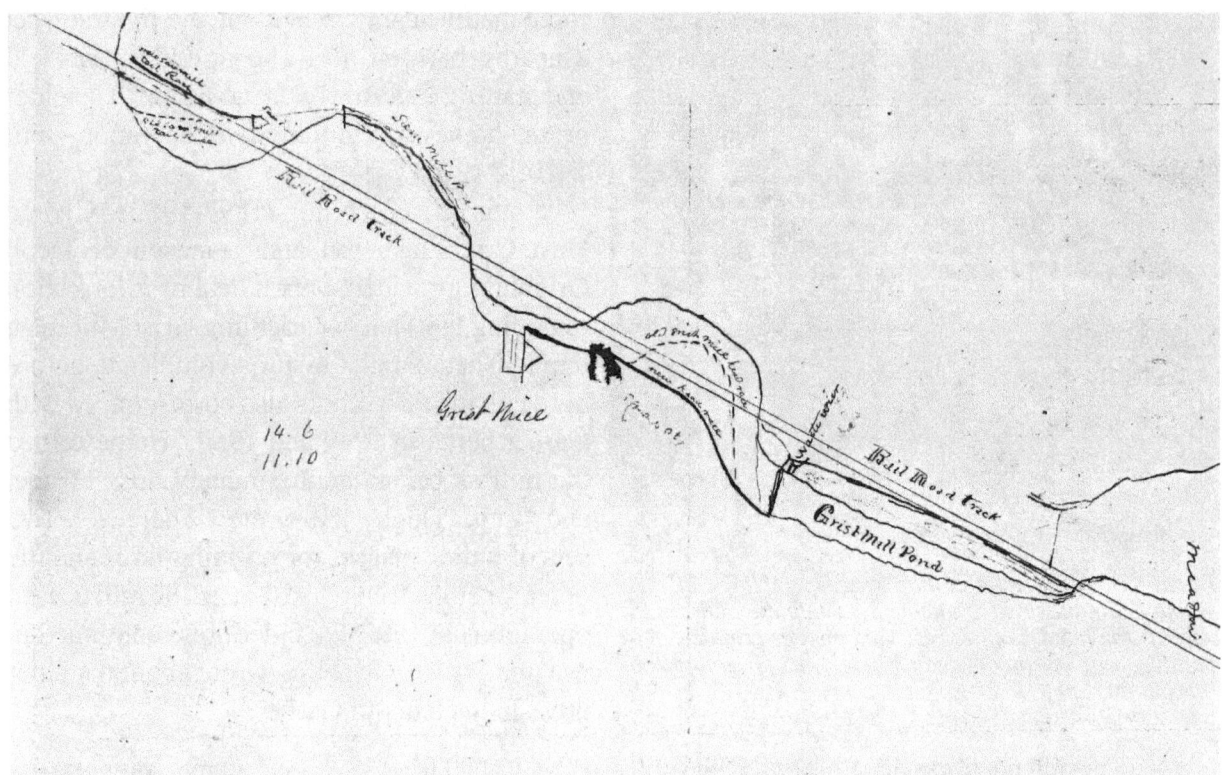

Figure 14. In a letter to Garber on January 11, 1950, L. B. Griebling wrote: I have made a map from memory of the millponds, races, bridges, etc., showing the location before and after the railroad was built. All of these races are still clearly visible except a short section north of the mill which was filled in.

He described in detail the 20-foot waterwheel in a letter to Garber on October 14, 1949.

> The water wheel was mounted on a wood shaft approximately 30 inches in diameter and about 26 feet long. Inside the mill was the main bull gear mounted on the same shaft, which was about 12 ft in diameter. This gear was completely made of wood except the teeth, which were cast in sections and bolted to the rim.
>
> The above bull gear meshed with a bevel pinion 30 inches in diameter, which was keyed to a vertical shaft, which extended to the top of the mill. Immediately above the bevel pinion was a spur gear about 12 ft. in diameter and made of cast iron, except the teeth which were of hard maple. This gear meshed with four 12 inch pinions which drove the buhrs, a corn crusher and a corn sheller."[38]

The old gristmill came to a quiet end on a warm summer day in 1920. As the Grieblings worked the fields, a loud rumble was heard. The mill, by then leaning badly, simply collapsed into a pile of rubble. The family salvaged some timber and burned the rest. The last water-powered mill in Troy Township was no more.

David Miller Saw and Turning Mill

George Miller, born in England in 1789, immigrated to America and set roots in Mansfield in 1830. A skilled carpenter and millwright, he settled in the deep valley on what is now Marion Avenue just west of Graham Road. By 1838, he built a dam on a small stream in the valley and built a sawmill that had a turning lathe. It was an unusual combination, but Miller furnished much of the lumber and building stock used in the area, and the lathe enabled him to turn furniture legs, spindles, and columns.

In 1850 he turned the mill over to his son, David, who ran it until the dam washed out in 1864. It was never rebuilt. The remains of the dam are still visible today. Since the dam took its water directly from the stream, no headrace was needed. Main access to the mill was from Bell Road and the mill itself was south of Marion Avenue down a long lane past the beautiful 1871 Miller house; only recently expanded. This unnamed stream continues to wind its way down to the Clear Fork near Owens Road just below the dam.

McConnell Saw Mill (Orweiler Road Saw Mill)

Early Auditor's Records list this mill in the southwest quarter of section 32 by Joseph McConnell & Others. This mill was located at the bottom of the big hill below the old Boy Scout Camp on the small stream near the bridge. At one time John Carter was involved with this mill. No other information on this particular mill has been located.

The Noah Watson Tavern, Grist Mill, and Saw Mill

Noah Watson, half-brother to Amariah Watson, the founder of Lexington, wrote a letter to Jabze Cook on January 8, 1858, in which he stated:

> I, Noah Watson, certify that I helped build the first two cabins in the vicinity of Lexington, and also did a job of clearing on Amariah Watson's first field, commencing on about the 8th of March, 1812. I also entered the southeast quarter of section 7, range 18, township 20, in which I now live, and commenced in 1813.[39]

As one of the very early settlers in Washington Township, Noah, along with a number of other early settlers, was presented with a special axe. With brothers Amariah and Samuel, Noah volunteered during the War of 1812. Watson owned the land that is now part of the Gorman Nature Center, and he built his cabin across from what is now the entrance to the Nature Center. In the 1830s he built a water-powered sawmill in the deep channel of the small stream just north of his home. Once the sawmill was running, Watson added a "small cracker grist mill" to supply the distillery used for his Washington Township inn.[40] It is not known when Noah began operating the distillery, but records show that between 1843 and 1845, he built a larger

Figure 15. Noah Watson

20 x 40 foot two-story frame tavern building that stood until 2000.

Watson was a deeply religious man who saw little conflict in running a distillery. Early tavern laws required tavern keepers to provide food and drink for man and beast. Those that stayed the night at the tavern received one charge that included bed, a meal, one glass of whiskey, water, and feed and stable for one horse. There would be additional charges for more drinks, food, or extra animals.

Noah Watson, the half brother of Amariah Watson, was a soldier, doctor, farmer, and tavern keeper. It is not known what medical training Dr. Watson may have had.

Watson's tavern was a popular stopping place for teamsters and drivers. After Watson's death in 1863, the operations of the mill and the tavern ceased, and in 2000 the old tavern was torn down. The tavern site is now covered in weeds and brush. The millsite, no longer recognizable, was on the south side of Terman Road, at the bottom of the hill.

Figure 16. The Watson Tavern as it appeared in 1906. The original tavern was a log building of course. The new tavern, as seen here with the Mishy family, was built between 1841 and 1842.

Figure 17. Taken in 2000, this shows the tavern as a well built home shortly before being torn down. Now it is a weed- and brush-filled site. A piece of history lost.

Alex W. McConnell Carding & Fulling Mill

Built in 1843, the Alex W. McConnell mill was located south of Lexington on the west side of State Route 42 in the valley just south of Kings Corners Road. The small stream there powered McConnell's mill as well as the Jacob King Saw Mill, located downstream from McConnell. Little information is available pertaining to these mills. The mills were eventually abandoned, probably because of insufficient water. The old mill building was later moved east to Schmidt Road and converted into a residence.[41]

Jacob King Saw Mill

As indicated above, the Jacob King Saw Mill and the McConnell mill shared a common water source. King, also known as "Squire" King, owned a water-powered sawmill southeast of Kings Corner Road and U.S. 42 as early as 1838. Sources indicate that the mill was near the bridge that crossed the same stream that powered McConnell's carding and fulling mill. By 1868, the property had passed to Jacob's son Samuel, and the road and intersection took on the name "King's Corner," a name still used today.[42]

Washington Township

The Strausbaugh Mills

John Strausbaugh built both grist and sawmills on the Clear Fork in 1865 and 1866. They were located down a long lane from the present intersection of Vanderbilt Road and State Road 97. The lane to the old Strausbaugh house, which is still standing, led to the mill, crossed the river, and continued onto the Mill Run Road. The road was abandoned after the mill closed, as there was no bridge.

Not much information about the Strausbaugh Mills is available, but Garber was able to acquire some interesting information from two interviews with Harry Palm, one in December 1946 and another in September 1949. In 1946 Mr. Palm told Garber that the mill was located on land then being farmed by a Mr. Murray. The dam built for use by the mill was a ford for crossing the stream. In addition, Mr. Palm told Garber that the customary toll, or grinding fee, at the time the mill was in operation, for making flour or meal, was one bushel of grain for every eight bushels delivered to the mill for grinding.[43]

Garber met with James Hiskey, of Lexington, on August 19, 1949. Mr. Hiskey was 90 years of age and recalled many details about the mill. It was 2 ½ stories, about 30 x 30 feet in height and depth and had two sets of buhrs. In addition, the dam was between 6 and 7 feet high, with the mill adjacent to the dam and the forebay connecting right from the dam. The tailrace was not more than 100 feet. Mr. Hiskey also stated that a turbine was eventually installed, but he was unable to specify the date. He stressed that although Strausbaugh was the owner, Benny Kaughman who

Figure 18. John Strausbaugh installed a Leffel Co. turbine when his grist and sawmills were built in 1866. A cast iron turbine was more efficient and durable than a wooden waterwheel.

was then "one of the best millers in this section," operated it for various periods of time for about 10 years. Another miller and expert stone dresser, whose name Mr. Hiskey could not recall, also operated the mill at times.[44]

Harry Palm, in his second interview with Garber on September 20, 1949, told him that the "Strausbaughs had an ice house that they filled each winter with ice cut from above the dam." Mrs. John Strausbaugh was known as "Tood," and Harry Palm, as a boy, would take his wagon and go to the mill where "Tood" sold him ice. He then delivered ice to his customers. In all of Garber's notes on mills, Strausbaugh Mill is the only mill ever associated with an ice house.[45]

Mr. George O. Neal lent Garber a letter from the James Leffel & Company in which they confirmed that a 48-inch, Leffel Standard, Left Hand Turbine was "furnished to Mr. John Strausbaugh in 1866."[46]

George Marshall Grist Mill, Saw Mill & Distillery

This early mill was located in SE ¼ Section 31 on the old road from Lexington to Bellville before Route 97 and Interstate 71 altered the road system. The mill was on Kings Corners Road on the west side of 71. In response to an inquiry about a Boy Scout trip along the B & O Railroad line in the late 1970s, Garber made the following comments regarding the history of the Marshall Mill. He wrote:

Figure 19. The Strausbaugh home was along the old road just above the mill. After the mill was closed, the road was abandoned, leaving the house at the end of a long lane.

The millrace (seen) diagonally across the field was for the Marshall Mill, erected by David Phelps. The old Phelps Mill stood on the opposite side of the creek, just above the bridge. A few rods above the bridge, the mud sills for the dam were still to be seen a few years ago. A small house has been erected where the Phelps cabin once stood. In 1933, I dug out a portion of the old mudsill, it was black walnut, and after several years of drying in my father's home, I had a nice box made for my desk, and several picture frames for which I am most proud. You see, both of these early mills were erected by my great-great-great grandfather.[47]

In separate notes, Garber referred to an agreement between David Phelps and Colonel George Marshall. Marshall wrote Phelps: "in consideration of the sum of four hundred dollars to him in hand paid by the said David Phelps (the receipt is hereby acknowledged and forever acquitted and discharged the said David Phelps, his heir's executors and administrators) hath granted bargained, (etc) … the NW ¼ of Section 29, in Township 20 or Range 18."[48]

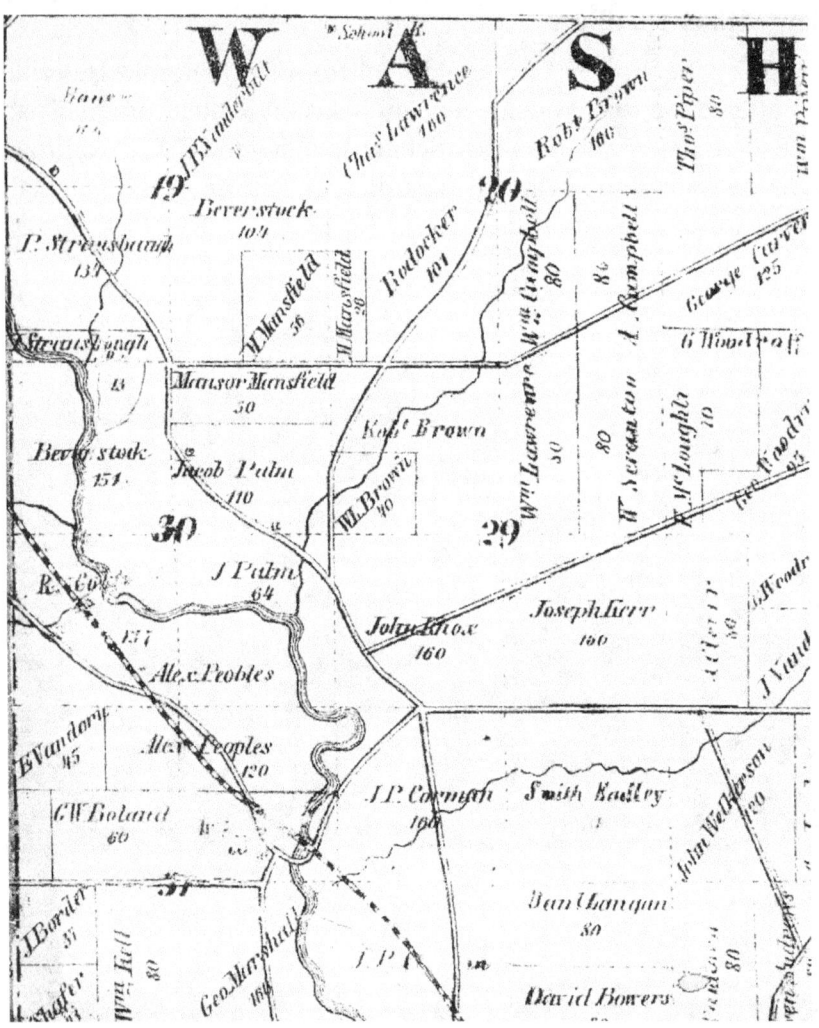

Figure 20. *The Clear Fork Snakes its way across the southwestern corner of Washington Township. The 1856 map shows the approximate location of the Strausbaugh Mill in the north and the Marshall Mill.*

Given that in 1817 the established price for millwrights in construction of a double-framed sawmill was $100.00; for a double-geared gristmill, $300.00, it is likely that Phelps received his land from Marshall for the sum of $400.00 paid in hand. With the signing of the above agreement, Marshall became owner of the saw and gristmills on April 18, 1821.[49]

On September 20, 1949, Harry Palm told Garber that the Marshall Mill was small, only 1 ½ stories with one, possibly two, sets of buhrs. The feed or gristmill was about 20 x 25 feet and the sawmill was about 25 x 30 feet. A wood wheel, 7 or 8 feet in diameter and the water race, only 3 or 4 feet, was the only power ever used. The mill was torn down in the early 1900s and the lumber used to build a barn on the Harry Palm farm.[50]

By 1881, Jerry Tinkey had taken ownership of the mill and placed an advertisement in the *Bellville Star* on October 13,

1881, stating, "Jerry Tinkey is putting in new waterwheels and preparing to ground grain feed and meal."[51] On January 1, 1882, C. E. Crain purchased Tinkey's property of 40 acres and a sawmill for $4,500.00. Crain continued to invest in the mill and advertised in the *Bellville Star* that he had added "to his machinery a first class corn sheller."[52] The sheller was used to remove the grain from the cob.

The Stump Mill

Little is known of the origin of this flour mill. Tax records indicate that the mill, built in the 1860s by the partnership of Shafer & Shafer, was located on the east side of the Clear Fork along the south side of present day Mock Road, west of Route 97. In 1872, Adam Shafer sold 106 acres, and presumably the mill, to Israel Stump for $7,000, a price that indicated a well-built mill doing a good business. Stump changed the name to "Stump Mill," and it was identified as such through the years, even though the ownership changed. It was a flour mill with two sets of buhrs, one for flour and one for rough grinding corn meal, distillery mash, or animal feed. No sawmill was connected with it.

The *Bellville Dollar Weekly* and *The Bellville Star* provide a timeline on the history of the Stump Mill. For example, in the April 12, 1872, issue of the *Bellville Dollar Weekly* there is an announcement that I. C. Stump, who had bought the Shafer Mill, was now "prepared to do custom work of all kinds." Not all went smoothly, and on September 12, 1873, an announcement appeared in the *Bellville Dollar Weekly* that Stump would have the mill up and running "in a week or two, it having been idle on account of breaking down."[53]

1873 was a difficult year for Stump. He announced in the September 12, 1873, edition of the *Bellville Dollar Weekly* that he had installed "an improved Thomas Leffel Turbine Waterwheel in his mill." The mill had either suffered a broken waterwheel or else the waterwheel had to be replaced because of age. The average wooden waterwheel had a life span from 20 to 25 years. Floods, headrace debris, or winter ice all contributed to the wear and tear on a waterwheel; and for whatever the cause, Stump decided to sell. An announcement in the *Belleville Star* (later changed to Bellville) on July 10, 1884, identified the new owner as W. H. Ward. Ward advertised that he was prepared to "do all kinds of grinding on short notice."[54]

The Stump Mill was drawn into what was locally known as "The miller's war of 1884." W. W. Cockley and investors had built a large, steam-powered, 500-bushels-a-day roller flour and supply mill in Lexington next to the railroad. W. H. Ward took possession of the Stump Mill on July 14, 1884, and, less than a year later, it sold at a Sheriff's Sale to Captain D. W. Wilson for $1,750. Wilson held it only for a few months, and on September 10, 1885, he sold it to George Ridgeway. When it next changed hands is not clear, but in May 1888, A. E. Lee was the owner, and he promised that repairs were being made. Other owners included J. R. English, A. G. Faust, and A. E. Shafer. In January 1894, Shafer promised to do grinding on all days except Mondays and Tuesdays; but the end was not long in coming. Garber noted that "Charley Palm's father lived on the Stump Mill property around 1910, and it was he who tore down portions of the mill between 1912-1915, as needed."[55]

Local water-powered mills in the Clear Fork Valley faced enormous competitive pressure. The Rummel Mill below Butler claimed their stone-ground flour was superior to the Cockley Mill. The Plank Mill, above Butler, converted to a new process roller system and claimed they had the best product. The Cockley Mill, accused of adding alum to their flour to make the bread rise better, denied doing so in the local newspapers. At the same time the Stump Mill's head gate was damaged by vandals, and the Crain Mill, east of Bellville, was leveled by a suspicious fire. Ultimately, technology won out, and Cockley's Mill and eventually the railroad put the county water mills out of business.

Figure 21. Zent-Fitting-Bowers-Shaler-Garber Mill. Taken in the late 1800s, this photograph shows the Zent-Fittiing-Bowers-Shale-Garber Mill in the late 1800s, about the time a steam engine was added. The 25-barrel-a-day mill had a long history before burning in 1895. Note the railroad train on the right, behind the mill.

The Zent-Fitting-Bowers-Shaler-Garber Mill

The Zent-Fitting-Bowers-Shaler-Garber Mill is a historian's jigsaw puzzle. The mill and millsite had a long list of owners and operators covering nearly a century. Each generation recalled and recorded their time in the mill. The mill was located between the bottom of the Bellville Cemetery hill and the Bixler Road–Route 97 intersection along the Clear Fork on the north side of Route 97, not far from the present bike trail. Nothing remains that would indicate a mill had ever existed there.

Jacob Zent Sr., from West Hanover Township, Dauphin County, Pennsylvania, moved west with his family in the early 1800s. He acquired considerable land in Ohio and, in his will (dated December 1, 1808), he left all of his personal estate to the children of his son John Zent (also known as John Zent Sr.). John was to have use of the land during his lifetime. He arrived in Richland County sometime in 1810 and was the third settler in Jefferson Township in 1812.[56] Garber, in his research, concluded that Joseph Zent's son, John Zent Sr. built the mill in

1814. Typical of frontier construction, it was probably a log cabin, but by 1830 it was no longer in operation.[57]

A mill existed on this land for nearly one hundred years, and the trail of ownership is a convoluted one. John Zent Sr. was unable to pay off the debt incurred in the original purchase of the land. Jacob Zent Jr. made full payment to the General Land Office in Canton, Ohio, for the purchase of the NW ¼, Section 9, Township 19, Range 18 on June 12, 1832. He ultimately acquired the land by paying off the debt and acquiring quit claims from the children, sons and daughters-in-law of John Sr.[58]

Once he acquired clear title to the land, Jacob sold the property to James (Jesse) Holley (or Holly) in 1835. From the time the original mill was built, ownership of the property changed hands several times.[59] Mills were often known by the name of the current owner, and when the title changed, so did the name of the mill. Among the owners of the original Zent Mill were F. M. Fitting, Isaac Bowers, Frank L. Shaler and Benton Garber. According to the deed records, Fitting bought the Zent mill in 1845, and in 1847, he tore down the old Zent Mill and built a new, larger one that he sold to David Bowers in 1852. Bowers' son, Isaac, took possession of the mill in 1864.[60]

An announcement in *The Bellville Star* on March 18, 1882, stated that David Shaler had purchased a "part of the Bowers mill." By October, *The Bellville Star* reported that repairs were underway at Shaler's Mill.[61] Shaler struggled to keep his mill in operation. A flood occurred in November 1882 when the B & O Railroad filled part of the creek, backing up the water in the Whitcomb Dam. It would be the end of November before the mill was back in operation.

One evening in 1886, Shaler's wife went to the mill to call her husband home for supper. As she walked by some chickens and ducks, one of them flew up to her face. Startled, she stepped back, and her foot landed on a round rock. She fell and broke her hip.[62]

In January 1888, the combination of rain and melting snow resulted in another flood that took out part of the dam and the bridge. That was it for the Shaler family. *The Bellville Star* reported on January 12, 1888: "The Shaler family is closing up their affairs in this neighborhood preparatory to moving to Pennsylvania in which state they make their home. Their many friends in this vicinity regret that circumstances render such a move advisable as they will be greatly missed."[63]

Jacob Silas Garber, D. W. Garber's father, told him that Benton Garber, who had purchased the Fitting Mill, had ordered machinery from Nordick-Marmon & Company. Garber was unable to pay for the equipment, and Nordick-Marmon took possession of the mill. They sent a man by the name of A. L. Walker to run it. Jacob Garber had provided lumber to be used in reconditioning the mill but the mill burned before it could be put into commission.

E. L. Brentlinger, in an interview with Garber on March 22, 1952, told a most interesting story involving A. L. Walker, the manager of the Fitting Mill for the Nordike & Marmon Company. Walker was definitely a ladies man. "He became involved with the wife of Ed Switzer, who was quite a 'clipper.' Ed Switzer warned Walker to stay away from his wife. Walker and Switzer's wife persisted in their activities, and Switzer shot Walker. Walker died because of his wounds, but no action was ever taken against Switzer."

The Nordick Marmon & Company also had problems. In February 1889, part of the mill dam washed out, making it impossible to run. In September 1892, Benton L. Garber again was the owner of the mill.[64] He continued struggling to make ends meet, and on Friday, January 4, 1895, the mill burned to the ground, cause unknown. In June 1895, he sold his property, including the old millsite, to A. A. Douglass for $2,300.

Of all the owners of the Zent-Fitting-Bowers-Shaler-Garber Mill, Benton L. Garber met a most tragic end in Chicago, where he was working as a traveling salesman. On the evening of March 24, 1897, he left his room at the Dearborn Hotel to go to the theater. Later that evening, he was found in an alley, a gun lying by his head, his coat and vest opened, and his pant pocket turned inside out. He had been robbed and shot in the head.

The week before Garber's mill burned, the Cockley Milling Company announced the opening of a new grain elevator in Bellville and that they "were in readiness to pay the highest price for grain, seed, wool and salt. Farmers could exchange their grain and depend on getting good flour as can be made from wheat."[65] Competition from the Cockley Mill in Lexington and the even larger national firms like General Mills and Pillsbury spelled the end of the small country mills.

This is a brief timeline of the major owners of the mill: the Zent family owned the mill for approximately 20 years, the Fitting family for about 7 years, and the Bowers family for about 8 years. During each of these time periods the mill took on the name of the owner. Between 1866 and 1882 there appears to have been three other owners of the mill, and in 1882, Michael Stuff, then owner, sold the mill to Helen Shaler.

Figure 22. Benton L. Garber

The Bellville Planing Mill

The Bellville Planing Mill was located at the edge of Bellville on the north side of the Clear Fork. Most of the information on this mill came from interviews conducted by Garber and from newspaper clippings that he either had, or from transcriptions that he made from an original source. The original builder is not identified. According to *The Richland Star*, Otis Howard took ownership of the Planing Mill in late 1865. In addition to custom sawing and turning, he also manufactured revolving hay rakes and bedsteads; often selling as many as 500 rakes a year between 1865 and 1870. In 1867 a plane was added and the business continued under the name of O. Howard & Son. As business grew, they added new machinery, and in 1870 a brick building was erected that housed an engine used when there was insufficient water.[66]

Otis Howard was a farmer until he began to manufacture churns in 1860. He continued his business until he purchased the sawmill on the creek across from the Bellville railroad depot. Howard not only operated the sawmill but also a planing mill and turning machinery. He continued to run the business until 1875, when his son, I. W., succeeded him. Otis returned to making churns.[67]

In February 1881, the Marshall Railroad Bridge between Bellville and Lexington was destroyed in a flood. Trains were unable to pass for nearly a week. The dam that powered the mills was also damaged by the water and ice, effectively closing mill operations until repairs were made.[68] By mid-June 1881, I. W. Howard and his brother (H.W.) were working together and had purchased a steam run muley sawmill. Business there was steady.[69]

In spite of the problems that water-powered mills faced throughout their history, it was not all work and no play. Occasionally, a mill would host a social event. Garber cited a newspaper dated August 1877, in which four men were arrested at the sawmill in Bellville for a late night party that involved playing cards, drinking, and gambling. When they were found guilty, their lawyer appealed their case and won by proving that the mill was outside the village limits. This just goes to show that even back in 1877, a good lawyer was worth his weight in gold!

The Moody Mill

After retiring in the early 1940s, Garber returned to his hometown of Bellville. There he focused on his passion for water mills in Ohio, especially those near where he grew up. The Moody Mill, in particular, was of great interest to him because it was the last water-powered mill to operate in Richland County. Garber often visited Mr. and Mrs. George O. Neal, the last owners of the mill. The history of the Moody Mill is long one, beginning with the original mill built by Reverend

Figure 23. Undated photograph of the Moody Mill (Belleville Flour Mill). Originally a fulling and carding mill, later it was converted to a gristmill. As can be seen, the headrace, a forebay, provided ample water for the mill. When rebuilt in 1900 by Hoy Shaffer and his father, the top half story was removed, and the entire mill building rebuilt a few feet further toward the hill and away from the race. (Copy of the original photograph given to Garber in August 1949.)

John Moody in 1831 and lasting until the Neals closed its doors for the last time on January 29, 1952.

Originally a carding and fulling mill, it was not successful, and Reverend Moody had it converted to a gristmill.[70] It was an expensive investment, and Rev. Moody attempted to dispose of it in 1832. The following appeared in *The Western Sentinel*:

> Notice for Sale, or Rent. The Mill property opposite the town of Bellville, in Richland County. There is now in operation a Saw Mill, Fulling Mill, and Carding Machine.
>
> If not disposed of, I wish to employ a hand to attend to the Carding Machine the present season. None need to apply who cannot give satisfaction as to morals, industry and a knowledge of the business.
>
> March 24, 1832.   John Moody[71]

Although not able to sell the mill at this time, Moody's influence in the community continued to grow, and he was "considered one of the best men that Bellville ever contained, [and had] opened a store and the usual trades and avocations to the village were well represented."

> Reverend Moody gave much to his community. During a period of famine in the 1830s, Reverend Moody did not hesitate to reach out to the needy. His farm did well during the famine and Moody had an abundance of crops. When his neighbor's crops failed and people approached him to buy grain for bread, he would ask them "Have you money to pay for it?" If the customer said yes, he was told to go elsewhere. If, on the other hand, the customer had no money, they were given well filled sacks and told to come back if they needed more.[72]

In 1837 Moody sold the mill property to the partnership of Thomas Parks and Washington and Charles Strong for $10,000. For a brief time the mill operated under the name of Strong & Parks. They had added a sawmill in a separate building. *County Auditor's Records* reveal that the Moody's Mill had been converted to a gristmill. Because of deed and mortgage problems, the mill returned to Moody. Moody died on September 11, 1838, not long after again taking possession of the mill. He was 38 years old.[73]

The mill property changed hands many times between 1838 and 1859, when it finally came under the ownership of the Strong and Waring partnership. Like those before them, they ran into financial troubles, and in 1864 the mill and property were sold to Dr. Niles Whitcomb and partners, Alexander and William Menzie, at a Sheriff's Sale. That partnership floundered, and at a Sheriff's Sale in 1869, Dr. Whitcomb became sole owner for $6,150. Dr. Whitcomb employed men to run the mill, and he returned to his medical practice.

Between 1869 and 1886, there were numerous advertisements or announcements pertaining to the mill, announcements that often referred to problems. Clearly, keeping a mill in operation was a challenge. For example, in the July 24, 1874, issue of *The Bellville Weekly,* it was announced that "Dr. N. D. Whitecomb's mill is at present not running on account of building a new forebay." On September 11, 1874, also in *The Bellville Weekly,* there was an extensive report on the refurbishing of the mill.

Mill Running.

> Dr. N. D. Whitecomb's mill, which has been stopped for some weeks undergoing repairs, is now running and has the capacity for doing double the work it did before. The Doctor has spared no expense to make a good job. He secured the services of Levi Hiple, who as a millwright is acknowledged to be second to none in the State; an inspection of his work is all that is

necessary to convince anyone of this fact, as for our part we have not seen any machinery anywhere of the kind that run anymore exact than this does. The mill has essentially been repaired as follows: the dam has been repaired, the head race has been cleaned out, which took no small amount of hard labor....There is an entirely new forebay, which is a large one and very tight, and which contain a forty-five inch turbine wheel....Mr. John Simpson has charge of the mill and is responsible for the grinding. Mr. S. has been in this vicinity for the past eleven years.... Mr. Simpson does business on a true basis, and he guarantees satisfaction in every instance.[74]

In January 1885, Whitecomb had a stroke and died in May 1886. John Simpson leased the mill from his widow, and just over a year later, in March 1887, he purchased the property at an estate sale.[75] Simpson made improvements to the millsite between 1887 and 1890. In the August 7, 1887, issue, *The Bellville Star* observed that:

The mill has been transformed from an old, dilapidated looking building to a comparatively new building, freshly painted and indeed a credit to the town. A new fore-bay and the necessary repairs on the dam has made the power equal to that of steam. New machinery has been added and the old all repaired and made as good as new.[76]

As the 20th Century approached, competition between mills that produced the stone ground buhr flour and the "New Process" roller ground flour increased. It was a topic often debated in the local newspapers. In 1890, Simpson bowed to the competition and installed the "Roller Process." *The Bellville Independent* announced on May 1, 1890, that the Simpson's Bellville Mills had:

...completed and placed in my mill the latest and best improved Roller Process, built and put up by the Case Company of Columbus, who guarantee to make as good a flour and give as large a yield as any mill in the country....I have retained one buhr for grinding Graham and Buckwheat meal, and one for chop and corn as formerly.[77]

John Simpson died in 1894, and ownership of the mill passed to his son, John E. (J.E.) Simpson. J. E. and his wife Elizabeth sold the mill to David L. Parker in late June or early July 1898. Parker, in turn, sold the mill to William Lanehart and F. W. Lanehart in September 1903, and in January 1909 title to the property transferred to F. W. Lanehart.[78] How long Lanehart owned the mill is not clear, but in 1914 W. B. Rutherford and his wife Carrie Elizabeth moved to Bellville and bought the Bellville Flour Mill. When Rutherford died in 1923 the mill remained in the Rutherford family. It is not clear who managed the mill between 1923 and 1933. Garber noted that the mill closed for an unspecified period in the early 1930s.

In January 1934, John M. McPeek and Dallas Williams leased the mill from Mrs. Rutherford with the option to buy. They spent their first five weeks cleaning and repairing the equipment and white washing the interior. Unfortunately, like many of the previous owners, success eluded them. The announcement of the closing of the mill appeared in the December edition of *The Bellville Independent*.

The Bellville Milling Co. under the management of John S. McPeek for the past eighteen months has discontinued business. The mill has been operated during that time under many adverse conditions, including several floods that did considerable damage, and when Mr. McPeek was offered a position as a traveling salesman for a well known feed concern, he accepted the position. The poor condition of the local wheat this year due to the many rains the last six weeks, according to Mr. McPeek, would make flour making very difficult as much of the wheat could not be used at all. The cost of having good wheat shipped was prohibitive.[79]

Once again the mill returned to the Rutherford family. George Craft, in an interview with Garber on February 10, 1948, stated that:

Figure 24. A rare view of the Moody mill showing the Alexander & Zent stone quarry to the right and the mill with the large opening where the railroad passed through to get to the quarry. To alleviate the danger of fire the tracks were later laid around the mill.

Figure 25. The foundation for the mill warehouse addition was captured in another rare post card photograph. The date is unknown but is believed to be around 1900 - 1908.

A man named Wolford bought the mill from the owner named Rutherford and paid $9,000.00 on the purchase price of $12,000.00 when he lost it. After Wolford went bankrupt Rutherford regained possession of the mill and sold it to a partnership firm named Morse & Ellis, people that came from the east. After a time, they found that they were unable to carry on and lost the mill back to Rutherford. George Neal bought the mill from Rutherford.[80]

Neal bought the Bellville Mill in April 1944, after a flood took out the dam at the Kanaga Mill he was running at Butler. By 1948, George Neal had repaired the mill, put in a new forebay and turbine and cleaned out the headrace. He turned on the water and ground the first flour on August 3, 1948. Garber and his wife Vera received the first bag of flour from the now renovated water-powered mill.[81]

Neal and his wife Clara lived in a second-floor apartment in the mill along with several cats that handled mouse-control duties. Clara was a small woman and the only employee. She deftly handled big bags of feed and wheeled them around with apparent ease. She generally wore dresses

Figure 26. An early but updated picture of the Moody Mill shows the headrace and forebay at far right which provided ample water for the mill. In 1900 the mill was rebuilt and modernized by Hoy Shaffer and his father. In rebuilding, the top half-story was removed and the entire main building was rebuilt a few feet further toward the hill and away from the race.

made from colorful feed sack material. This printed cloth was popular with frugal farm wives who sewed aprons, dresses, children's clothes, and other items from a variety of feed bag patterns. Chicken feed sacks were the most sought after by the fashion conscious.[82]

Neal spent most of his life as a miller and millwright. At one time he was the head miller at the huge Hanley Milling Company in Mansfield, working under Jerry Hanley. His career took him to a number of mills, and the Bellville Mill or "Neal's Mill" was saved through his skill and

Figure 27. The Moody Mill was also known as the Bellville Roller Mill as late as 1947. Purchased by George O. Neal in 1944, he and his wife Clara operated the mill until it closed in 1952. The white-trimmed second floor windows in the warehouse section were added when the Neal's created living quarters in the old mill.

effort. Rated at 50 barrels a day with a storage capacity of 8,000 bushels, it came to a sad ending in 1952 when the State of Ohio rerouted Highway 97 along the Clear Fork straight through the mill. Garber recorded the demise of the last operating water-powered mill in Richland County in an article entitled "Bellville Mill, Oldest Industry, Is Closed Down For The Last time" published in *The Bellville Star* and *Tri Fork Press* on Thursday, February 28, 1952. In part he wrote:

> The pioneer mill at Bellville, perhaps the oldest industry in Richland County, closed down for the last time on January 29, when George O. Neal, the miller, shut off water to the turbine; it marked 122 years of almost continuous operation. With few brief interruptions for repairs and changes in ownership, the mill erected in 1830 by Rev. John Moody has been running continuous since that time.
>
> It was erected by Moody as a carding mill, with a saw mill attached, one of the earliest enterprises of this kind on the Clear Fork. But it was not a success. In 1830 Bellville had a population of 173, Lexington 69, Newville 77 and Perrysville 9. The population was entirely too small to support profitable operation and the number of sheep inadequate to provide wool necessary to run the mill except for brief periods. In 1832 Moody tried to sell the mill but was unsuccessful. There were then seven grist mills in operation within four miles of Bellville, but in face of this stiff competition he converted the establishment to a grist mill. Moody's genial personality and ability contributed to his success and he continued to operate the mill until 1837 when it was sold.

The Bellville Mill was always a busy activity and as the village grew so grew its trade. It continued operating as a buhr or stone mill until 1890, the last along the Clear Fork to accept the change to the roller and "New Process System" of milling. Even then the owner, John Simpson, was reluctant to convert completely to the modern system. He retained two buhrs, one to make graham and buckwheat flour and one for corn meal and coarse grinding.

The sale of the mill to the State to make way for highway improvements has not brought happiness to Mr. and Mrs. Neal. Neal, a miller for 42 years, has never engaged in any other occupation and finds no pleasure in dismantling an old land-mark. Farmers throughout the area and adjoining counties have brought their grists to be ground at the mill. The Neals wish to express their appreciation to these people for their fine patronage. The mill will soon be gone; it will soon be sold and torn down; the mill race filled in and a new highway built.[83]

Although the city of Bellville was unable to save Neal's mill, they did pass an ordinance on September 3, 1951, that included an understanding that the State Highway Department would not remove the existing dam over the Clear Fork and that the dam would remain in its present location. Unfortunately, the old milldam was destroyed several years later when several people advanced the theory that the old milldam race was the cause of Clear Fork flooding. As a result, the dam race was torn out. Nature proved these people wrong and the Clear Fork today continues to flood as it always had. Perhaps saddest of all is that the last generation that remembers water-powered mills in Richland County is slowly fading away.

LeFever Saw and Carding Mill

Baughman in his *History of Richland County* wrote that "John LeFever, an early Richland County pioneer settled in Bellville about a half mile below Bellville, where he built a sawmill and a carding mill."[84] LeFever's mills were located along the Clear Fork a few hundred feet south of what is now the Bellville sewage treatment plant on Durbin Road. Exactly when the mills were constructed and how long they were in operation is not clear, but tax records indicate their construction was sometime around 1840. The 1839 tax records confirm that LeFever had a sawmill in operation. His

Figure 28. Clara and George O. Neal.

sawmill probably preceded the carding mill that was in use in 1843. By 1856, the mills no longer appeared on the Jefferson Township map, and no traces of the mills remain today.

Garber interviewed Tom Zigler in Bellville, on August 13, 1949. Zigler said that he had spoken with Ben LeFever, a direct descendant of John LeFever, who told him that there had been a cane mill and that the carding machines had been removed and a water-powered cane mill installed. He also thought that a cider press was also in operation.[85]

Honey Creek Mills

Honey Creek is a small winding feeder stream running south along the present day Honey Creek Road from State Road 13, then east to Stoffer Road and the Gatton Rocks where it joins the Clear Fork. Three mills were once located along Honey Creek, but because of the drop in the water table, none lasted for more than a few years. All three were on the 1856 map but were not on the 1873 map.

In 1821, a man by the name of Cornell built a gristmill "about a half mile below where the creek crosses the Old State Road (Ankneytown Road)." A pottery plant operated in the same location as the Cornell Mill.[86] Johnson Howard built a sawmill on Honey Hill between the two state roads that operated until the early 1870s. Samuel Heron had a mill on the east side of Route 13. He also purchased the Marshall Saw Mill, located about a mile up the central branch of Honey Creek.[87]

Heron's first mill, a gristmill built along what is now State Road 13, was a small mill built of logs and most likely an undershot mill. Located not far from the Johnson Howard sawmill, the Heron Mill was a disaster. Once completed, Heron opened the water flow to the waterwheel, but it did not turn. Heron had his wife "walk the wheel," but the wheel refused to turn, and the mill never went into operation.

Heron had tried to save money by not hiring a competent millwright and instead used house carpenters. A mill has to be built using exact mathematics, balanced correct gearing, and the necessary plan of water power for the wheel. The lack of knowledge on the part of the carpenters led the mill to be a "duster." Word spread to the other mills and especially to the millwrights who were a tight knit group of men who refused to touch it. The mill stood silent for many years.

Later, Calvin Robinson purchased the property, and for several years used the water impounded by the dam for washing sheep. Once washed, shearing had to wait until they were dry. Clean wool was more valuable and brought a better price. Sometime in the late 1880s, Calvin Robinson tore the mill down and used the timber for firewood.[88]

The Greenwood-Crain Grist & Saw Mills

The Greenwood Mill was of particular interest to Garber given that some of the earliest owners were distant ancestors to the Garber family. Anna E. Angust was 91 years old in December 1951 when she was interviewed by Garber. After the war of 1812, her family settled on a portion of Honey Valley along Honey Creek not far from where it merged with the Clear Fork River. According to Anna, there were still Indians in considerable numbers when the family settled into its new home. They soon discovered that the Indians had a hidden site where they dug or mined raw lead in considerable quantity. The Indians told the settlers that the lead was located on Greenwood hill but they would not tell them where. Anna's father, George Angust, told her that he had searched on several occasions but was never able to locate the lead.[89]

The Greenwood Mill was built on the south side of the Clear Fork just west of the present day iron truss bridge at the junction of Gatton Rocks Road. David Phelps, a millwright from New Hampshire, built the mill around 1825-1827. It was one of the earliest mills in that part of the county. A sawmill was probably built first and soon followed by a larger gristmill. Richard and Elmina (Phelps) Oldfield lived there from 1827-1834. Two of their children were born there; Anna on January 25, 1827, and Cordellia on April 17, 1832.

Anna married Lyman Andrews in 1845, and they settled in Bellville on Huron Street. In 1917 Anna wrote a brief history of the Oldfield family entitled "Memories of Long Ago." Peggy Mershon, who writes wonderful articles on local history, was kind enough to send the author a copy. Garber had copious notes on the Greenwood Mill, but Anna's stories were about her family and the conditions in which they lived at the mill when she was young child. She wrote, "Another memory of early days when we were still living in an old cabin with its great fireplace and puncheon floor one cold, windy winter night the fireplace was blown in and we children had to be taken to a neighbor's until Father could rebuild it."[90]

Figure 29. The Greenwood-Crain grist and sawmills were located on present day Stoffer Road across the bridge at the base of the steep, winding hill. The remaining half of the 1816 Greenwood Mill is on the far right. The miller's house that later burned, is on the left. (This post card is from the Garber collection.)

David Phelps transferred the mill to Daniel Leedy in 1838. He did not operate the mill but employed or leased it to others to operate it for him.[91] Jacob Garber told his son, D. W., the story of a man who had drowned when his loaded wagon slipped off the side of the muddy road. He and the wagon went down the steep bank into the Clear Fork River on the road that went from the Bellville Bridge towards the old Fox place and on to Greenwood Mill. Jess Swank, the grandson of Daniel Leedy, told Garber of another accident that involved a wagon that was leaving the Greenwood Mill loaded with heavy barrels of flour. It was a large Conestoga-type wagon pulled by a double team. A bridge had not yet been built, and the team was forced to ford the river. The load was apparently too heavy for the double team, and as the front team scrambled up the bank, the second team was dragged off their feet. Only the skill of the driver prevented the horses from being lost. It was not until March 1883 that the remains of the bridge that had been destroyed previously by a flood was removed. In May 1883, a foot bridge was completed.

Figure 30 and Figure 31. These are sandstone buhrs. Garber photographed them in the late 1940s. The sandstsone buhr in Figure 30 appeared in his book Waterwheels and Millstones, published in 1970. These are primitive stones of rough texture. They measure 23 inches in diameter and are roughly 5 inches thick.

Garber's mother, Maria (Swank) Garber received a letter from Roy Leedy, who wrote to her regarding the Greenwood Mill. Leedy wrote:

> I have this entry in a notebook from Uncle Aaron B. Leedy: 'Grandfather Daniel Leedy bought the Greenwood Mill about 1830 including a quarter section of land. The Mill was built by Daniel Phelps and had nigger head buhrs. Grandfather drove to Pittsburg and brought back French buhrs, and put the mill in good repair. He then made sale and did well in the deal. The two sharpers had grandfather buy back the mill in partner with them but these men cheated him out of all his shares and so involved him in debt that he had to sell some of his land to pay out. He borrowed funds from his brother Abraham Leedy, to hold a prized 160 acres, which he paid back about 1863.[92]

Sometime before 1838, David Phelps sold the mill and mill property to Daniel Leedy, who did not operate the mill himself; but employed or leased the mill to others who operated it. In 1844 Salome Leedy, Daniel's widow, sold or mortgaged the mill property to Jackson and Beach of Bellville. Christian Frederick moved into Jefferson Township in 1856 and assumed control of the Greenwood Mill. Frederick put in both a carding machine and a sawmill.[93]

Shortly after the Civil War, the mill was cut in half – literally down the middle. One half was moved across the river by George Tinkey, who converted the building into an up-and-down sawmill with a cabinet shop and cider press. A large mill, it had two stories above the water line, with one run of buhrs for buckwheat and one for corn meal. Tinkey, a carpenter, built the covered "Pickle Bridge" near Bellville. C. E. "Ed" Crain bought the mill in 1882 and ran it until June 1885 when it burned under mysterious circumstances. Arson was suspected but never proven.

What remained of the 1819 Greenwood Mill stood near the roadside for over a century, the oldest mill in Richland County. The grandfather of Richland County mills came to a sudden end in 1978, when a large tree opposite the mill fell and destroyed the building. Ten years later, in 1988, the ancient miller's home across the road, occupied by the Steven Wade family, was destroyed by fire.

Figure 32. Garber took this photograph in August 1947. It is a flinty granite buhr that was roughly 40 ¾ to 41 inches in diameter and roughly 7 ½ inches thick. Garber believed that once the buhr broke, it was later used as a stepping stone.

Figure 33. The Greenwood Mill was of special interest to Garber since one of his ancestors, David Phelps, built it. This photograph shows what remained of the Greenwood Mill after conversion to a barn. This picture was taken from the hillside.

Feeder Streams in Perry and Jefferson Townships

The Shauck Mills, Perry Township

The Cedar Fork had its beginning west of Johnsville, and its flow increased as it moved through the valley along the present Bellville-Johnsville Road to where it joined the Clear Fork just west of Bellville seven miles away. John Shauck was one of the earliest settlers in what became Perry Township. He came from York County, Pennsylvania, and bought nearly all of section five (636 acres) in Perry Township on December 13, 1811, for $1,119.37. Shauck was one of the eleven men who organized Perry Township in 1816. He served as a Major in the Pennsylvania militia and when he left Pennsylvania, he followed an Indian trail to his new land. By the 1820s, his sawmill, the first one on Cedar Fork was in operation, and in 1844 his son, Elah Shauck, added the gristmill.

These Shauck mills were a considerable undertaking. A headrace, nearly a mile in length, brought water from the small stream that was the beginning of the Cedar Fork branch. The water reached the sawmill before the gristmill that was on higher ground above the marshy valley.

In the late 1860s, Samuel Wagner and his brother were in a merchandising partnership, Wagner and Brother in Johnsville. They retired from that business in 1879 and became sole owners of the Shauck Mills. They purchased a one-third interest in the mills in 1873, an additional third in 1874, and they completed the purchase of the property in 1876. As a result, they owned a gristmill, sawmill, two dwellings, and eight acres of land. By 1876 the gristmill, originally built in 1844, was run by steam power. It had three runs of buhrs and ample room for merchandise and storage.[94] Interviewed by Garber in August 1947, Mrs. Charles Sowers told him, "Elah Shauck,

Henry Shauck, and Charles and Arthur Shauck ran the mill until they went bankrupt. A local group purchased the mill and Frank Keifer ran it until it burned sometime in either 1906 or 1907."[95]

Figure 34. This photograph was taken around 1900. The man in the buggy on the far left was Jim Bishop. On the step is Ben Perry, fireman for the mill; Frank Keifer, miller, is in the doorway; in the wagon with his 8-year-old daughter, Daisy Reed, is teamster John Reed. The mill, together with the adjacent sawmill, burned on January 13, 1907. The mill was originally water-powered, but as the land was cleared, the water table dropped, and a steam engine was added to supplement power during the dry season.

Life at a mill could be dangerous for those who lived there and those who went to the mill on business, including the children who played nearby. One such "close" call was reported in the *Bellville Star* on July 17, 1884.

> A little daughter of Mr. Judd's fell in the mill-race last Tuesday at Shauck's mill and came very close to drowning. She with a little associate was playing at the water and fell in. The other child who is about four years old gave the alarm, and her companion was rescued after sinking the third time. It was thought that life at first was extinct, and had it not been for the timely arrival of Lee Richardson who was in the cemetery near by, and heard their scream, she would never have been resuscitated.[96]

The Eby Grist Mill

Located on the east side of Algire Road a short distance south of the bridge at the intersection of Mock Road was the Eby Mill. The mill, built in 1837, remained in operation for thirty-seven years. Mr. Roy Thuma, in 1947, owner of the old Eby farm, met with Garber on May 1st that year and pointed out the location of the mill. Nothing remained of the building and only a depression where the mill once stood could be found. The location of the millpond that fed and stored water for the mill was evident. Today it is located across the street from where the mill originally stood. The mill office, torn down many years ago, was a small building with hand-hewn support beams inside, and probably had been an integral part of the mill itself.[97] The millpond and headrace are now farm fields. Eby Run, the small stream on which the mill was located, emptied into the Cedar Fork further south.

Corbett's Saw Mill, Grist Mill, and Woolen Factory

The water for the Corbett Mills, located on the east side of Algire Road just north of Bellville-Johnsville Road, came from two branches of the Cedar Fork. The main branch to the north was dammed and water diverted into the smaller south stream to provide greater volume to the head of the mill. The mill building remained at its original location until torn down in the 1950s. The first building on the Corbett site was a sawmill built in 1830 by Thomas Phillips. In 1835, a gristmill was added. In 1848, Mr. Frairie purchased the mill and installed a carding machine and general woolen machinery in 1849. John Corbett took possession in 1876.[98]

Corbett was born in Clarion County, Pennsylvania, on April 28, 1830. He left there in 1850 and moved to Columbus, Ohio. He worked in Delaware County as a carpenter. In 1876, he moved to Richland County where he managed the Perry Woolen Mills for the next twelve years.[99] The Perry Mill ceased operations around 1888. Around that time Corbett relocated to Lexington, Ohio,

Figure 35. The Corbett Mill was located on Cedar Fork, a branch of the Clear Fork River.

Figure 36. Photo of the Corbett Mill taken from the opposite end.

where he again worked as a carpenter. Up until 1888, the Perry Mill manufactured cashmere, blankets, sati nets, flannel, and stocking yarn. By 1888, the mill could no longer compete with the larger, more efficient eastern manufacturing businesses moving into the area. After the equipment was removed, the old mill was used as a barn.

The Hanawalt Grist Mill

This mill was located in Perry Township at the junction of present day State Route 546 and the Bellville-Johnsville roads. Originally, it was on the north side of the Cedar Fork just east of the present bridge. After the mill closed in 1906, it was relocated, and today it is one of only two water-powered mills remaining in Richland County. In January 1812, John Frederick Herron purchased the northeast quarter of section eleven (160 acres) for $316.00 or $2.00 per acre. It was a choice piece of land in a fertile valley. Herron made improvements that increased the land's value by building a mill. He hired Peter Weirwick to do carpenter work while he went to Baltimore to procure millstones. The mill was a log-cabin mill and the machinery consisted of a "waterwheel, shaft, and master wheel which articulated with a trundle-head that ran the stone. The gearing was made of wood."[100]

Francis Baughman purchased the quarter section of land where the Herron Mill stood in 1833. His son Francis and his wife arrived in Richland County and moved into a log house near the mill. The Baughman family lived in that home for several years and ran the mill until 1833 when John Hanawalt purchased it. He arrived in Perry that year.[101] After purchasing the mill, then known as the Herron Mill, Hanawalt tore it down and built a frame mill the following year. Two runs of buhrs and a corn crusher were installed. That mill was destroyed in a fire on March 20, 1855, but by the fall of 1856 a new mill was in operation.[102]

Hanawalt was well liked in his community and active in local affairs. After the Civil War, he actively supported The National Grange of the Order of Patrons of Husbandry, a new, fraternal organization that promoted the economics and political well-being of the community and agriculture. Hanawalt was a charter member of the Richland Grange, and he added a second story to his home to serve as a meeting place by the Grange membership.[103]

Levi Heiple, a well-known millwright, married Leah Ann Hanawalt, on September 23, 1857. With the exception of six or seven years, the Heiple family lived on the Hanawalt property. Levi took over management of the mill when John Hanawalt relinquished the day-to-day running to him. The mill remained in the Hanawalt family until 1906, when Levi Heiple and his wife sold their property and moved to Oklahoma to be near their children.

For seventy-three years, the Hanawalt mill stayed within the family. Once the mill changed ownership, it was moved across the road and up on a hill, where it served as a barn for many years. Jack Gleckner and his family bought the barn in 1953 and converted into a home. They sold the house to Mark and Barb Berry, who remodeled it in 1981.

Figure 37. This barn was originally the Hanawalt Mill. As of May 1947, Garber stated that the "old mill building was in an excellent state of preservation."

Figure 38. The Hanawalt Mill is one of only three mill buildings left in old Richland County. Eventually it was remodeled and made into a home.

Throughout Garber's notes pertaining to the Baughman Mill, there was also much information related to John Chapman, better known as Johnny Appleseed. According to the Baughmans, Johnny Appleseed had an early nursery "down in the lot by the spring run."[104] Appleseed had planted his nurseries before the Richland lands were sold and was present from time to time to sell seedlings to the arriving settlers. There is little doubt that the Herron and Baughman families knew Johnny Appleseed, whose scattered nurseries covered a wide area of Ohio, especially along the forks of the Mohican River. He generally planted his apple seeds in the fertile ground of a river valley. The Baughmans planted an orchard from seedlings purchased from Johnny. The "spring run" was within easy walking distance just east of the Herron-Baughman-Hanawalt mill and emptied into the Cedar Fork.

The Baughmans improved their fruit by grafting, a process not approved of by Appleseed. Many of the early farm orchards in the county owe their origins to this simple, kind, and eccentric

Figure 39. The Hanawalt Grist Mill (in center) was photographed in the 1880s. In 1951 Mrs. Dora (Bowers) McDaniel identified Curt Gross on the left with the shovel and Gene Rinehart. The boys fishing off the bridge are unidentified. The mill was later moved after it closed.

Figure 40. Millrace for Hanawalt Mill. The dam, not seen in this picture, was located almost directly to the right of the point from where the picture was taken. Photograph taken by Garber in May 1947.

wanderer. The headrace for the Baughman-Hanawalt Mill was a long one and could be seen over the bank along Baughman Road. Garber photographed the millrace, still visible today through the thick brush and trees that line the road.[105]

Shafer Saw and Oil Mill

Little is known of the Frederick Shafer Mills that are located between the Cedar Fork and the Bellville-Johnsville Road just a short distance east of the Mill Run Road intersection. According to tax records, the mills operated from the late 1830s until sometime before the Civil War. The millsite was marked on the *1856 Richland County Map* but not on the 1873 edition. It is not known why it ceased operation. Like many of the pioneer mills, it may have fallen victim to floods, fire, or it was simply abandoned. No information on Shafer or his mills is found in Garber's notes. Several mills in southern Perry Township were on streams that meandered in a southern direction to the North Fork or Owl Creek, ultimately arriving at the Kokosing River.

Worthington Township

The Myers-Kanaga-Plank Mill

Upon completion of the American Revolution, the frontier quickly moved westward to the Ohio River. Border counties were rapidly settled by migrations to the Northwest Territory. Encouraged by the enactment of the Ordinance of 1787 as well as by the added security of Major General Anthony Wayne's successful campaign against the Indians in 1794, the number of settlers moving west surged. This rapid increase in settlers and the cultivation of the land resulted in a growing demand for skilled craftsmen. Among those especially needed were millwrights and millers.[106]

Figure 41. Jacob Myers Sr.

Jacob Myers, born in Northumberland County, Pennsylvania on Sunday, August, 11, 1782, was the son of Frederick and Elizabeth Wrick. He grew up in the atmosphere of the mill, the millrace, the constant sound of water tumbling over the waterwheel, and the hum and vibration from the millstones. His earliest recollections were of those of mill activities. At the age of twenty one, on January 5, 1804, he was married to Sara Coleman, daughter of John Coleman, in Belmont County, Ohio. His understanding and familiarity of how a mill operated served him well. Following his marriage, he worked as a miller. His was an exacting trade, and he was called upon regularly to repair a water mill, a head gate, dress millstones, make a new cog for a wooden gear, or replace broken flights in an elevator—tasks that often required the ingenuity of a millwright. By 1815, he was a confident, experienced millwright and miller whose services were often in demand.

Casper Langal of Columbiana County, Ohio, planned to build a mill on land he owned on Apple Creek in

Wayne County, Ohio. An ambitious man of considerable consequence, he journeyed to Belmont County and met with Jacob Myers. He arranged for Myers to build a mill on Apple Creek. With title to several hundred acres of land on the Clear Fork of the Mohican River in Richland County, Langal proposed a transfer of some of his land on the Clear Fork to Jacob Myers, in exchange for the construction of both a sawmill and a gristmill on Apple Creek.

Myers spent time at both the Apple Creek location and on the Clear Fork, surveying millsites and estimating the millwright problems involved in Langal's proposal. Myers signed the agreement on July 10, 1816. This agreement marked a turning point in the fortunes of Jacob Myers and his family. The Apple Creek sawmill was completed by December 1, 1817, and lumber produced was used in the construction of the gristmill. Building the sawmill first and then the gristmill was the normal process in developing a mill enterprise on the frontier.

The building of the gristmill was a more complicated procedure than the building of a sawmill. It was the real test of a millwright. *The Young MillWright and Miller's Guide* by Oliver Evens was the primary source of instruction of the miller; but it was only a guide. The millwright developed his ability and his reputation through experience and by solving the many problems that inevitably occurred. Myers delivered his completed mill to Langal on December 1, 1818, the agreed upon date. The Langal Mill was 2 stories high and 30 by 26 feet, and it was a monument to Myers's workmanship. Upon completion of the Langal Mill and when it was running, Myers turned his attention to building his mill on the Clear Fork.

Figure 42. Myers-Kanaga-Plank Mill.

The bottomlands of Richland County, along the Forks of the Mohican, equaled any land in the state for richness and the growing of crops. The countryside was heavily timbered when the Myers family arrived. The hill across the creek was covered with dense hardwood forest. Wintergreen Hill, rolling off to the south and west, was colorful with dogwood, sassafras, spruce, and hemlock that provided the timber needed for the construction of a mill.

There was not, however, a satisfactory water supply for household use except from wells dug by the Myers family. Almost directly across from the mill, a cold spring flowed from the base of a large rock ledge. To access this stream, it was necessary to ford the creek that was shallow enough for the women to wade across when the weather was good. They would often do their washing in the shade of the overhanging trees. On the hillside above the spring was an orchard planted by Johnny Appleseed, and as late as 1915, a few of the original trees, gnarled and broken with deep roots and enormous trunks, were still bearing fruit.

Myers Mill was a large one, by far the largest on the forks of the Mohican at the time of its completion in 1819. It measured 45 by 45 feet with 2 ½ stories above a full basement where machinery and other equipment were stored. To obtain the needed water power to run the mill, Myers built a dam across the Clear Fork, about one-eighth of a mile upstream. The gristmill waterwheel was six feet in diameter and eight feet wide, and the main shaft was octagonal and twenty-four inches in diameter.

Figure 43. Myers-Kanaga-Plank Mill Dam.

At the time Myers constructed his mill, only the north branch of the Clear Fork provided sufficient water for all immediate demands. A few rods west of the mill lay a large island containing three to four acres of fine bottomland. It divided the Clear Fork into two streams of equal volume that rejoined almost directly back of the mill.

Myers Mill was the center of community activities, and as Myers' business expanded, it became necessary to operate day and night. Too often he was unable to operate the mill the needed number of hours because of insufficient water power. As a result, he purchased the water rights and privileges on his land from his neighbor, John Gatton. Myers then built a second dam upstream near the head of the island. Erected in 1831, the additional dam forced water into the north channel and into the millrace, significantly increasing the water power available.

As protection against spring floods, Myers diverted the millrace, which was one-quarter of a mile in length, northeast for some distance away from the creek. There was a twelve-foot head of water for operation of the gristmill with its four runs of stones and the up-and-down mulay sawmill. Located west of the gristmill in a separate building was the sawmill that operated independently of the gristmill. Dual gates controlled the diversion of water to either or both mills as needed.

The delays caused by the diversions occurred because of the demands on the mill, but they afforded an opportunity for the exchange of news and information on the progress in the nearby settlements. Myers built a blacksmith shop a few rods north of the mill and built additional houses for use of the blacksmith and for a miller, whose services were required in the busy season. Bed and board was always available for the itinerant traveler or for the farmer delayed, pending his turn at the mill.

By the early 1830s, Jacob Myers was quite successful and highly respected within his community. A deeply religious man, he became interested in the newly found Mormon Church, and he converted to Mormonism sometime in 1833. By September 1833, Myers had become "the presiding elder in the Worthington branch, with 24 members in good standing."[107] Church records reveal that on January 29, 1834, Myers was baptized into the Church and subsequent records show that he was ordained an Elder while attending a Church conference on July 6, 1835.[108]

Figure 44. The wheel may have been as tall as eight feet. The men are standing in front of the flume head gate. Note that the buckets that would have been attached to the wheel are missing, indicating that the photograph was taken shortly before the mill was torn down in 1947.

The Mormon Church did not sit well with area Protestant congregations as they began losing members to the Mormons. Local ministers pounded their pulpits, condemning Joseph Smith, the Book of Mormons, and the whole Latter-day Saints movement. Myers faced much criticism and loss of longtime customers at his mills; but he remained committed to his new Church and, when Joseph Smith issued a call for all Mormons to gather in Missouri, Myers heeded that call. He sold his mills and captained a wagon train west.[109]

Figure 45. There were two sources of water power, one for the gristmill and one for the sawmill. This is one of the gates used to control the water in the headrace or possibly for draining the headrace. The stream behind it appears to be the headrace rather than the Clear Fork.

Figure 46. This is a photograph of one of the two timber milldams. The ends of the logs and the wood deck on the right side extend into the stream. Mr. Garber took these photographs in the late 1940s.

Figure 47. Elam Plank and his wife Mary. Elam operated the mill with various partners from 1883 until his death in 1911.

Figure 48. The Myers-Kanaga-Plank Grist Mill was located outside Butler on Route 97. This 1900-era picture shows the road bridge over the forebay at the entrance to the mill. The entrance to the present day bridge on Route 97 passes over the millsite.

Myers sold his mill in March 1834 to Joseph Kanaga of Newville, Cumberland County, Pennsylvania. Kanaga arrived on horseback carrying $10,500 in cash and took over his new venture. He successfully operated and maintained the Myers Mills, known as the Kanaga Mills until his death in April 1843. Following his death, his wife leased it for several years until their son, Israel, took over the operation and, with the aid of a miller, ran it for the next ten years.

In 1862 Jonathan Plank purchased a half interest in the mill from Israel Kanaga and, eventually after a couple of partner changes, bought the entire mill. He and his son, Elam A. Plank ran the mill until Jonathan retired in 1884. Elam, with a variety of partners who came and went, continued to run the mill until he died in March, 1911. During the Plank ownership, the mill was known as Plank Mill. It enjoyed a good business reputation and a loyal customer base but faced stiff competition from the Rummel Mill south of Butler and the Greenwood Mill, located upstream from them.

In April 1904, a terrible flood hit the Clear Fork Valley. The covered bridge at the mill was swept from its foundation and carried downstream with such force that the B & O railroad bridge was knocked two feet from its abutment. The mill flooded, as did three other mills nearby, with up to three feet of water.

There were several owners and operators over the next ten years; but the mill had been idle for quite some time when George Craft, in 1922, placed it back into service for a new owner,

Figure 49. Two major floods, the first in 1903 and the other in 1913, did considerable damage in the Clear Fork Valley. This photograph shows the damage to the headrace. The 1913 flood took out the bridge in front of the mill.

Mr Evans from Ross County. In 1925 Croft bought the mill and ran it until April 1942 when he sold it to George Neal. Neal would be the last owner. He ran the mill until March 11, 1944, when a major flood washed out the lower dam. Jacob Myers had built it well; but its time had finally come, and the 123-year-old mill was abandoned.[110]

The Myers-Kanaga-Plank Mill was a favorite of Garber. He often stayed with his grandparents for various periods as a boy, and he spent hours playing in and around the mill. His grandparents lived on a farm next to the mill, and he often told his friends and family members of those treasured memories. He fondly recalled how he and his childhood friends walked across the Clear Fork on stilts and climbed the hillside above the mill to "steal" a few apples from an orchard planted from seedlings from Johnny Appleseed, an orchard known locally as the "Appleseed orchard."[111]

The Miller Saw Mill

The history of the Miller Saw Mill is somewhat vague and confusing. Built in Independence, Ohio, (later renamed Butler), it is shown on the 1856 county map just across the bridge on present day Route 95 at the edge of Butler on the east side of the road and the north side of the Clear Fork.

According to a brief announcement in *The Richland Star* on April 11, 1878, "Martin Miller's saw-mill burned to the ground last Tuesday evening, caused by two much fire after sawing that day." The mill was rebuilt, and in a brief report in *The Richland Star* on April 10, 1879, it was announced that, "Martin Miller had his sawmill in operation again. He has added water power."

The Butler Axe Handle Company evolved from the Miller Saw Mill, and later it became the Richland Handle Company.[112] No photographs of either Miller's Mill or the Butler Ax Handle Factory have been found. Figures 50 and 51 are of the Richland Handle Company.

Figure 50 and Figure 51. These photographs of the Richland Handle Company were taken sometime between 1909 and 1919. Steam had replaced water power then, and the smokestack can be seen in the far left in Figure 50. Two of Mr. Garber's brothers and a sister worked at the plant for short periods. (Photos provided by the Butler-Clear Fork Historical Society.)

The Rummel Mill

The Rummel Mill was located about a mile northeast of Butler just off State Route 95 on Benedict Road. Garber often referred to the Rummel Mill as an "infant mill" because it was the last water-powered mill built in Richland County. David J. Rummel purchased the land along the Clear Fork in 1850 from Jacob Armentrout, who had built a sawmill there in the 1840s. Rummel saw an opportunity at that location because the Sandusky, Mansfield, and Newark Railroad was to be built through Independence (later known as Butler). A sawmill was needed to produce the lumber necessary to construct a gristmill, and Rummel believed that the coming railroad would open a market for shipping flour.

Figure 52. This photograph of Rummel Mill was taken before 1890 when it was still powered by a waterwheel nearly 20 feet in diameter. It was housed in the small addition on the right side. The covered bridge on the left was replaced in 1909.

In 1853, Rummel, who came from a family of millwrights, built a huge 33 by 42 foot, 4-story building with a basement at the river end. A nearly 20-foot waterwheel powered three sets of buhrs that gave the mill a 40-barrel a day capacity and offered a variety of products. A low dam and nearly one-thousand-foot-long mill headrace carried water to both mill wheels. Rummel prospered, and his mill was well received.

A separate cooper shop for the manufacture of wooden barrels stood just north of the sawmill,

Figure 53. Garber took this picture of the cooper shop in August 1947.

across the road and sluice bridge. Garber noted that the shop did not have a water-power connection but was a separate industry connected with the early operation of the mill. With its up-and-down blade, the shop was kept busy as the operation often ran twenty-four hours a day in peak seasons.

Milling was not without its problems, however, and inevitably there were setbacks. The Clear Fork River regularly flooded, causing water damage that sometimes reached the first floor. At other times there would be a shortage of water. In 1879, low water and a broken wheel shut the mill down for repairs. In September 1880, the peak season for the mill, it was reported that "A piece of floating timber found its way into the waterwheel of Rummel's Mill, stopping the machinery suddenly and doing considerable damage."[113] Each of the rotating millstones weighed nearly a half ton or more and could not be quickly halted without tearing the wooden gearing to pieces.[114]

Figure 54. This photograph of one of the two mill dams for the Rummel Mill was taken by Garber in August 1947. It was a well-made concrete structure. Little remains of it today. Periodic floods have erased most millsites and dams all along the Clear Fork.

Despite difficulties of an unpredictable nature, Rummel was a successful millwright and miller. By 1879, he shipped railroad carloads of flour to Baltimore, in addition to that sold locally in Ohio. Crown Jewel flour, wheatlet, germ, and gluten flours were the main products produced, but the mill also ground corn, oats, barley, and rye. By the late 1890s, the Crown Jewel brand was shipped in large quantities, and hired help was needed at the two Rummel mills and the cooperage.

Although the Rummel family retained ownership for many years, they rented out the mill on occasion. For example, in the May 7, 1885, issue of *The Bellville Star* it was announced that

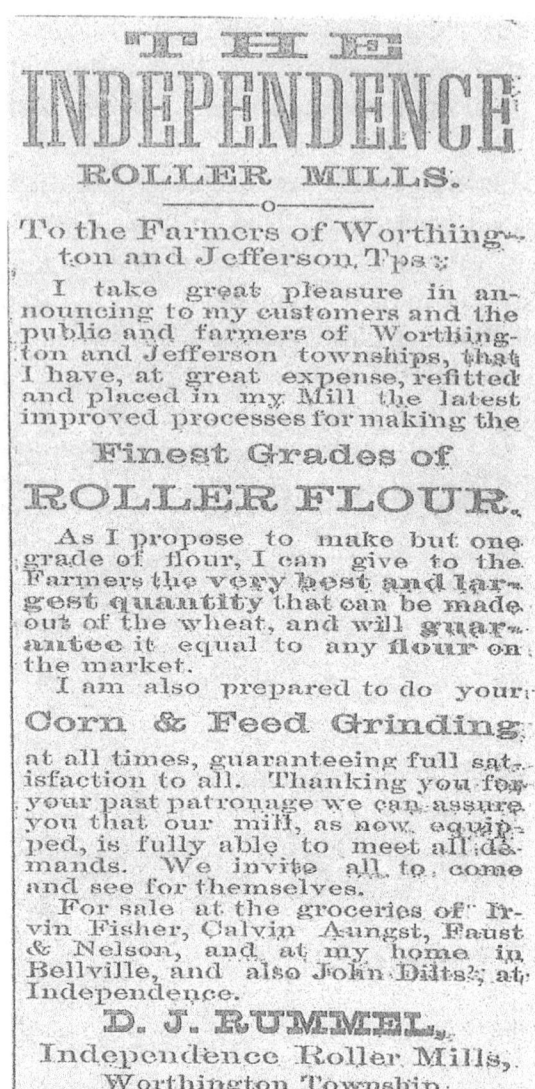

Figure 55. Advertisement for the Rummel Mill in the Butler Enterprise on Dec. 4, 1890.

Figure 56. Undated photograph of O.B. Rummel and his wife.

"J. H. Weigel, an experienced miller from the Hoosier State, has obtained control of the flouring mill of D. J. Rummel, below Independence."[115] And, in a subsequent issue, *The Bellville Star* stated, "Mr. J. H. Wiegel, who has rented the Rummel mill near this place is giving good satisfaction with his work."[116]

David J. Rummel retired from the mill and spent his last years in Bellville. His son Orlandus B. Rummel took over management of the mill and ownership after his father's death in 1903. In 1890, Orlandus (often addressed as O.B.) updated the mill equipment and replaced the wooden waterwheel with two turbines.

O. B. Rummel's personal life certainly had its ups and downs. He and his wife, Mary E. Garber (married November 24, 1867) had five children. At some time during his marriage, O.B. became involved with Hattie McClelland; the Rummel housekeeper who lived in the mill for many years. O.B. had no trouble living part time at the mill with Hattie. Discreetness was not a part of their relationship, and Hattie on occasion would accompany O.B. into Butler where they no doubt caused more than a few eyebrows to be raised and tongues to wag. Divorce was still relatively scarce in those days. Mary and O.B. reconciled, at least before the public, after he purchased her a rather large diamond ring.[117]

For a while, G. P. Blystone and O. B. Rummel were partners, but O. B. later regained full ownership. Val McClelland, brother of Hattie McClelland, O. B.'s mistress, either rented or owned the mill for a brief period. In 1908, Stitzel & Nau of Loudonville, Ohio, purchased the Rummel Flouring Mill at Butler, and Ed Stitzel operated it.[118] By the end of 1915, Ed Stitzel, then the sole owner, sold the mill to S. L. Myers.[119] In a letter sent Garber by Hal McCune on March 2, 1981, he wrote: "Walter Eisenbach was the last to operate the mill, then under the name O'Shannon Mill. This was during the Depression and it only served as a feed mill. It ceased operation in 1933, due to a lack of customers."[120]

Doctor Benedict then purchased the property and lived in the mill house across the bridge. During his ownership, Dr. Benedict hooked up a generator to one of the two turbines and generated part of his electricity. Because of World War II and labor shortages, Benedict put off building maintenance, and the mill began to show its age. The basement end near the Clear Fork began to settle in the 1880s, and the mill was reinforced. Floods between 1890 and 1913 further weakened the supports and damaged the bridge next to the mill.

In 1974, Marge Metcalf, who then owned the property, hired Amish workers to repair the building, but little was done after the initial work. A new owner, Evan Adams, tried unsuccessfully to have the mill placed on the National Register of Historic Places; and with the help of the Butler-Clear Fork Historical Society, he organized a volunteer group to clean up the building. Despite

Figure 57. This second floor shows the clutter after the mill had stopped operation. The bin at the rear center was the hopper for bran. The hopper bin to the left was for "middlings" and to fill sacks. The hard-to-see shaft through the floor with the wheel on top in the rear was the water control for the turbine. The round can near the front hanging from the shaft held the handmade RPM meter, and the chute front left fed bran roughage into a feed grinder.

Figure 58. This photograph of the fourth floor of the Rummel Mill was a maze of elevators (vertical box-like enclosures), chutes to lower floors and the top head gearing of the mill elevator. Whole and ground grain from the first floor were lifted to storage bins on upper floors and fed by gravity to the shipping and milling equipment below.

these efforts, flood waters on July 2, 1987, again reached the first floor, destroying all that had been accomplished in the efforts to clean up and restore the mill.

In 2003, the weakened foundation gave way, and the wall nearest the bridge collapsed, exposing the grain elevators and equipment. Later, part of the roof collapsed leaving half of the mill standing. Still later, a controlled fire and a bull dozer completed the destruction of the Rummel Mill. Along with the Myers-Kanaga-Plank Mill, the Rummel Mill had a long, productive history in Richland County, and like so many treasures of the past; its memory is rapidly fading. Much of the original mill equipment was donated to the Wolf Creek/Pine Run Grist Mill restoration project near Loudonville, Ohio, where it can be seen today.

Old pictures of the mill show the covered bridge that crossed the Clear Fork at the millsite. A number of covered bridges still standing at various locations in the county were lost in the flood of 1904. The big covered bridge at Rummel's Mill, originally built by Albert Rummel, was sold to Atho Simmons, who removed it and replaced it with a smaller iron structure that crossed the Cler Fork to the sawmill.

Figure 59. This post card of the Rummel Mill and the covered bridge were a gift to Garber from his brother Clark M. Garber.

Figure 60. As seen here, Rummel Mill died a slow death over many years.

Garber in a letter to Carter on January 9, 1978, wrote:

> The pre-1913 picture of the Rummel Mill is a treasure. Perhaps I have told you in the past but when I was a boy, perhaps eleven or twelve, my father sent me to this old mill on horseback with a sack of corn to be ground. The number of times I visited this mill prior to 1913, when the covered bridge washed away, would be difficult to estimate, but it too was lost in the 1904 flood."[121]

The Zimmerman Powder Mill

Samuel Lewis, the first settler in Worthington Township, established his home in the northwest quarter of Section 1. It was Lewis, who in the spring to 1818, built the first blockhouse used for protection of settlers against roaming Indians. Peter Zimmerman, one of the first five pioneers in Worthington Township, settled on the northwest quarter of Section 16 and built the first powder mill on the Clear Fork. Gun powder was essential to survival on the frontier. Not only was it necessary to secure food; but without it, settlers were vulnerable to Indian depredations and rogue whites who sought to gain money the easy way. Because of the need for powder on the frontier, Zimmerman created a successful business.[122]

Details on the Zimmerman Powder Mill are scarce. Records show that the mill was located in Section 16, which was reserved for school lands by the county. Yearly rental proceeds supported the schools in the township. His mill was located on the Clear Fork south of the Butler-Newville Road. Although Garber did not cite his source, he did make the following notes: "The Zimmerman Powder Mill was doubtless an undershot or tub mill. It was located at the site of the dam for the Herring-Calhoun-Files-Gilliland Mill a quarter mile further downstream. There was no millrace for the Zimmerman Mill, the power being taken direct from the dam."[123] In all likelihood the Zimmerman Mill was a log mill and when it went down is not known. It did not function for many years and quite possibly may have fallen victim to one of the annual floods or a fire.

The Winchester Mills

There are a few people still living around Butler and Worthington Township areas who still refer to the town of Winchester as being "just down the road." Garber did considerable research on the history of Winchester, the mills, and the people who lived in the valley. Winchester was located northeast of Butler, just off Route 95 where the Butler-Newville Road crosses the Clear Fork. The town was on the east side of the Clear Fork, and the mills on the west side. Today, the only house still standing where the Winchester Mill had been is across from the present bridge at that site.

Figure 61. Although not dated, this early photograph of Winchester shows the mill on one side of the Clear Fork and the "town" on the other side. Not much remained of Winchester at the time of this photograph.

Garber's research on the Winchester Mills appeared as the first article he wrote for the *Mansfield News Journal* in May of 1956, entitled "Calhoun Grist Mill Tragedy Nearly Repeated in Razing." It was Noble Calhoun Sr. who founded Winchester and laid out the town. Christian Wise, born in 1810 in Baltimore, Maryland, was a well-educated pioneer teacher. He was active

Figure 62. The Winchester mill was 40 x 60 x 52 feet high and was thought to be one of the largest frame buildings in Richland County at one time. At the time of this photograph, the building was used as a barn.

in the Dunkard Church, where he served as Bishop for several years. He was also the Surveyor of Richland County for twenty years, and it was he who surveyed the town. On April 2, 1845, he received ten dollars for "laying out the town of Winchester."[124]

Noble Calhoun Sr. was an experienced miller. He, John Herring and Jacob Manner were co-owners of the Winchester Mill, each having a third interest. John Herring's interest was probably in lieu of payment for having helped construct the mills; which began in 1842. John, Jacob, and David Herring, sons of John Frederick Herring, founder of Newville, Ohio, were all partners at various times and all apparently participated in construction of the mills. Between 1844 and 1847, the mills operated under the name Calhoun & Company.[125]

Baughman, in his 1908 *History of Richland County*, wrote that the mills built in Winchester, known as Calhoun's Mills, included a gristmill, sawmill and a carding and fulling mill. The land on the west side of the Clear Fork, where the mills were, was too rough and uneven for a town site. The town was actually platted on the east side of the Clear Fork where at least six houses were built. Among the businesses that sprang up were a general merchandise store, a blacksmith shop, a cooper shop, a shoe shop, and a weaver's shop.[126]

David Herring and his wife purchased the property where the Zimmerman Powder Mill had been located, near the town of Winchester but further upstream. When Herring purchased the land, the powder mill no longer existed; but the dam that Zimmerman built was still there and was used by Herring to provide the water needed to power the large sawmill and woolen factory that he built.[127]

At the time the mill was built, it was the largest framed building in Richland County. David Herring, John Frederick Herring's youngest son, built the Winchester mills in 1840 and ran them for several years. A carpenter named Clapper, from Newville, was married with a family of seven children. He was employed to help in the building of the various mills in Winchester. Considered an excellent carpenter, one day he reported to work intoxicated and careless. Somehow, he caught his head under a heavy beam as it lowered into place on the east side of the building. The beam came down with such force that it crushed Clapper's skull and his brains squirted into the trail race below.[128]

Herring shipped part of his products by flat boats launched from Perrysville or Loudenville. They drifted down the Mohican River to the Ohio River, then to the Mississippi River and, eventually to New Orleans, where they sold their goods. On the return trip, Herring sailed to New York, where he bought needed goods and then returned to Winchester via the Erie Canal, Lake Erie, and finally by stagecoach or wagon. It was a lengthy, risky trip but profitable. Herring got into financial trouble when he cosigned a large note for a friend who could not pay; leaving Herring with the debt. In an effort to save his mills, Herring shipped flour to a firm in Detroit where he arranged for them to retain their payments to him until his last shipment of flour had arrived. Once that final shipment was paid for, Herring planned to draw the whole amount being held in his name to pay off the debt. Unfortunately, the Detroit company went bankrupt and Herring lost everything.[129]

In 1856 the mill was converted from a gristmill to a woolen mill. In the years that followed, there were a number of owners and partnerships. S. Clapper & Co. purchased the

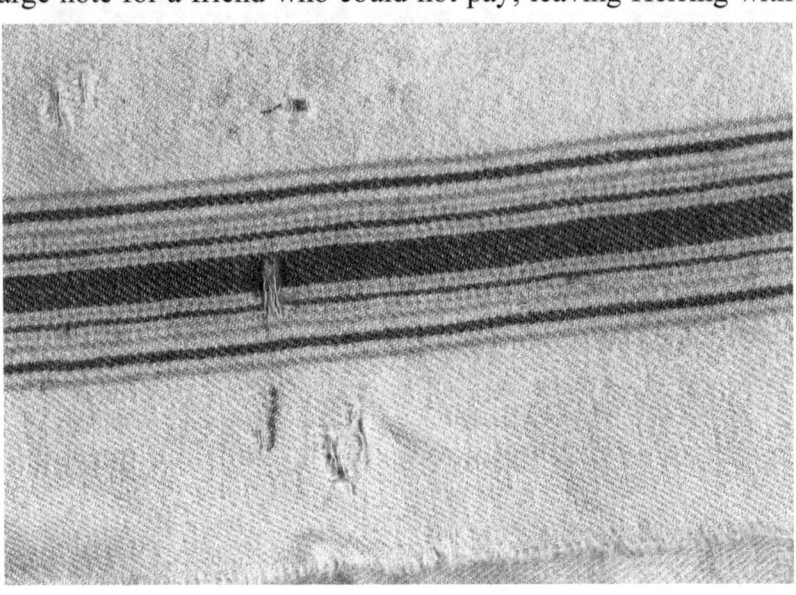

Figure 63. The Butler-Clear Fork Valley Historical Society provided the photograph of this wool blanket produced by the Winchester Mill. The mill turned out numerous cloth products from local grown wool. When in operation, the mill employed a number of young women. It ceased operation in 1890.

Herring Mill in the summer of 1868 and changed the name to Eagle Woolen Mills. They advertised that they were open for business in the June 10, 1868, issue of *The Mansfield Herald*.[130] By 1873, ownership had passed to John Files. Files advertised in the *Bellview Dollar Weekly* that they were producing "Cloths, Flannels, Jeans, Cassimere, Blankets, Yarns, and all kinds of Woolen Goods."[131]

In June of 1878, the partnership of Alexander and Zent bought the mill. They retained ownership of the mill until 1883. That year, the Gilliland Brothers took ownership and announced in *The Bellville Star* in June that they were "now ready to buy wool and do custom work."[132] They intended to run the mill to its full capacity and the brothers sought to increase the size of their business by constructing a large building that would support their mill. They sought community support and local funding, but they were unsuccessful.[133] Neither Bellville nor Independence could raise the necessary funds needed to upgrade the mill.[134]

Despite this setback, the Gilliland brothers continued operations. They employed 10 to 12 people; but by 1890 the mill ceased operation. Deroscus L. Calhoun became the new owner. His son, Homer, in an interview with Garber in June of 1949, stated that after the mill closed, he helped pack the mill equipment and ship it from Butler, Ohio, to Wisconsin, where it was installed in a woolen mill there.

With the equipment removed, the mill served as a barn for nearly 50 years. For a short time there was some thought of turning the property into a skating rink; but the location was too remote and the idea quickly dropped.[135] In March 1884, Thomas Hannon purchased the woolen factory on the west side of the Clear Fork.[136] Hannon lived in Winchester, and in June 1884, he sold his

Winchester home to T. E. Mix. Mix disassembled the house, moved it to Bellville, and reassembled it on the lot, which became known as the Mix property. With the relocation of the Hannon home, only one house remained in Winchester.[137]

Garber interviewed Mr. and Mrs. Floyd Norris, owners of the property upon which the mill stood in August 1947. According to Mr. Norris, the mill was built in 1840. Officials making a survey in the area of Pleasant Hill Dam determined that the mill was 40 x 60 feet and stood 52 feet high. There was also an up-and-down sawmill near the main woolen building. Both were water powered from the same millrace. Mrs. Norris stated that the gristmill ceased operation because the flour and meal picked up the scent of the wool.[138]

A storehouse was built and managed in connection with the mill. In 1947, it was still in its original location, but had been converted to a dance hall for old-fashioned square and round dances that were held under Mr. Norris's direction. These dances were held often during good weather. At the west end of the hall a nigger-head buhr had been placed in the ground as a stepping stone for the entrance to the building. The stains from the Clapper tragedy could be seen as long as the mill was still standing. One of Noble Calhoun's descendants showed it to Garber.[139]

Garber interviewed Homer Calhoun and Mrs. Cora Stull on June 14, 1949. Mrs. Stull worked at the woolen mill for eight years from 1879 to 1887, from the age of 15 to 23, until she got married. Her co-workers included Ida Smith, who later married Charley Gilliland. Ida was a helper on the spooling. Mina Greer ran a spooling machine. Cora Smith married John Shoemaker who also ran a spooling machine. Cora Fike married a Stull who ran three carding machines. John Fry ran a spinner. John, Austin, and Charley Gilliland were employed where needed. John worked wherever needed and helped in supervision. Austin was a dyer, and Charlie did trucking and hauling and helped inside as needed. Their father was the boss.[140]

Mrs. Stull also commented on how her work was "real work." Her hours were from 7 a.m. to 6 p.m. with a half hour for lunch. Her work required constant attention and did not allow her to sit down at all. For this eleven-hour workday, she received fifty cents a day. After "a long time," she received an increase, and after eight summers of work and after she married, she received $3.50 a week for six days work.[141]

Mrs. Floyd (Calhoun) Norris, daughter of D. L. Calhoun, with her husband owned the mill property in 1953. In an interview with Garber in March 1955, Mrs. Norris said:

> The old covered bridge stood at the location of the iron bridge that was replaced following a breakthrough of the bridge about 60 years ago. Manuel Teeter was crossing with a threshing machine when the floor of the bridge collapsed, dropping the threshing machine into the creek. Teeter went in with it. Following this, the entire structure was so weakened that it was impractical to repair it and the present iron bridge was built. In January 1904, a heavy flood carried it away from its foundation and into the stream. It was rebuilt and the abutments were raised about one foot. In the flood of 1913, however, it was again carried away and the abutments were raised an additional two and one half feet.

> In the 1913 flood the water was over the sills of the first floor windows of the mill. The stock, horses and cattle were all taken out about midnight but about 4 a.m. Mrs. Norris looked out her bedroom window and saw the water was over the posts of the road below the house and called her husband. He quickly dressed and with the aid of his brothers, saved the cattle and horses which had been placed in the barn, somewhat higher. To rescue the animals it was necessary to wade into the barn chest high and lead them out. Some eighty head of sheep and two or three hogs were lost however.[142]

In September 1953, Wilbur Floyd Dall and his wife purchased the Winchester Mill property from Mr. and Mrs. Norris and immediately took possession. Garber met with Mrs. Dall on May 18, 1955, in what was his last interview on mill history in the Clear Fork Valley. She told him:

> At this time the mill is partly dismantled, the top, and a portion of the upper floor having been removed. Mrs. Dall stated that on April 15, 1955, Mr. Maurice Hettinger who had arranged to tear down the old mill had his leg broken while working removing timbers. Work has since been discontinued pending Mr. Hettinger's recovery and possible return to the task, although it is uncertain whether he will continue the job.[143]

The place where Hettiger broke his leg was eerily close to the site where Clapper had been killed while building the original mill. As pointed out earlier, blood stains from that accident could be seen for many years. Although the mill no longer stands, traces of the long race can be seen below the beginning of Wilson Road and along the Butler-Newville Road. The mill itself was across the road from the lone house in the valley.

Figure 64. The Watts sawmill and woolen factory, located south of Newville on the Clear Fork was captured on canvas by Jeanie Griffin at the request of Garber.[144] The Watts sawmill was one of several built by Frederick Herring.

Figure 65. The Butler-Clear Fork Historical Society provided this photograph. It is believed to be the old Watts Mill near Newville. It was probably located on a feeder stream and not the Clear Fork.

The Watts Saw Mill and Woolen Factory

Perhaps this was a father and son operation, as both mills were operating at the same time. These mills were built by millwright Frederick Herring. The southern mill was built as early as 1812 or 1813. This was one of the first, if not the first, water-powered mill built in Richland

County. Specific facts are few, but it is evident that Thomas Watts was a man of means and a land speculator who could afford to hire a millwright.

The Watts Mills continued in operation until some time after the Civil War. Nothing remains of these mills, and Garber was unable to find much information on the mills or the Watts family. The Watts Mills appear on the 1856 maps, although incorrectly located; but by 1873, they are no longer identified. Located in a rugged part of the Clear Fork Valley, both mills may well have been destroyed by floods. Noah Watts was listed as the last mill owner.[145]

Figure 66. Photograph of the Herring Mill looking across towards the location of the town of Winchester. During construction of the mill a man was crushed under the beam just above the third window from the right on the second floor. Garber took this photograph and the one in Figure 67 in August 1947.

Figure 67. This millstone was from the Herring Mill and was located at the entrance of the old "store building." It was used by the mill before it was converted entirely to a woolen mill. The buhr was 36 inches in diameter.

The Herring Grist and Saw Mills

The same Frederick Herring, millwright and early land owner in Worthington Township, purchased the southeast quarter of section three (160 acres) in May 1814. A year later, he purchased the northwest quarter of section ten. As a millwright, he built the mills for the Watts family that were described earlier. Herring laid out the town of Newville on his land near the mills he built. He chose the name Newville after his old hometown in Pennsylvania. The surroundings in the Worthington Township were similar to those in Pennsylvania.

On Christmas day in 1823, Herring ran the following advertisement in *The Mansfield Gazette:*

Public Sale of Lots in the Town of Newville

The subscriber will offer for sale at public auction on Wednesday the 10th day of March 1824, that pleasant situation on the Clear Fork of the Mohicken (sic), at Herring's Mill in Richland County, which is handsomely laid off in town lots for that purpose. Newville is situated on the north side of the Mohicken within ten miles where it is navigable, on a state road leading to Mansfield to Shrimplin's Mill, 12 miles from the former and 20 miles from the latter place.

It is surrounded by a fertile and healthy country abounding with good timber and never failing springs. It possesses the advantages of wholesome water, and an abundance of building stone of superior quality may be obtained in the immediate vicinity. The Mohicken is a large never failing mill stream and on it at this place there are excellent sites for mills and machinery. The mill at this place now in operation does altogether the most extensive business of any one in the county.

Frederick Herring[146]

Another advertisement in the *Mansfield Gazette* suggested that Herring had built a second mill across the Clear Fork from his first Newville mill. It read:

> The subscriber having taken that excellent Carding Machine which for two years had been run by Mr. Craig, near Herring's Mill, on the Clear Fork at the Mohicken, in Worthington Township; he offers his service to the public, and assures them that their work shall be done in the best manner and on the shortest notice. Those who bring their wool from a distance shall, if possible, have it to take home with them.[150]
>
> He will receive in part payment the following articles of country produce, at market prices, to wit: Hides, Tallow, Beeswax, Wheat, Rye, Flour --- Butter, Flax, Linen or Cloth, Bacon or Sugar, or any other articles that may be agreed upon. Jonathan Pearce, Worthington Township.[147]

Unfortunately the passage of time has made it difficult to trace all of the owners, operators, or exact locations of many of these early mills. History is based on fact or at the very least, interpretation based on information available at the time. Mills were built and often rebuilt. Ownership changed. The mills were leased, rented, or sold. For example, five months after the above advertisement appeared in September 1824, another advertisement appeared in the *Mansfield Gazette* stating:

> The subscriber informs the public that he has taken the new fulling mill lately erected at the town of Newville, at Herrings Mill on the Clear Fork of the Mohicken, where he intends on carrying on the Fulling, Dying and Dressing in all its various branches. The works are so constructed that work can be done in all season of the year. Cloth will be taken in the following places, viz at R. McCombs Store, William Downey's Tavern, and M. Kelly's Tavern in Mansfield, and returned to the same place when done. Each piece of cloth left at any of the places must be accompanied with the owner's name, also the color and dress that is wanted. The subscriber flatters himself, for his long experience and attention to business, to share a portion of that patronage.[148]

This advertisement raises questions. Did Jonathan Pearce give up in four months and Benjamin Smith assume ownership, or were there two competing mills? Frederick Herring, the mill builder, still owned the land. The 1853 township plat book shows two mills using the same dam across the Clear Fork from each other. To add to the confusion are these comments from *The Brinkerhoff Scrapbook* in the *Ohio Liberal*, 1869-1870:

> Worthington Township Mills. The township abounds with fine springs. Never failing streams flow into the township as follows; Clear Fork of the Mohican, which runs six miles in the township, on the stream are the grist and saw mills of Robert Zueyr, first erected by Jacob Myers, also a mill built by John Piper, now a saw and planing mill owned by Redick and Secrist; a mill built by Jacob Armentrout, now a grist and saw mill owned by David J. Rummel; a large grist and saw mill built by David Herring at Newville, now abandoned. The other streams are Shields Run, on which there are three saw mills, Simmons Run with one saw mill.[149]

Much change had taken place since Brinkerhoff completed his scrapbook. Today Slater Run enters the Clear Fork from the south after it passes just east of Butler. On the 1856 map, however, it was identified as Gold Run. There was also the small stream that runs north of Bellville, in Jefferson Township, which was also known as Gold Run and sometimes as Deadman's Run. There were some individuals living along or near these streams and the Clear Fork who prospected for gold with little success. Andrew's Run is a small stream that passes through the Village of Butler from the south and then joins the Clear Fork. Possum Run, once known as Slater's Run, enters Washington Township from the northeast and empties into the Clear Fork at Newville. All these streams, regardless of the names they went by, had mills on them at one time or another. These name changes clearly add to the confusion as to where and when these various mills were located.

Frederick Herring died in the summer of 1832. Ownership of his land and mills passed to his sons David and Jacob. It took fifteen years for Frederick Herring's estate to settle. There is no clear reason as to why it took so long. Questions as to land ownership, unsold town lots, mill ownership, and leasing contracts may have had something to do with it.

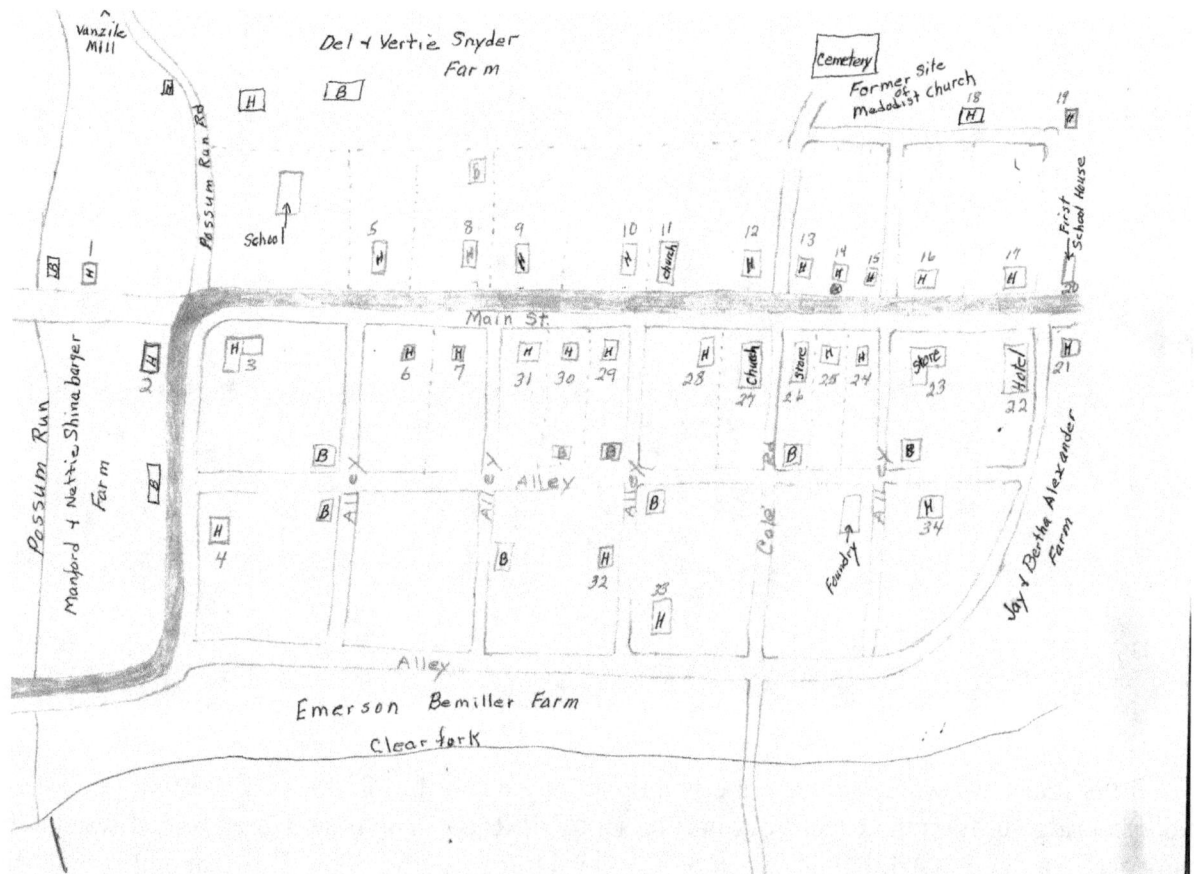

Figure 68. Map of Newville with the names of the residents still living in the city in the late 1920s to the mid-1930s. The town was abandoned in anticipation of a dam that would have flooded the area. The dam was completed in 1938, and to this day the town site has never been flooded. Map provided by the Butler-Clear-Fork Historical Society.

Newville was founded in December 1823 on the north and southeast quarters of Section 3 on the Clear Fork near the site of the first mill Herring had built. Herring built a second mill in Newville on land owned by the Garrett family of Mansfield and was in operation in 1880.[150] The sequence of ownership here is also confusing. Early maps and ownership records are not clear. Mr. E. E. (Ebb) Lime, who lived in Butler in 1957, provided some insight into the original Herring Mill in an interview with Garber. Lime, born in 1876, grew up in Newville.[151] He was 82 years old when he met with Garber.

Lime recalled fishing from the old dam site for Herring's Mill as a boy. His descriptions of the millsite and of the dam were accurate according to Garber. He stated that the dam was 400 or 500 feet downstream from the old covered bridge and the mud drills, and other timbers of the dam were still in evidence. He recalled that the Herring Mill had burned down, apparently by a malicious individual who was never discovered. According to Lime, an arsonist started the mill, and when running and the buhrs turning rapidly, he threw a log chain in the buhrs causing sparks and resulted in the fire that destroyed the mill.[152]

Figure 69. Newville in the late 1800s or early 1900s. Note the telephone poles.

In his interview with Garber, Lime mentioned a covered bridge located near where today's modern bridge crosses the Clear Fork on Pleasant Hill Road. The old covered bridge was badly damaged in a flood in April 1904, when one of the abutments gave way. The dam and early mills were all downstream from the bridge. In the summer of 1936, present and former residents of Newville gathered for a homecoming. It was their final gathering. Two years later in 1938, the Pleasant Hill Dam for flood control was completed, and Newville was no more. Buildings still standing in Newville were torn down because government engineers told them that the new Pleasant Hill Dam would flood the town. As of today, however, the town site has never been under water.

The Alexander Saw Mill

Robert Alexander and his wife moved to Washington Township from Maryland in 1826, and bought 447 acres along the Clear Fork, northeast of Newville and near the township line. His son,

Robert Alexander Jr. owned 240 acres of that land as late as 1880, "on which there was a fine sawmill." Built between 1844 and 1853, the site of this mill is now under the waters of the Pleasant Hill Lake. Little is known about the Alexander family or their mill.[153]

Daniel Teeter Saw Mill

The Teeter Saw Mill was located on Possum Run in the northeast corner of Worthington Township near Teeter Road and just off Possum Run Road. Located upstream, it is unlikely that the mill operated for many years. Unfortunately, like many of the small, isolated mills, little information is available. Once the timber had been cut near these mills, the labor required to move logs a long distance was neither practical nor cost effective. Mills like the Teeter Mill would have stood idle much of the time and eventually abandoned. [154]

Henry Foults Saw Mill

Like the Teeter Saw Mill, the Foults Saw Mill was located between Synder Road and Swigart Road, near the "S" turns. Like the Teeter Mill, once it was no longer economically feasible to haul logs to the mill for cutting, or the power to turn the wheels was reduced or eliminated because the water table had dropped, the Foults Mill stood idle. Today nothing remains, and the location of the mill cannot be determined. Mills were taxed separately from land, and a notation in a tax record or a mark on an early map was the only indication of their existence. Mills, like the Foult's Saw Mill, the Alexander, and Teeter Mills that were often located on smaller feeder streams, were short lived because of their location.[155]

Samuel Graber Carding Mill

Located at the western edge of Newville, on Possum Run just before it joined the Clear Fork, was the Graber Carding Mill. Little information on this carding and woolen mill is available, but there were two woolen mills, one gristmill, and a sawmill in Newville or the immediate area in the 1840s. The Winchester Woolen Mill was just upstream. Newville, located on hilly country, was more profitable for raising sheep than for crop farming.[156]

Rocky Point Mill (Van Zile Mill)

The Rocky Point Grist Mill was built by Frederick Herring between 1817 and 1820 for a man named Thomas Watts. No original documents or records have been located, but the mill was just upstream from the Graber Mill, about a half mile or so west of Newville on Possum Run just west of the State Route 95 intersection. The rock outcropping at this location gave the name Rocky Point to the area.

Originally known as the Watts Mill, it was owned by Ebenezer Lee who operated it from 1854 to 1864. The *1856 Map of Richland County* shows the mill property in the name of E. Lee. Mrs. Charley H. Lee, in an interview with Garber, stated that Ebenezer participated in the Underground Railroad. She said that Charley's father, James Albert Lee, often told how Charley's grandfather, Ebenezer, would "take a plate or containers of food to the mill early in the morning and again in the evening; and that upon those occasions the children in the family were not permitted in the mill."[157] When Charley was nine years old, he remembered that his father, James, would often leave early in the morning or late at night and drive away without letting anyone know his destination or the purpose of the trip.[158] In 1864, Lee sold the mill to John B. and C. B. Rinehart. They ran the mill quite successfully for several years and did well enough that they bought 60 acres of land adjacent to it. The *1873 Andreas Atlas of Richland County* shows the mill property in Rinehart's name. J. B. Rinehart sold the property in the fall of 1874, and he and his family moved to Ada, Hardin County, where he purchased an interest in a steam mill. It turned out to be a bad investment, and Rinehart lost most of what he had acquired over the years. He spent the rest of his life in Ada and died there in 1879.[159]

Rinehart and his wife, Mary (Stump), had ten children, five sons and five daughters. Their son, I. S. Rinehart was born in a mill at Amkneytown, Knox County, on September 1, 1838. At the time of his birth, there had been no other dwelling suitable for the family. I. S. was truly a child born to be a miller. As soon as he was old enough to be of any service, his father began to teach him the trade. I. S. followed in his father's footsteps. Soon he, too, had a very good reputation as a miller.[160]

As late as 1878, the mill was known as the Rinehart Mill. An advertisement in *The Richland Star* stated "The Rhinehart (sic) Mill, near Newville, is being completely repaired, and as soon as in running order, it will be offered for sale."[161] From the records examined and Garber's notes, it is not clear who owned the Rocky Point Mill between 1874 when Rinehart sold it and 1884. Millers faced a myriad of problems: loss of water power, poor crops, fires, floods and severe winter weather. Records show that the Rocky Point Mill was in operation in 1881, and that Reinhart faced severe winter problems. An announcement in *The Richland Star* stated: "Our grist mill is frozen up, and has done no work for more than three weeks."[162]

In 1884, another announcement in *The Richland Star* declared, "Mr. Strickler is pushing repairs on our flouring mill with a great deal of energy. We think the right man has gotten hold of it." It is not clear who Strickler is. Records show that there was a Mr. Strickler who had operated a woolen factory in Newville in 1859. Perhaps it was the same man.[163]

Figure 70 and Figure 71 Van Zile Millstones. These are two millstones that Garber bought. They were in his backyard until he moved to California in 1970.

The Rerick Atlas of 1896 showed the land then in the name of W. Garrett. According to Garber's notes, Bill Wallace owned the property for a short period. Orlando Van Zile bought both the property and the mill in 1896. He would be the last operator, and the mill became known as the Van Zile Mill. In 1938, long after the mill ceased operations, Garber took his camera in hand and recorded the decaying mill. He met with Orlando on several occasions and kept notes of their meetings. He purchased the pair of millstones shown above from Orlando and wanted also to buy a set of wooden bevel gears.[164]

Garber wrote in his notebook:

> In August of 1938 I again visited the mill a number of times to see about the stones I had purchased. I was able to buy the gears from him for $1.00 for the pair and obtained the following history of them. Jesse Van Zile, a millwright and grandfather of Orlando, had built the Wolf Mill about three miles from Loudenville, on the Hayesville pike, and the gears had been used in this mill. The gears had actually been made by Isaac Van Zile, great grandfather of Orlando, and Jesse had obtained them from him to use in the Wolf Mill. The gears were left by Jesse Van Zile at the old house on the Hayesville Road out of Mansfield and Orlando had obtained them there and installed them in the Van Zile Mill at Newville, and used them on a shaft before obtaining cast gears.
>
> The old mill, in disuse for many years, has numerous relics of old milling activities. In an effort to move the large stones I had purchased, the top stone was hoisted with an apparatus provided for the purpose. Between the stones was found a considerable quantity of buckwheat, the last grain to run between the stones, buckwheat flour being the product.

Figure 72. Although undated, this Rocky Point Mill on Possum Run appears to have been taken in the 1890s. Garber often visited this mill before it was torn down.

Perhaps twenty years ago at the beginning of the war [World War I] a heavy flood washed out the bridge at Possum Run Road that crossed his mill race. The county commissioners, instead of replacing the bridge, filled the race entirely stopping his supply of water for power purposes. Orlando Van Zile employed an attorney, Thomas McCrary to represent him for damages, all deeds and papers pertaining to his property were turned over to McCrary. McCrary entered the army and during his absence his wife is supposed to have destroyed the papers. The suit was brought and successfully prosecuted and the county was forced to pay a judgment of $4,000.[165]

The handmade wooden bevel gears that Garber bought for a dollar were a prized possession for many years, and he delighted in showing them to visitors in his library. A tooth had broken on one of the gears, and the skill of the millwright was evident. A hand-carved replacement had been inserted, not unlike the technique a dentist would use to replace a missing tooth. The gears, part of Garber's mill collection, were sold to the Velvet Ice Cream Museum in Utica, Ohio. Unfortunately, the old mill housing the museum was destroyed by fire on April 29, 1989, and Garber's mill collection, along with many other mill artifacts, were lost.[166]

The Manner Grist Mill

Jacob Manner, born in Berkeley County, Virginia, on December 9, 1804, moved with his parents to Green Township, then located in Richland County (now Ashland County), in the spring of 1812, and purchased a farm where an old gristmill stood. Jacob and his father remodeled and repaired it and ran it for many years.[167] The Manner Mill was located on Switzer's Run, just across the border in Monroe Township, downstream from Malabar Farm Park. Located in the Muskingum Conservation District, the mill was torn down after the State acquired the land for a water control project.

In the 1840s Jacob Manner purchased an interest in the Herring Mills. It turned out to be a bad investment, and he lost approximately $2,500.00. According to Graham's *History of Richland County*, Manner built three mills and remodeled and repaired a fourth. Three of these mills were located within the boundary of Richland County, and the fourth in Summit County.[168]

Garber was a good friend of mill owner and third generation millwright Guy Kister of Millbrook, Wayne County, Ohio. Kister had records and account books of his father and grandfather that indicated that Jacob Manner was a contractor and not a millwright as indicated in the following letter from Manner to George Kister.

Perrysville, O, Sept. 13th 1870

Mr. George Kister, Esq.
Sir

Yours recd. Your answer is not altogether satisfactory as I intend to propose to Stamens to start a mill up for so much and I necessarily will have to know somewhere what it will cost to tear down and put it up again. So I will know how to make my proposition to Stamens please tell me immediately by return mail what it will cost to tear down and put up again. So I will know how to make my proposition to Stamens please tell me by return mail somewhere near what it will be worth, you can make your calculation, say for tearing down and building up again considering that it will all do again to go up just as it is with the addition of one run of new buhrs.

Make careful calculation and tell me immediately.

Respectfully, Jacob Manner[169]

As indicated earlier, the life span of most of these old mills was limited. Rotting timbers and machine vibrations could literally shake an old mill building to pieces. Others were lost to

Figure 73. This Manner Mill photograph by Louis Griebling was taken about 1913-1914. The metal flume to the water mill is still intact although the mill had not been in use for many years. The mill was built with a heavy sandstone foundation. Note that the loading platform has been removed from the front of the building.

flooding, trees fell on them, and still others were victims to lightning strikes. It was not uncommon to tear down an old mill and rebuild it on the same foundation, reusing salvaged machinery where possible. Owners constantly made changes, upgraded equipment, or enlarged the mill capacity.

Garber spent many a weekend tracking down old mills, probing the millsites, and prowling through the dilapidated, often collapsed buildings. He was forever seeking undiscovered treasures, and whenever possible, interviewing whomever he encountered that he thought could provide some insight to the mill in question. In 1946, 1953, and 1957, he interviewed three such old-timers in his search for information on the Manner Mill. On December 10, 1946, he interviewed "Old Mr. Darling" of Ankneytown who stated that he could not recall the Manner Mill having been used in grinding meal; but he did recall a sawmill in operation in conjunction with the mill.[170]

On June 23, 1953, he interviewed Elmer E. Wigton, age 91, who commented: "The Manner Mill had a sawmill in operation when (he) was a boy but the gristmill had been discontinued."[171] After an interview with E. E. (Ebb) Lime on March 23, 1957, Garber noted that Lime disagreed with Mr. Wigton, regarding the gristmill being in operation. Lime, born in Newville, had lived there until 1941. According to him, "the Manner Mill continued to grind feed until the flood of 1913, and afterward a cider press continued to operate until the death of Marion Manner, when the

Figure 74. Marion Manner, son of Jacob Manner, was the last to operate the mill. (Photograph from the Garber collection.)

Figure 75. Garber found this toll dish at the time the Manner Mill was being torn down.

press was sold to Vernon Butler who moved it to his farm and made cider.[172]

In October and November 1951, the Manner Mill homestead, the miller's house, just east of Newville, was torn down. In October of that year, Garber visited the site and took photographs and made notes of his observations. The front portion, constructed of mostly massive oak logs, was in a splendid state of preservation. In the attic he found a number of old medicine bottles, some that predated the Civil War, and he also found a toll dish that was round and flat and secured with old handmade square nails or brads. In the bottom of this dish was carved the date 1827.[173]

Figure 76. The date 1827 is carved in the bottom.

The Schrack Grist Mill and Oil Mill

The Schrack Mills also intrigued Garber. They were located on Pleasant Valley Road on property now known as the Malabar Farm State Park. Malabar Farm, the home of the famous Ohio author Louis Bromfield, is today one of the most visited landmarks in Richland County. Charles Schrack came to Ohio from Centre County, (now Clinton County), Pennsylvania and purchased the northwest quarter of section 34 (160 acres) in November 1815. He chose this particular site because he believed it would support three separate mills, and eventually it did. All three mills were built on Switzers Run upstream and north of the Manner Mill. All of the Schrack property eventually became part of the farm owned by Louis Bromfield and included the old brick house built and occupied by David Schrack on the main Lucas–Newville Road. Bromfield purchased the mill property from Clem Herring.[174]

Figure 77. The old Charles Schrack homestead had a store of sorts in the walk out basement. This picture, from a postcard, was taken shortly before the house was torn down and replaced with a modern ranch house, much to the disgust of Louis Bromfield.

Garber interviewed Lena May McGrew, the great granddaughter of Susan Schrack, in 1946. She told him that Susan Schrack "died on the old Schrack place and was buried on April 18, 1821. It was necessary to cut a road to the knoll south of the house where she was buried. On that day [April 18, 1821] everything was covered with sleet."[174] On December 7, 1946, Mrs. McGrew took Garber to the Schrack cemetery at the top of the knoll overlooking the reach of Switzer Run and the farmstead to the north. At the time of their visit, it was found to be in excellent condition. Garber noted that Bromfield "has had it fenced with rail fence and it was discovered that Bromfield's father and sister had been interred in the southeast corner of the cemetery."[175] Mrs. McGrew also pointed out the original sites of the still and oil mill that Charles Schrack had built soon after settling on his property.[176]

Schrack had a sawmill, oil mill, and a cooper shop in operation by 1839, and in 1841, he built the large gristmill. He was also a blacksmith and had a shop next to the mill. The family homestead, a two-story frame house built on a small knoll had a walkout basement that was a county store of sorts. A distillery downstream rounded out the family endeavors. Schrack Mills was a busy place and the hub of the valley community. The schoolhouse, built of sandstone, was across the road from the mill and called the Sandstone School.

Figure 78. In 1841 Charles Schrack built this gristmill to compliment the sawmill and oil mill already in operation. At the time this picture was taken the mill was turbine powered as the flume (with the man standing on it) feeds a column of water to the turbine below. The date of the picture is unknown.

The two-and-a-half-story gristmill stood on a heavy sandstone foundation. The overshot wheel turned two sets of buhrs and had a bolting system for manufacturing flour. With family and hired help, Charles Schrack had a very successful enterprise. Following his death in 1860, Samuel Graber purchased the gristmill and ran it from 1864 until 1872. It is not known who operated the mill from 1872-1874. In 1874, Graber sold the mill to the partnership of G. W. Pervine and Andrew Parr. As part of the agreement to sell the property, Pervine and Parr could not deny access to the grave yard, the gristmill, the mill lot, and the water. These privileges were to remain with the mill.

Four years later, in 1878, ownership of the mills passed to Adam Berry and Cyrus Herring, who lived on adjacent farms. It is not clear from Garber's notes when David Rose purchased the mill, but he operated the mill until 1894, when tragedy struck his family. The Roses had two children, a son named Walter, who helped in running the mill, and a daughter Celia, also known as Ceely. John A. Tucker, who taught at the Valley Hall or Sandstone School in the late 1890s, met with Garber in July 1951 and told him that: "The Rose girl was a pupil at the Sandstone School, and although 13 years old, she was still in the beginner's class, because she was 'slow to learn.'"[177]

Although Ceely was not particularly attractive, and the boys at school had little to do with her, she was infatuated with them. She was especially attracted to Guy Berry, who lived on a nearby

Figure 79. The remains of the dam for the Schrack Mills can still be seen along Pleasant Valley Road just before the entrance to Malabar Farm.

farm. He was five years younger than Ceely, and she visited him almost every day. She told her parents that she was going to marry Guy. Her parents and her brother Walter refused to allow her to see Guy, much less marry him.

Ceely was not to be denied! On June 24, 1896, she laced their breakfast with Rough on Rats, a poison heavily laden with arsenic. Her father, on June 30, 1896, was the first to die. A few days later, on July 4, Walter died. Her mother, Rebecca, recovered and began to talk about leaving the area. Ceely, determined not to move, again laced her mother's food with rat poison, and she died on July 19, 1896.[178]

Miss Lavine Andrews was a neighbor of the Rose family. She had visited the family shortly before they were murdered and appeared as a witness at the trial. She testified, "Celia was always a queer girl, but it was hard for us to believe she was capable of premeditated poisoning of her own mother, father, and brother."[179] Celia was the main suspect in the murder of her parents and her brother; however, without a witness to her actually poisoning them, it seemed that she might be set free. The authorities arranged for Cora Davis, a childhood friend, to visit her in jail. Celia confessed to Cora who testified against her at her trial. Celia was found not guilty by reason of insanity and confined to the Toledo State Hospital. In 1915, she transferred to the new Lima State Hospital for the Criminally Insane. She remained there until her death on March 14, 1934, one day after her 61st birthday. No one claimed her body, and she is buried in the hospital graveyard.[180]

With the murder of the Rose family, use of the Schrack Mill rapidly dwindled. Garber interviewed Mr. Mergert in March 1959. Mergert told him that Dell Schrack operated the mill for sometime, but for custom or feed grinding only. The ownership of the mill had transferred to Clem Herring and Dell Schrack worked for him. Mergert also stated that George Berry built the new house on the site of the original Charles Schrack home.[181] It was a brick ranch style home but Louis Bromfield did not like it. He wrote in *Pleasant Valley*:

> Once there had been on the Fleming [Schrack] place a lovely old house, long and low with a gallery along the southern side. It was one of those happy houses which appeared to have grown out of the earth itself. That house had a soul but with neglect it had rotted slowly until the owner at last found it no longer livable. He pulled it down and in its place built the ugliest house in the valley.[182]

The small, neat, white-framed miller's house is next to the road in the valley below the farm buildings. The Schrack Mill was across the stream from the former Rose miller's house. The saw and oil mills were also across the road and downstream. The oil mill ground flaxseed, which was then pressed to produce the linseed oil used in paint and varnish. After pressing, the flax cakes were used as animal feed. No traces of the mills remain, and only a portion of the mill dam can be seen upstream along Pleasant Valley Road.

In 1939, Bromfield moved to what he later named Malabar Farm. He bought four adjoining farms and began transforming the old Anson farm house, expanding it into what is now known as the "Big House." His agriculture writings and his interest in rebuilding the worn out farmland of Malabar Farm through scientific contour farming and crop rotation brought back much of the beauty of Pleasant Valley. Because it was too steep for pasture and mowing, Bromfield had a bulldozer brought in and leveled off the last vestiges of the steep millrace that had once fed the mill owned by David Ross. The Schrack Mill is nearly forgotten, but the legacy of Louis Bromfield lives on, as does the ghost of Celia Rose.

The William Thompson Saw Mill

The Thompson Saw Mill was on Switzer's Run upstream from the Schrack Mill near present day Rider Road. When Thompson bought the quarter section, it was unimproved and heavily forested. By 1832, he had a sawmill in operation. Thompson was a hard worker and in time acquired additional land in both Richland and Ashland counties. He served in the war of 1812, raised a family of eleven children, and died October 13, 1877, at age 84.

Not much is known of the Thompson Mill, but it continued in operation through the 1840s. It is difficult to trace the exact location of the mill today, although it must have been near the intersection of Rider Road where it crosses Switzer's Run. Neither the 1856 or 1873 maps show the mill location. No trace remains today. Being so far upstream, it probably was not in operation very long.

John Shield's Saw Mill

This mill was southeast of Butler on Slater Run near Wheat Craft Road just south of the intersection of Brokaw Road. Built on a small stream, it had sufficient flow to power a sawmill, and according to the tax records, it was still operating into the mid-1840s. Little else is known about the Shield Saw Mill.

Daniel Teeter Saw Mill

The Teeter Saw Mill was also located on Slater Run just outside Butler on Route 97 near Wheat Craft Road. The mill is shown on the 1856 map. Teeter had earlier lived in Newville where he ran a sawmill and was involved in milling operations at other locations.[183]

The Richland Axe Handle Factory

Andrew's Run, a small stream, passes through downtown Butler, past the Three Crosses Methodist Church and the Butler-Clear Fork Valley Historical Society's preserved log cabin. Today it flows along a recently straightened stream bed next to Route 95. The exact location of the sawmill is not known, but the factory was north of the grain elevator and an undershot wheel would have been used. John Piper had a sawmill in the 1830s, and on the 1856 map and tax records, he owned the mill on eight acres just north of the factory. This sawmill may have been one of those built by Jacob Myers, who was known to have built several mills in the area.

The sawmill was used until it could no longer keep up with the demands of the expanding plant. Then a steam-powered saw was added to the factory. The library at the Butler museum has a history of the plan written by an unknown author on yellow tablet paper.

> Richland Handle Factory - 1904-1919, owners Harvey Solmon with connection with his brother A. J. Solmon who owned the factory got the government contract for the handles. They made handles for mattock, hatchets, adze's, picks, sledge hammers, cant hooks. We have one report during the building of the Panama Canal 1907-1914. In 1906 one railcar load of handles was shipped to the Canal Zone every day. Like the furniture factory, the woods around Butler were filled with hard woods, especially hickory which was a very hard wood for making these handles that had to be strong. When the hickory was exhausted here, they got it by train from Arkansas. The building set across from the old depot along and in back of the elevator. At it peak production 36 Butler men worked 60 hours a week for 35 cents an hour.[184]

The Bedford Axe Handle Company moved to Butler in 1901, no doubt because of the hardwood in the area. In 1909 a large steam boiler was added to power their expanding plant, but the owners were aware that the timber supply was dwindling. The depression took its toll, and in 1939 the company, faced with delinquent back taxes, was forced to close.

Samuel Brallier Saw Mill and Carding Machine

The site of this mill is now under the waters of Pleasant Hill Lake, just a short distance above the dam. Garber had no information about this mill, but tax records revealed that it operated into the mid-1840s. Brallier owned 575 acres of rugged land in the Clear Fork Valley that provided an ample supply of timber, at least for a while. It is another mystery mill, and it and the people involved are lost to the ages.

Thomas McMahan Grist and Saw Mill

The McMahan Grist and Saw mill was located in what is now the Mohican State Forest, beyond the south end of the dead end Road C 939 or south of the southern part of Road C 917, on the river, deep in the Clear Fork Valley. Graham, in his *History of Richland County* wrote that "One of the earliest mills in Hanover Township, Ashland County, was that of Thomas McMahan on the Clear Fork, erected in 1834."[185] Knapp, in his *History of Ashland County*, wrote: "There are only two privileges used upon it [the Clear Fork] in Hanover Township – the McMahan Mills which include two pair of buhrs and one saw, and a sawmill owned by James Coe, which runs one saw."[186]

By the 1870s, ownership of the McMahan Mill passed to Daniel Yarnall. Hill, in his *History of Ashland County* wrote that McMahan's "mill being two miles south of Loudenville, has three runs of stones and grinds on the new process."[187] Dr. Robert C. Paul, 80 years old and a practicing physician since 1892, met with Garber in June 1950. Garber stated that he had a "clean memory and an alert attitude and considerable interest in old mill projects."[188] Dr. Paul shared the following about the McMahan-Yarnall Mill:

> When 20 years old, Dr. Paul accompanied his father, John A. Paul, to the Yarnall Mill [McMahan Mill] on the Clear Fork. The father operated this mill from 1881-1883. They moved there from the Springville Mill in Wayne County. John Paul was a miller by trade, at the time they moved there [to the Yarnall Mill]. It was in a rundown condition and had not been operating for some time. The floods had reached the first three feet on the first floor of the mill and Yarnall, John A. Paul and the son Robert C. lived in the old Hibbard Tavern, batching it for some months while cleaning and conditioning the mill. Dr. Paul said he certainly learned how to fry potatoes while he was living with Yarnall and his father. He described the mill as 33 x 50 feet. He also stated that the mill faced away from the creek.[189]

Dr. Paul described an incident that Yarnall recorded as a drawing on the wall of the mill. It took place on the hog back hill, or knoll, across the creek:

> One evening when it was pleasant, a woman that lived on Horsetail Run, walked up to the crest of the hog back for exercise and to view the sunset. Standing on top she was outlined by the sun, and in profile she presented a picture for comment – she was pregnant and about her term and Yarnall viewing her, sketched her distorted figure on the wall of the mill where it long remained – with resultant frequent comment.[190]

Dr. Paul also told Garber about the time he was working on the third floor of the mill and his coat or jacket caught in a pin in the upright shaft, and he was saved, probably from serious injury, by Yarnall jerking him out of his coat.[191]

Garber also interviewed Harry Cannon of Loudenville in September 1949. His father, John Cannon, purchased the property not for the mill but for the farmland around 1890. There was considerable good timber remaining on the farm but the land was generally poor. The Cannons had moved from near Big Prairie in Holmes County. John Cannon never actually operated the mill. Harry, who was 18 years old at the time, learned how to operate it from Mark Ernest, the old miller. Harry did custom grinding only, making graham, buckwheat, etc. He marketed his cornmeal in ten pound bags, under the name of "Cannon's Corn Meal."[192]

Harry recalled that he used to go swimming in the forebay, and copperheads were very numerous. On one occasion he released water into the forebay to raise the water level and jumped in for his swim, and a copperhead swam towards him, head up, ready to strike. Harry scrambled out just in time to escape the snake. Copperheads were so numerous that he gathered up a number of them and had them penned up at the mill.[193] The mill was torn down in 1897 or 1898 by John Cannon, and the material used to build a barn which he subsequently lost in the flood of 1913.

William Garrett Saw and Grist Mills

The Garrett Mills were on the Clear Fork, about half a mile upstream from the junction of the Black Fork. Garrett first had a sawmill in the mid-1840s. He later added a gristmill. Already on his property were a sawmill and gristmill that were located further down on what is now Wally

Road. A search for information on the Garrett Mills turned up little, but they were still operating in the early 1870s. Garber had no information on these and other mills below Pleasant Hill Lake. These were the last mills downstream on the Clear Fork when it joined Black Fork and formed the Mohican River.

Nicolas Flaherty Saw Mill

The Nicolas Flaherty Saw Mill was located on the southwestern part of Hanover Township along County Highway 3475 where it crossed a small spring-fed stream. Pine Run meanders in a northeastern direction until it empties into the Clear Fork a few hundred feet from where the Black Fork joins and the two form the Mohican River. Built somewhere around 1843, the Flaherty Saw Mill had disappeared by 1861.

Jessie Eyster (Oyster) Grist Mill and Saw Mill

The Eyster (Oyster) Mills were also located on Pine Run downstream, somewhere in Mohican State Forest, west of the dead end of today's Township Road 3264. The mills first appeared in the 1843 records and were still in operation in 1861. Detailed information on these mills has not been located to date.

Edward Lipset Saw Mill and Oil Mill

This was an unusual combination of mills. Oil mills were quite scarce in the early days. They were set up to mill flax seed to extract the linseed oil used in paint and as a thinner. The mill was located along Township Road 3275, which follows Pine Run, and before the intersection of State Route 3. This is another one of those mystery mills. We know that it was there but no history of it has been located.

Section 2

Water-Powered Mills on the Black Fork of the Mohican River

Less good from genius we may find

Than that from perseverance flowing

So have good grist and hand to grind

And keep the mill a-going -

Robert Burton 1576-1640

Water-Powered Mills on the Black Fork of the Mohican River

The Black Fork is the longest stream in old Richland County. Beginning just north of Ontario it proceeds in a zigzag course north through Shelby where it turns east, passing the small town of Ganges. From there, in a meandering fashion, it heads southeast towards Charles Mill Lake and on to Loudonville. Numerous small feeder streams contribute to its existence in the northern part of the county where the terrain gradually becomes less hilly to the north. A number of millsites were located along these feeder streams, but they did not survive long once the land was cleared and the water table dropped. Because many of these water-powered mills operated for short periods of time, the exact locations are difficult to pinpoint.

Garber did not have access to early county auditor's records that are now in the author's possession, consequently, many of the early mills on the upper Black Fork escaped his attention. In the 1830s and 1840s mills and distilleries were taxed separately. Records listed the owner, the section of land, the mill type, and the year taxed. Many of these mills, particularly the sawmills, did not endure long, and their history is often difficult or impossible to find. Nearly one hundred and seventy years of farming and floods have erased the existence of most of these pioneer mills.[1]

Springfield Township

The Joseph Runyon Saw Mill

The Runyon Saw Mill was located just south of the spring-fed Walker Lake in Springfield Township, north of Ontario. The lake is on the north side of Walker Lake Road, but the mill dam was along the south side, just 200 feet east of the drive into the Oak Tree Golf Club. The remains of the dam can still be seen next to the road. It was eight to ten feet high and impounded about an acre or so of water. Today the Black Fork stream is small and in a deep, narrow ravine. The sawmill may have taken its water directly from the dam, and it is possible the mill sat where the

Figure 80. The remains of the dam for the Runyon Saw Mill are on the south side of Walker Lake Road. It crosses the small beginning stream of the Black Fork about 200 feet from the entrance to Oak Tree Golf Club. Only half of the rather high dam remains.

roadway is now, as no headrace or mill location is visible north of the road. The deep ravine shows the scars of periodic flooding and bridge replacement.

Runyon owned 160 acres in the southwest quarter of section 9 in 1844, where the mill was located. His was the first mill on the Black Fork and was at an elevation of 1329 feet above sea level. The stream below the dam passes through the ravine and drops over 100 feet in the next mile. From there, five miles north to downtown Shelby, the Black Fork only falls an additional 100 feet, accounting for the town's frequent flooding. Further details on the Runyon mill are lost to the pages of history. As seen today, the upper stream is so small that one can easily step across it in springtime. This was the furthest mill upstream on the Black Fork.[2]

E.P. & E. Sturges Grist Mill

The Sturges Mill was also located in northern Springfield Township. It was on the stream north of Springmill West Road, about half a mile east of the Rock Road intersection. This mill was probably an investment by the Sturges brothers who were not millers. The actual builder of the mill and who operated it is not known. It is unlikely that the Sturges brothers were involved in its construction, but they were financial backers when it was built in 1842-43. By 1848 the property had been sold to James Purdy, an early Mansfield lawyer and businessman. The stream volume would have gradually diminished as the land was cleared and the water level dropped. It is doubtful that it operated for very long. The mill is not shown on the 1856 map, and little is known of its existence, although the Purdy family still owned the land then.

The Sturges' background is interesting. Eben P. Sturges was born in Fairfield, Connecticut, in 1784, and at the age of fourteen, he embarked on a sailing ship owned by a relative. His goal was not to become a seaman, but he discharged his duty so well that by the age of sixteen, he was made first officer. By the age of twenty-one, he was master and part owner of the ship. He commanded the merchant vessel "Madisonia" on a trip from South America during the War of 1812, and was captured by the British and imprisoned in Kingston, Jamaica.

After suffering prison hardships and yellow fever, he was paroled and returned to the United States. He gave up the sea, and in 1812 he came overland to Zanesville with a stock of goods that he intended to sell in northern Ohio to General Harrison's army camp. Because of the difficulty he faced traveling overland and the ongoing Indian situation, he decided to remain in Mansfield where he opened the first business in a rude log cabin.

Figure 81. Eben P. Sturges wss headed north during the War of 1812 when Indian troubles stopped him in the tiny settlement of Mansfield. He opened the first store there and with his brother Edward were the financial backers for building a mill in Springfield Township.

In 1820, his fourteen-year-old brother Edward rode over the mountains on horseback. The two formed a partnership, E. P. & E. Sturges. The business thrived. Their investments included not only the mill, but stock in the Mansfield & Sandusky Railroad. The railroad reached Mansfield in 1846, and it was a shipping boon for local flour, grain, and produces that brought much needed cash to Sturges retail businesses. The railroad, however, was a financial failure for stockholders, paying a dividend only once in 1853.

Edward Sturges left the partnership in 1863, and with several new investors, went into the banking business. This new firm continued until it merged into the Richland National Bank. Both Sturges brothers were active community and church leaders.[3]

Nathan Tompkin's Saw Mill

This mill was on the eastern branch, near the beginning of the Black Fork, south of Toledo Junction, and on the north side of Springmill West Road. Two sawmills were located along this small feeder stream that today contains only a small quantity of water. This mill was listed in the *1832 Auditor's Records*, but it was gone by 1839.[4]

The Jacob George Saw Mill

The George Saw Mill was located near the Tompkin Saw Mill, and it, too, was gone by 1839. Nothing is known about the mill except its location, and it must have suffered from lack of water as well. The George Saw Mill, the Tompkin's Saw Mill, and the Sturges Grist Mill were all located near each other on that section of the Black Fork. The land south of Springmill West Road had more potential for mill dam construction. The 1856 map shows a pond near the south side and early roads had been laid out to go to mills. The north side is wide, level pasture land with a shallow stream bed. No sign of mill works is evident today, but they were probably somewhere along that road.[5]

Figure 82. This now small stream once supported the above mills. In the early 1800s the volume of water was greater but land clearing, the falling water table, and spring floods may have led to their demise.

Richland County

Richland County was the largest county in the state before 1847. When the local populace clamored for nearby township seats for voting, Crawford, Morrow, and Ashland Counties were created from parts of Richland County. Jackson Township was created out of the eastern part of Sharon Township, four miles wide and six miles north to south. Two miles of Sharon Township remained, and two miles west of Old Vernon Township were added, making Sharon Township four miles by six miles.

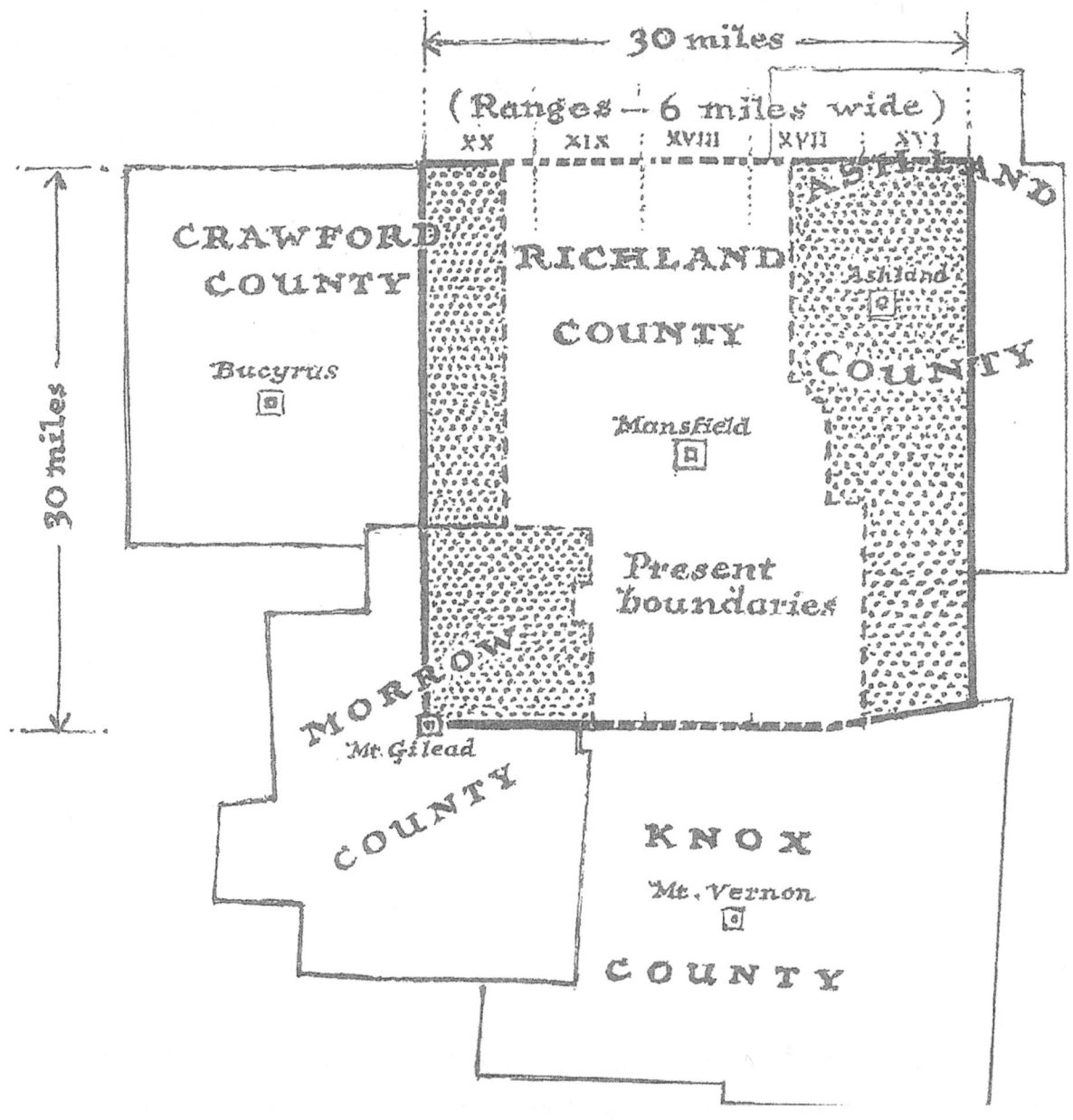

Figure 83. This map shows the results of boundary changes made to Richland County in 1847.

Jackson Township

The Leppo Saw Mill

Located on the west side of State Route 39 just south of the Amoy Road junction, the Leppo Saw Mill was along the Black Fork some distance west and behind the Abraxas Treatment Center. No road to that mill area is evident, as farming and modern construction has erased any trace. The mill started operation in the late 1830s and was still shown on the 1856 and 1873 maps, indicating it was far enough downstream to have sufficient water for continued operation. Sawmills generally did not require the volume or head of water that a gristmill did, because manufacturing flour required greater power to operate the associated machinery. Little information has been found on John Leppo. When Jackson Township was created in 1847 out of the eastern half of the original six-mile square Sharon Township, John Leppo was one of the first trustees elected.[6]

Joseph Cotterman Grist Mill and Saw Mills

Joseph Cotterman Grist Mill and Saw Mills were a short distance downstream from the above mentioned Leppo Mill. The Cotterman Mills were somewhere along the Black Fork west of Route 39, just north of the Springmill Road and Amoy West junction. The mills were listed in the *1839 Auditor's Records* but were gone by 1844. They were evidently abandoned due to insufficient water, burned, or damaged by floods.[7]

The Abbott Grist Mill

The Abbott Grist Mill is a bit of a mystery. The only information on the mill came from H. Dale Kuhn of Shelby. He recalled that the mill was on Gamble Street, Highway 61 in Shelby. In a 1951 interview with Garber, Kuhn stated that the Abbott Mill was originally a gristmill. It was a log structure about 20 x 30 feet, 1 ½ stories high and was on the east side of Gamble Street at the "Tube Works Run," which probably supplied the water power. The mill was torn down about three years before. Kuhn believed that it may also been known as the Coltman Mill.[8]

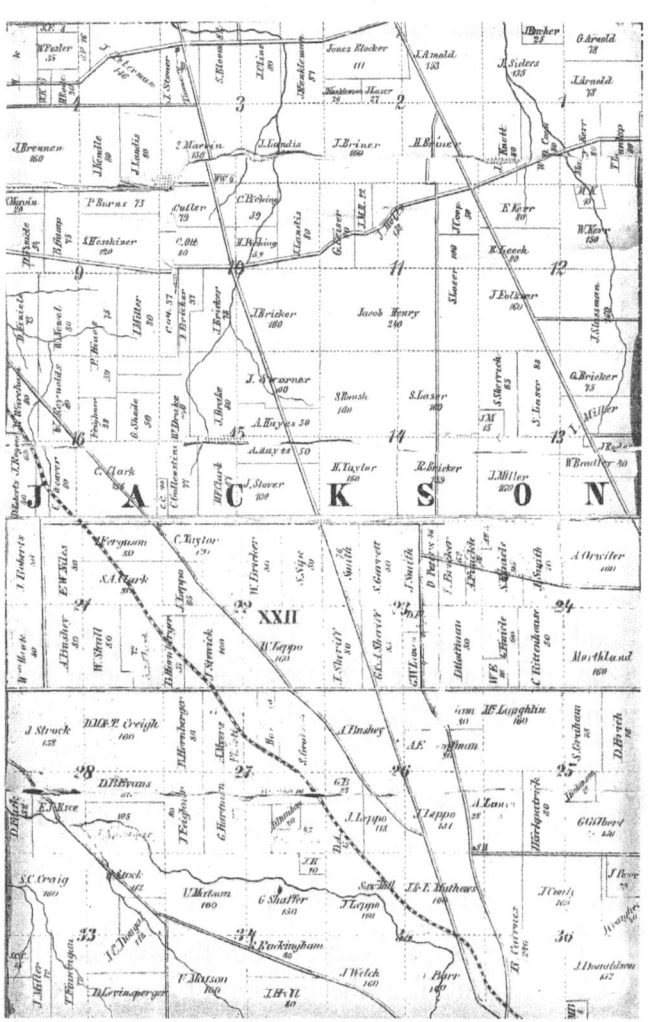

Figure 84. Map of Jackson Township.

Clapper and Orewiler supposedly had their woolen factory in this building in 1873, but Garber questioned this. An 1872 advertisement in the Shelby newspaper was for the sale of the carriage works owned by Sheffler & Barkdall, another for the Duncan Mill, and still another for the Clapper and Orewiler woolen factory. Additional research is required to determine what went where.[9]

James Kerr Grist Mill

The Kerr mill was in the very northern part of Jackson Township, located on the south side of the Shelby-Ganges Road slightly less than a mile east of the Bowman Street Road. According to Graham's *1880 History of Richland County,* James Kerr erected the first and only gristmill in Jackson Township on Richland Run in the northern part of the township on section 1 in 1830. Mr. Urie was the first miller, followed by William Kerr, son of James Kerr. William was still living on the place in 1880. The old mill was taken down in 1853, and Kerr used the timbers in construction of a barn. The old millrace could still be seen. The territory was not well supplied with water, and although a few mills were erected from time to time, few were ever in operation. Spring Mill or the Gambles Mill at Shelby were frequented by most of the settlers.[10]

Garber interviewed J. C. (Chalmers) Dunlap in 1952. Dunlap, the grandson of James Kerr who erected the Kerr Mill, was 89 years old at the time.[11] Garber noted that Dunlap's hair was coal black and thick as a school boy's, and Garber found him to be mentally alert. Dunlap refrained from making any statement about the mill unless he knew that it was accurate. Dunlap described the mill as a small one, about 25 x 30 feet, 1 ½ stories tall. It was located on the east side of Richland Run about 35 rods south of the existing highway. The dam was ¼ mile to the south and about 5 or 6 feet high, and water was collected in a pond about 2 acres in size. The mill used a bolting system to manufacture flour. In 1863, the year Dunlap was born, the mill was torn down. Dunlap confirmed that James Kerr owned and operated it for a time and that William Kerr, a son, later owned and operated it.[12]

The Briner Saw Mill

The Briner Saw Mill was located in northern Jackson Township, east of the Kerr Mill on Leatherwood Creek which flows in a northeasterly direction to the Black Fork. John Briner moved to Jackson in 1831, and sometime in late 1830s he operated a sawmill on the south side of the Ganges Road just a few hundred feet east of the Bowman Road. The Leatherwood Creek is a small stream today; the first one east of Bowman. Although the mill had disappeared by 1843, the property was then owned by John Briner Jr.[13]

Sharon Township

John Kerr Grist Mill and Saw Mill

These mills were located along the west side of Striving Road, roughly half way between Myers and Stein roads, near the Jackson-Sharon border. John and James Kerr were probably related, as both had mills built around 1830. Records are not clear, but it appears that Joseph Coltman built two water-powered mills along the Black Fork at "an early time." One may have been the Kerr Mill. The other was built about a half mile south, along County Road 314 south of Stine Road.

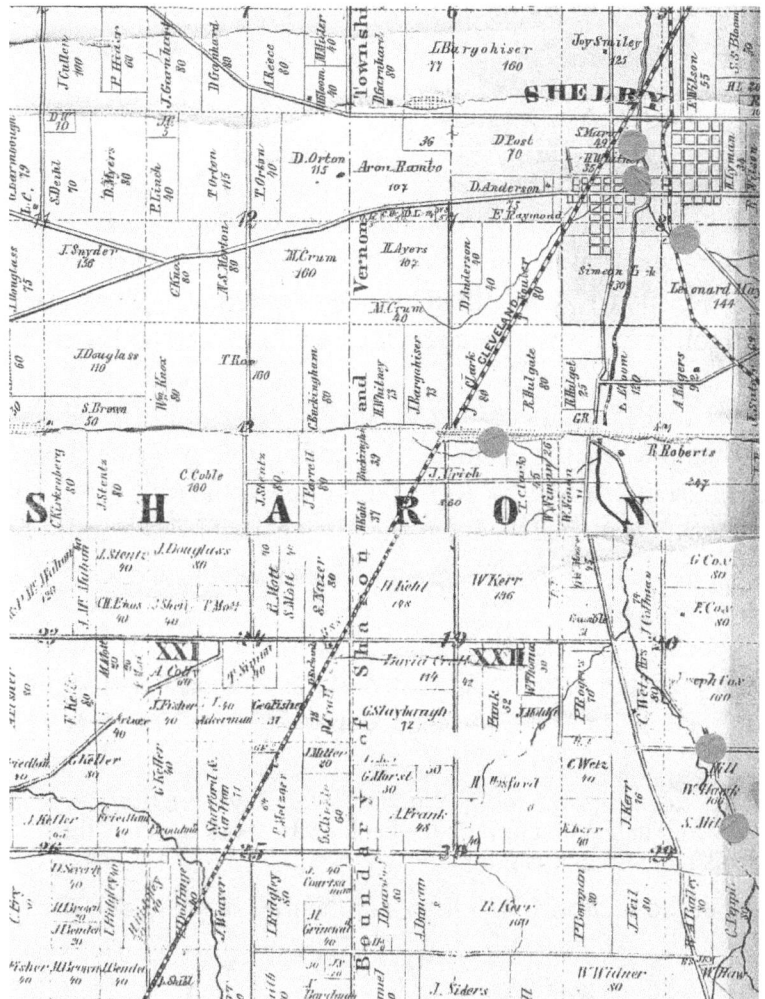

Figure 85. Partial 1873 Sharon Township map showing approximate mill locations along the Black Fork and feeder streams.

Coltman had a reputation as a "mill builder." This is another mill puzzle of who built what, where, and when, but it is unlikely that there were four mills in the same area.

"John Kerr came to Sharon in 1826 and settled in section 29, where he erected a gristmill in 1829, and in 1833, a sawmill. David Kerr was the first miller in the gristmill. In 1875 it was destroyed by fire."[14]

In 1952, Garber interviewed John Kerr and his wife, who were then living at 198 West Main Street in Shelby. At that time, Kerr was 90 years old. He was not related to the Kerr family originally associated with the Kerr Mill. However, his wife was a granddaughter of William Hawk, who was an owner and early operator of the mill. She stated that her grandfather had operated the mill for many years; but she did not know if he was operating it at the time it burned. Mrs. Kerr was very definite in describing the location of the gristmill. She located it as about halfway from the barn to the sawmill. The sawmill was at the head of the road, about a quarter mile south of the Hawk home, then occupied by George Wills. At one time her father, Jacob Hawk, operated the mill.[15]

George C. Hawk, in an undated interview with Garber, recalled that the mill dam was located on the line at the south of the farm property and was fully eight feet in height.[16] Garber noted that the depth was understandable because the natural flow of water was not enough to afford much power. The *1856 Richland County Map* shows the sawmill at the bend of the road, about a quarter mile south of the crossroads of the Willis home.

In February 1955, Garber interviewed Daniel Sipe, who was 80 years old at the time. He was living on Rock Road in Shelby. Sipe's grandfather, John Strock, came to Ohio in 1832. Strock owned a farm but never farmed it. Instead, as a miller, he operated the Kerr Mill in Sharon Township and is believed to have operated it during the Civil War.[17]

In a visit to the site in 2013, Carter observed the stream running in a narrow deep channel near the bend in the road. In the distance, a wire fence, running from near the road in a westerly direction, had been built along the top of the old low mill dam. This low dam, plus damming of the stream, created a good-sized millpond. No evidence of a headrace or mill location was found, but an effort had been made to stop bank erosion by dumping concrete and rocks along the river, a common practice in several areas of the Black Fork where it twists and winds its way across the fairly level landscape.

The Coltman Mills

The Coltman Mills are sometimes confused with the Kerr mills. Unfortunately, the information Garber gathered does not clarify the issue. According to Graham in his *History of Richland County,* Joseph Coltman, known to be something of a mill builder from Martinsburg, Pennsylvania, settled in Sharon at an early date. He erected a horse mill in the southeastern part of the township. Later, he built two water-powered mills; one was located on the Post farm, and both were in operation for a number of years.[18]

When Garber interviewed John Kerr in 1951 at his home in Shelby, Kerr said that he had owned the farm and land in Sharon Township where the Coltman Mill was originally located; now "Archdeacon Acres." It was on Route 62, south of Shelby. Kerr did not recall the mill itself, but the millrace was very much in evidence when he owned the land. He filled in much of the millrace and the millsite proper. The mill, as he described it, was directly east of the barn close to the Black Fork. The Kerrs owned the property for ten years.

In March, 1957, Garber visited the general area where he thought the Joseph Coltman Mill was located. He spent some time in a cemetery located in the southwest ¼ of the southeast ¼ of section 17 immediately adjacent on the north of section 20. At the entrance of the "Coltman Cemetery," he discovered a plaque that reads:

> The head of the Coltman family in this township was Joseph Coltman who came here from Virginia in 1820. He and his son built a saw mill and a grist mill on the bank of the creek opposite this spot. Four generations of his descendants rest within this ground.[19]

Garber believed the cemetery to be in the section 17-20 line, and the mill opposite the site to be in section 20.[20]

Figure 86. The small, well-cared-for Coltman Cemetery is on high ground just above the road and only a few hundred feet from where the mill once stood on the opposite side of the road. No trace of the mill works remains.

Gamble's Mill

John Gamble laid out the town of Gambles Mills, and when a post office was opened there, he was the post master. Sometime around 1849 the town name was changed to Shelby. The Black Fork cuts right through the middle of town, often subjecting it to heavy flooding. The wide area of gently rolling land to the south funnels its waters through the middle of town during heavy storms, much to the dismay of the city. Plans by government agencies over the years to solve the situation have accomplished little.

Figure 87. The City Park in downtown Shelby is a mill hunter's treasure. The base cone from John Gambles horse-powered gristmill is displayed for all to see. The inside buhr stone is missing but a few feet away is a complete base and cone from another mill. It is extremely rare to find the complete set as many bases were carried off and used for flowerpots or lawn ornaments.

Figure 88. Millstone flower pot found in Galion, Ohio.

John Gamble, who came from New York, built the first mill in the township with logs, on the corner where Kerr and Marvin's drug store is now located. Horse power ran the mill. Those who brought their grits to the mill ground it themselves by hitching their horse or oxen to the sweep, and they bolted it themselves.[21] The Gamble Mill was in use until 1822. Then the mill was razed, and part of the material was used in the home of Mrs. Nancy Wolfe at 33 West Whitney Avenue and in the barn on the same property.[22]

Dale Kuhn told Garber in 1951 that the old cone buhr from the Gamble Mill still existed. George Rogers of Mansfield had the cone part, and it was about three feet across. The inner, or buhr part, was in the basement wall of the A & P store in Shelby.[23]

A record dated 1839 lists John and James Gamble as the owners of "one mill" with no location or type given. This could have been the horse mill, or they might have tried their hand at water power. Whatever kind of mill it was, it had a short life as no further mention is found, and there is no record of what became of the stone buhr.[24]

Figure 89. There are two small dams in Shelby's Seltzer Park and at least one may have replaced the pioneer dam for the Briner-Craner sawmill. Facts are lacking, but it is probable.

The Briner-Craner Saw Mill

This mill was located in the southeast quarter of section 9, along the small feeder stream that eventually flows through Seltzer Park. This mill did not last long, as it only appears once in the 1839 records and was gone by 1843. Ownership changed during that brief period. Streets and houses stand where a humble sawmill once stood. Two small dams are in the lower section of Seltzer Park. One of these newer dams might be on the site of the earlier Briner or Craner mill dams. There would have been sufficient fall of water to power a sawmill. No trace of a headrace is evident but time could have easily erased it. This is purely speculation on the authors' part.

The Wilson Saw Mill

Dale Kuhn provided important information regarding the Wilson Saw Mill:

> About the same time that the Gambles Mill was built, Eli Wilson built the Wilson Saw Mill, the first sawmill in Shelby, on the Black Fork at the end of Blackfork Street, now Central Avenue. According to Dale Kuhn, the old mill dam was located behind the old town hall or mayor's office. The millrace ran up toward the Tube Works Creek, as it was called in 1934. The mill operated for many years. In 1829 John Kerr built a gristmill, and in 1833, another sawmill. A remnant from one of these old mills, Shelby's first industry, is an old millstone that was presented by Will Dick and resides in the school yard.[25]

Figure 90. School yard millstone – the millstone from an early gristmill rests in the lawn of the former Shelby High School. There is some question whether it was from the Wilson or Cline mill in the Shelby area.

The Heath Brother's Grist Mill

Garber's notes on the Heath Brothers were extensive and broken into three mills: Heath's City Mills, Lowrie-Heath Mill, and the Heath Mills. His personal notes went as far as 1951, and reflect notes taken from original sources, such as Graham's *History of Richland County*, as well as interviews with other individuals who were either descendants of Roger Heath or who recalled the mill in operation. Conflicting information from these interviews was difficult to unravel because there were two Lowries involved with the mill, David Lowrie and David L. Lowrie. Solving the mystery of the two Lowries was necessary in order to understand Garber's notes.

Garber's active research in mills ended with the publication in 1970 of his book by the Ohio Historical Society, *Waterwheels and Millstones – A History of Ohio Gristmills and Milling*. Since its publication, much additional research on water-powered mills in Ohio has been done. Much of the information that follows comes from the website of the Shelby Chapter of The Ohio Genealogical Society, who did an outstanding job in providing a history of the Shelby Mills.[26]

The exact date when David Lowrie arrived from Scotland is not known, but he was listed in both the 1860 and 1870 Federal census as a "Mill Wright" and "Miller." He was the owner of the "Shelby Centre/Center Mill" in the 1860s. The Shelby Chapter of the Ohio Genealogical Society noted that the mill was known at various times as the Centre, Center, and City Mills. When David Lowrie sold his mill is uncertain. According to Shelby newspapers, David L. Lowrie took possession of the Centre Mill sometime in the late 1860s, and he appeared in the 1870 census.

The last advertisement for David L. Lowrie as owner of the Shelby Centre Mills appeared in the July 22, 1869 issue of the *Shelby Chronicle*. On that day he sold half interest in his mill to John Sprague. One week later, on the 29th, he sold the remaining half. About this time the name changed from Shelby Centre Mills to Shelby Center Mills. Sprague was not a millwright or a miller. To fill that position, he hired a Mr. Haffstodt. Sprague retained ownership for several years, but sometime before the 1880 census he sold his mill to Samuel Haislet. Sprague was no longer listed on the 1880 census as a miller, but instead as a farmer.

Sprague made little effort to maintain his mill. Sometime about 1878, the Heath brothers, Roger and Henry, purchased it at a sheriff's sale and changed the mill name to Shelby City Mills. The brothers worked together for several years until Henry quit and relocated to Milton, Indiana, where he died in 1898. Roger continued to run the business, assisted by his son, Will. Roger died in July 1911, and his five sons inherited the mill. In November, George and Frank purchased the shares of the other brothers. Bert Heath, a traveling salesman for the mill for several years, turned that responsibility over to his brother Harry.

Figure 91. Roger Heath's Grist Mill was able to grind nearly 200 bushels of wheat a day by 1897. The barrel house was originally the water-powered mill but was converted to barrel making when steam was added to the larger structures on this post card photograph.

Figure 92. The building on the left next to the Black Fork was torn down in 2015. Builders thoughtfully used pilings for support in the event the stream bed widened. Note the distance from the stream to the top of the bridge railing.

Figures 91 and 92 are courtesy of the Shelby Historical Society.

Ownership of the mill passed between the brothers until 1913 when Bert Heath bought out his brothers and became sole owner of mill. By 1913, the mill was known as The Shelby Flour Mill. Because of growing competition of mills running on modern technology, production began to fall, and by 1919 production fell to that of 1911. By 1920, Bert Heath had reentered sales, and the Heath Mill faded into history.[27]

Garber, born in 1896, was fortunate to be of the generation that could reach back to those who built and operated many of the water-powered mills – especially those in Richland County, Ohio, where he grew up and where he returned after retiring from the Navy. He loved the water-powered mills and played in them as a child. His notebooks are rich with interviews with those who ran the mills, worked in the mills, or remembered them.

One example is an interview with Mrs. Susan. D. Inscho, a daughter of Roger Heath. Born in 1869, she was more than 80 years old when she met with Garber.[28] She remembered her father's mill and recalled that the old wheel was about 8 feet in diameter and about 4 feet wide and that it was still standing beside the mill when she was a little girl.

In a follow-up interview with Mrs. Inscho a month later, she confirmed that the mill was originally water-powered. She said that she worked in the office for six years, and she described the dam that supplied the water as being about a block from the mill where it stood a short distance above the bridge.[29]

Robert Sheffler, in another interview by Garber, also confirmed that the Heath Mill was originally water-powered. According to Sheffler, the barrel house, seen in photographs of the mill, was the original water-powered mill. He had no reservations at all that the barrel house was the original Lowrie Mill.[30]

Figure 93. The Heath Mill shown on the left was partially flooded when pictured during the 1913 storms when the water level was over the bridge. The Black Fork frequently floods the downtown and efforts to correct the situation have met with little success. Courtesy of the Shelby Historical Society.

Figure 94. This flood picture of downtown Shelby gives an idea of the amount of flood water that passes through town. The date was not recorded but it is believed to be 1913. Courtesy of the Shelby Historical Society.

Dale Kuhn told Garber a story about an old friend of his, who as a youngster, used to shoot ducks on the millpond upstream about a block above the mill. Once shot, the ducks floated down the spillway where they could be fished out without difficulty.[31]

McClure's Mill Site

The McClure Mill Site represents an interesting bit of mill history as the mill that never was. Judge James McClure and Thomas McClure purchased two parcels of 160 acres each in Sharon Township sometime in 1814 and 1815. Judge McClure bought what is now the north half of downtown Shelby, and the two together owned the land in what is now the south end of town along the river, south of the cemetery. This latter parcel is probably the one that became known as "McClure's Settlement."

Graham, in his *History of Richland County* described Judge McClure, who was well acquainted with the country, as acting as a guide for immigrant settlers coming from the South through the

McClure settlement at Bellville. He showed them choice quarters of land in different parts of the country. Just after the War of 1812, McClure entered several quarters of land on the Black Fork in the southern part of Jackson Township. Because McClure intended to erect a mill there, it came to be known as "McClure's mill seat," but he never did build one. The first road in the township is said to be the cut from Mansfield to "McClure's mill seat." Later the road was extended north to where Gambles Mills were located in Shelby.[32]

The Duncan Mill

The exact location of the Duncan Mill is another mill historical puzzle. As early historians collected material for publication, interviewers of old-timers wrote down more "firsts" than "seconds" or "later." Stories sometimes conflicted, and in the case of Shelby, it is unclear whether the mills were actually in Shelby or near Shelby. Exact locations are difficult to pin down.

Auditor's Records of 1839 and 1840 list "Holland Duncan" and also "Duncan & Stikel," indicating partnerships. John A. Duncan was identified by Baughman in his *History of Richland County* as building the first water-powered mill on the Black Fork in 1839 where Whitney Avenue crosses the stream.[33] Later steam was added to power the mill.[34]

According to Robert Sheffler, Knapp took over the Duncan Mill and manufactured "Knapp Chairs" from 1853 to 1858. Many of these were prized possessions in old Shelby homes. Antonie and Gustave Longe acquired the mill in 1858 and converted the property into a woolen factory that they operated during the Civil War. The Shelby women (including the mother of Robert Sheffler whom Garber also interviewed), "picked lint" for surgical dressings for the wounded. Samuel Sheffler and Barkdall converted the mill into a carriage factory in 1872.[35]

Figure 95. The tallest portion of the building was no doubt the original mill. After the Civil War it was converted to a woolen factory, and in 1872 it became the Sheffler & Barkdall Carriage factory. It was torn down in 1920.

Samuel Sheffler learned the blacksmithing trade at Shenandoah after a few years of schooling. As then customary, he traveled about honing his skills in order to become a finished craftsman. An ambitious man, Sheffler ended up in Shelby in 1872 and purchased a defunct woolen mill. His industry and ability as a carriage builder became well known to all those within a 20-mile radius. By the 1880s, the Shelby Carriage works was prospering. It was the largest employer of labor in Shelby, employing 35 mechanics. Under the management of Samuel's two sons, Robert and Hamler, the Sheffler industry continued until 1937.[36]

The original Duncan Mill was torn down in 1920. Some of the large timbers were "red beech" which were not usually used in construction. The timbers were large, some measuring up to 24 inches square and were in excellent condition.

Plymouth Township

Because of the limited access to water in Plymouth Township, water-powered mills were few in number and were usually short lived. The first settlers had to travel miles to the nearest gristmill. Water sufficient to power mills was too scarce in the dry season. Eventually a number of horse mills were erected, and later steam was used for operating power.[37]

The Cline Grist and Saw Mill

The Cline Grist and Saw Mill was in southeastern Plymouth Township, at the bend of the Black Fork on the east side of State Route 61 and the south side of the Bistline Road intersection. Joseph Cline owned 320 acres in 1838 when the mill was built, and it was still in operation in 1844 but on 80 acres. These 80 acres later passed to William Cline. It is not known how long the mill was in operation, nor is there any information about the owners.

Figure 96. A very rare set of cone buhrs rests in the downtown Shelby Park. This set was from an early horse-powered mill evidenced from the three holes in the buhr or rotating stone. Few of these have survived as most were carried away or filled with rain water, froze and broke. The cracks in the base stone show such damage.

Dale Kuhn was a major source of mill information for Garber in the 1950s. Kuhn stated that the cone-shaped red-granite buhr millstone located behind the band stand came from the Cline Mill. Garber noted soon after that he had seen the stone there. The *1873 Andreas Atlas* shows that the property in question was owned by William Cline, and a mill is identified. A large millrace can be traced on the property at this time and follows the road north for some distance. No mill is shown on the 1840 or 1856 maps, indicating it did not last long. The Shelby mills were not profitable due to the water situation – from floods to low water.[38]

Cass Township

The Hershiser Saw Mill

The Hershiser Saw Mill was located on the north side of the Black Fork just inside Cass Township on the north side of Bistline Road. It was in operation from the late 1830s through the 1850s. The 1856 atlas map shows the Hershiser Saw Mill location but no other information has been found. Its location was far enough down the Black Fork to have enough water to power the mill.

The Brodley Saw Mill

Another early water-powered mill was the Brodley Saw Mill. It was located on the west side of Bowman about a tenth of a mile or so south of Miller Road where the Black Fork crosses. David Brodley started with a tannery in the early 1830s and added a sawmill a few years later. Both businesses were gone by 1841, but Brodley remained on his 80-acre farm. Why both business ventures failed remains unknown.

The Baker Saw Mill

The Baker Saw Mill was on the Black Fork on the north side of the Shelby–Ganges road, near the Ganges Five Points intersection. The southern loop in the river on the east side may have furnished enough fall of water if provided by an upstream dam. Whether or not such a dam existed is not clear. John Baker, a veteran of the War of 1812, settled on 160 acres in Cass Township in 1815. By 1831, he had built a water-powered sawmill, and by 1840 it had been abandoned. The short life of this mill was typical of many of these early mills. As the timber closest to the mill was cut away, the labor involved in moving large tree timber to the mill at ever greater distances resulted in ever-increasing costs. When possible, logs were dragged by horses or oxen in winter over snow; but ultimately higher labor costs or insufficient water power may have led to the demise of the Baker Saw Mill.

Figure 97. This recent photograph is from the 1818-era Staley Mill in Champaign County, near New Carlisle, Ohio. It is typical of early up-and-down sash mills which could operate the single blade by lifting the sash or frame with the cutting being done on the down stroke. A rachet mechanism advanced the log with each stroke. The last timber cut is still in place unfinished.

Figure 98. Sawmills were usually open on one side to facilitate rolling logs onto the saw carriage. The waterwheel was under the mill below the sash, and evidence of the headrace can be detected.

The Guykendall Grist Mill

The Guykendall Grist Mill, owned by Ross Guykendall, was located in the southern part of Cass Township, and it used steam and water power. It was in operation for many years.[39] Garber photographed the Guykendall Mill in 1951 and noted that "the old mill stood on the Black Fork, or perhaps a spring run, in Section 26, Cass Township." He added that the mill was moved to that present location and remodeled into a home on the farm then owned by Joseph Gevetz.[40]

Garber did not always record the locations of all of his searches and as a result, the original location of the Guykendall Mill is not certain; nor is the location of the Geyetz farm.

The Anderson Grist Mill

The Anderson Grist Mill was on the Black Fork, just northeast of London, where Fackler Road and Miller Road cross the Black Fork. The millsite was somewhere in that general area, but it cannot be pinpointed. Evidently, it was built by William Braden and in operation by 1831. By 1839 it had been sold to John Anderson. Both the mill and Anderson were gone by the early 1840s. Again, lack of sufficient water may have been the reason.

Blooming Grove Township

The Ganges Grist and Saw Mill

The history of the Ganges Grist and Saw Mill is quite interesting. Located in the southwest corner of Blooming Grove Township, the land was settled by William Trucks in 1812. Trucks laid out the infant town of Truckville, later Ganges. He sold off part of his land to George and Harry Ayers around 1829; but the history of Blooming Grove mill began as early as 1816.

The business, although a poor concern, was much better than none at all. The buhrs were manufactured from "nigger-heads." At the same time, they also erected a sawmill and a distillery, thus providing the three great needs of the time, flour, lumber, and whiskey. Unfortunately, because they stood on low ground where the Black Fork frequently overflowed, they ran only a small part of the year. The place developed a bad reputation as a resort of "bummers." When the settlers lost part or all of their grist, they stopped patronizing it.[41]

In 1825 Mr. Trucks built a water-powered mill on the little stream by his cabin. Because steam power was not yet an option at that time, the mill could only be used for a part of the year. Over the next fifty years or so, the mill was rebuilt several times and changed ownership several times as well. By 1880, steam power had been added and the mill was then operated by Snyder and Wolf.[42]

Between 1951 and 1963, Garber interviewed three men who shed some light on the last few years of the Ganges Mills. George W. Armstrong was 87 years old at the time of Garber's 1951 interview. His grandfather, Andrew Armstrong, operated the Ganges Mill for some years during the Civil War, but Garber did not note the specific dates.

Arthur W. Cox, 90 years old at the time of their meeting in 1952, moved to Ganges in 1890. He recalled that the Weaver Mill building was moved to the location at the turn in the highway near the edge of the village near where the old road originally led to the mill, either in 1888 or 1889. Once moved, the mill was only used for miscellaneous purposes. For a brief time Cox operated a blacksmith shop on the first floor, and the second was used as a meeting place for the local band organization.

According to Cox, "The old mill was of frame construction 2 ½ floors high and about 30 x 35 feet, not larger. About 1892,

Figure 99. The brick tavern at the edge of Ganges that once was part of the mill and distillery operation still remains although covered over with modern siding and additions.

a housewife was making soap in the old manner in her kitchen yard." Apparently the fats caught fire and spreading sparks caused the house to burn. Flames jumped from the house to the old mill building, consuming it as well.

In 1963, Ray Weaver was the present owner of the property where the Ganges Mill was located. He told Garber that what he knew about the mill came from information provided from the old residents who remembered it. The house he lived in was the miller's house, and it served as a tavern for farmers bringing their grist to the mill where they received both bed and board until their grain was ground. The old mill wheel was 14 feet in diameter.[43] There was evidence of the distillery that operated in conjunction with the mill, part of the mud sill of the dam, and evidence of the millrace could still be seen. Weaver showed Garber where the buhr was located in the foundation of the barn. It was red granite and measured 43 inches in diameter.[44]

When the barn foundation was rebuilt a few years ago the millstone broke in half and now rests in a flower bed along the driveway. The farm is now a good-sized apple orchard, and at this writing is operated by three generations of the Burrer family. The west part of the old brick tavern house was torn down when the road was relocated in the 1920s, because it was too close to the road. The remainder of the brick home was covered by siding. Several small additions have been made over the years.

Part of the mud sill of the dam could still be seen in 2013, fifty years later. The old headrace is still quite evident, although overgrown with trees. It was quite large and possibly also served as the penstock. The mill location was east of the old barn.

Figure 100. The 43-inch buhr that once adorned the bank barn wall broke in half when the barn was rebuilt. Both halves now stand guard in the Burrer family flower bed. The pink granite nigger-head cap stone with a center notch for the balance rynd is shown.

Figure 101. The remains of the mud sills for the dam are still visible after nearly two centuries. The headrace, although grown over with trees and brush remains near the millsite.

The Ayers Grist Mill

The Ayers Grist Mill appeared in the 1832 tax records with George and Harry Ayers listed as owners. Much about this mill remains a mystery as it was never found in records again. It was listed in the southwest quarter of section 31 just outside of Ganges. This might represent a change of ownership in the Ganges Mills or it might have been a separate endeavor. These county records are rather vague and exact locations are difficult to determine.

Stoner's Grist and Saw Mill

The Stoner Mill was located north of Rome somewhere along a stream called Ships Run. The exact location of this mill, built in the 1820s, is also difficult to pinpoint. It was one of the mills of particular interest to Garber. He had a long, very interesting interview with George Armstrong, a descendent of one of the owners.

The Stoner Mill, built by Jacob Stoner, was the second mill built in Blooming Grove Township. Stoner's mill was built on low, marshy ground, and like the Trucks-Ayer Mill, it was called a thunder-gust mill.[45] The low water in dry seasons kept the mill idle. With the arrival of the rainy season, the stream would overflow and the mill began operation. Patrons would scramble to see who would get their grist attended to first.[46]

Jacob Stoner and his brother John settled on section 22 in Blooming Grove Township in 1814. As late as 1880, the widow of John's son occupied the place. The Stoner name was well known among the pioneers. Wyandot Indians captured two sisters of Mrs. Stoner in 1791. Mary was nine and Margaret was thirteen when they were taken prisoner. Their story is recorded in several history books. Margaret was sold to the French and taken to Detroit. Mary was forced to live with the Wyandot and became part of the tribe. She married a Delaware, Abraham (Isaac) Williams, and they had a daughter, Sally, who was born in 1797. Sally came to understand a number of Christian Hymns under the influence of the Methodist Missionaries, and she spoke English as well as several Indian dialects, often serving as an interpreter for the tribe. Her mother, however, was treated badly by Williams, and she escaped eventually and returned to her father.[47]

Sally was married to a full-blooded Delaware named Solomon Journeycake (Johnny Cake) by Judge Peter Kenney in Richland County. They had a son named Charles Journeycake who was born on the reservation at Upper Sandusky just before the tribe moved west. He grew up to be an early Christian tribal leader, a Baptist Minister and was described as the last Great Chief of the Delaware Nation. His mother's faith gained from the Methodists at the Wyandot Reservation Mission was a great influence of his life.

Armstrong, in his interview with Garber, shared much of his family history, as well the history of Stoner's Mill. Andrew Armstrong, his grandfather, was a miller. He came to Ohio in 1802, with his parents when he was two years old. In 1822 his family moved to Richland County. Andrew operated the Urick Mill in Franklin Township for some years. In the spring of 1841, he moved into Blooming Grove Township where he operated the mill at Ganges for a considerable time.[48]

Figure 102. Solomon Journeycake was born on the Reservation near Upper Sandusky and became known as the last great Chief of the Delaware Nation.

Shortly after the Civil War, Andrew Armstrong purchased the Stoner Mill property and farm on Ships Run near Rome, making the deed out to Elizabeth Armstrong, his wife. Andrew continued in the milling business at this location until the operation of the mill was discontinued in 1876. George Armstrong confirmed that Jacob Stoner built the mill in 1828. He stressed that Stoner and Armstrong were the only owners and operators of the property. The mill was a frame building, and Samuel, Andrew's son and George's father, converted it into a barn in 1886.

No evidence of the mill remains at the site; however, George preserved a red-granite buhr 36 inches in diameter in his back lawn that was originally in the Stoner Mill. As he recalled, the stone was used in the basement as the foundation stone for a supporting timber. The mill measured at least 50 x 60 feet, three stories above the basement level with two runs of buhrs about 48 inches in diameter used in making flour. The buhrs from the old mill were sold to a miller at Shiloh where they were used in a steam mill.

As a boy George used the old silks from the flour bolting chests to make set nets for fishing after the mill was discontinued. Muskrats went through it, however, and it was quickly ruined for that purpose. Andrew employed a miller named Robb in the operation of the mill, and George barely escaped a thrashing from him. While playing with a gamin-stick (used to spread a butchered hog for dressing), George poked it down into the hopper to the stones to see what would happen. Caught in the act by Robb, he ran out of the mill attracting the attention of his grandmother. Learning the situation, she cautioned Robb that he was employed to run the mill and not to chastise the children.

The Gibson Carding Machine

The Gibson Carding Machine was in Blooming Grove Township in the mid-1840s. It would have been water powered. Unfortunately no location is given; and it remains another of the mill mysteries, raising the question of whether this was a new mill or an earlier mill that had been converted.

The McGaney & Eunick Carding Machine

The McGaney & Eunick Carding Machine is also listed in Blooming Grove Township, but again no location is given. It was in operation in 1845.

Franklin Township

The Urick (Eurick-Eurich) Grist Mill

In 1831, Christopher Urick and Benjamin Schiffles and their families accompanied Henry Backensto and his family from Dauphin County, Pennsylvania, to Franklin Township in Richland County, Ohio.[49] Urick built the only gristmill within the limits of the township about 1840 just north of Mansfield on the Black Fork, in the valley just east of the junction of State Routes 13 and 96. This intersection today is still prone to flooding from time to time. No doubt the mill was hampered by the same situation then.[50]

John Shatzer was born in Franklin County, Pennsylvania, where, at an early age, he apprenticed himself to Samuel Frederick to learn the millwright and the miller's trades. In 1844, he relocated to Granges in Richland County with his parents. In 1845, he rented the Urick Mill in Franklin Township, a mile south of the Shenandoah, on the Black Fork. He operated the mill for four years, until his lease ran out. Then he purchased a small tract of land in Jackson Township and moved his family to their new home. A year later, in 1850, he passed away, and his children were given homes with neighbors.[51]

Much of the mill property remained with the Urick family for many years. The 1846 records indicate a sawmill partnership of Cline & Urick. About the same time, J. T. Charles was listed as having a gristmill in the same area, and this may have been the old Urick Mill. A mill is still shown on the *1873 Richland County Atlas*. The mill evidently had a series of owners or leases, but how long the mill was in operation beyond 1873 is not known. According to the *History of Richland County* the mill was standing near the Black Fork where the road running from Mansfield crosses that stream. It was a local business owned by John Bell. A sawmill was connected with it for many years, but had long since disappeared.[52]

FOR SALE,

EIGHTY acres of land situate in Franklin township, Richland Co. with twenty-five acres cleared and  TWO  comfortable log houses. Also a

DISTILLERY

with 2 *Copper* Stills, one containig **112** and the other **56** gallons; **12** Mash tubs, **3** Singling kegs, and other necessary vessels, all which are nearly new, and will be sold on reasonable terms.

N. B. The above land and Distillery will be sold either separately or together to suit the purchaser.

ABRAHAM WURTS.
September 12th 1827.   n 2—7m.

Figure 103. The Wurts Distillery in Franklin Township was for sale in 1827. The services of a gristmill would be needed, and the setup would have been similar to the present day Staley distillery.

Figure 104. The rebuilt Staley Mill Distillery is now producing rye whiskey from the same recipe that was used from the 1820 era up until Prohibition in the 1920s. There are two original copper stills that produce whiskey for legal sale and has proven quite popular.

The steadiest customers for the gristmills were the distilleries because their grain had only to be rough ground. From information available, it appears that there were two such distilleries located near the center of Franklin Township somewhere along Linn Road.

Cline Distillery

Jacob Cline erected a distillery near his cabin on a spring in Section 17. This gave the earliest settlers a market for their corn and smaller grain that Cline purchased and made into whisky. Part of it was sent to the lake for shipment, but most of it was sold to the settlers at 15 or 18 cents a gallon. This was not the poison later retailed by saloons and drug stores, but honest whisky that would "make a man drunk but would not murder him."[53]

Figure 105. The Staley Mill, Miami County. Indian Creek provided the water power for this mill and dates back from 1818. A sawmill and a distillery stood at the same site. The mill siding has been replaced and painted. It is the oldest gristmill with original equipment still standing in Ohio.

Wurts-Clay Distillery

The following newspaper advertisement identifies Abraham Wurts as the owner of the distillery in 1827:

> For Sale, Eighty acres of land situate in Franklin Township, Richland Co. with twenty-five acres cleared and containing two comfortable log houses. Also a DISTILLERY with two copper stills, one containing 112 gallons and the other 56 gallons, 12 mash tubs, 3 Slingling kegs, and other necessary vessels, all which are nearly new and will be sold on reasonable terms. "The above land and distillery will be sold either separately or together to suit purchaser," Abraham Wurts, September 12, 1827.[54]

The land, the southwest quarter of section 18 of Township 22 in Range 18, 80 acres on Friends Creek in Franklin Township was conveyed from Wurts to John Clay in 1828.[55] There were other mills located in Franklin Township. Without question it was difficult for the early settlers to get their milling done. Gristmills were scarce because of insufficient water power, especially within in Franklin Township, so the early settlers had to travel a long way to get milling done. Most of the early mills were primitive by any standard. Promptness in meeting the needs of the settlers was all but impossible. The water that was available in Franklin Township was mostly stagnant and not able to furnish the required power. The few sawmills that were erected ran only occasionally. Frequent floods filled the races with dirt and debris that blocked the mill, requiring a great deal of expense and labor to keep them clear.[56]

John Ross built the first of these mills on Brubaker Run on section 21. Ownership passed to Jacob Whisler who ran this mill for several years. Another sawmill was erected by John Ralston around 1840 on the same stream on section 22, and he ran it for 8 or 10 years. Although other sawmills were built during those early days, all disappeared with no information remaining about their exact locations and owners. These old mills were left high and dry when the country was cleared and drained.[57]

Weller Township

The Osbun Grist and Saw Mills

These mills were located east of State Route 13, about a mile south of the Black Fork along Brubaker Creek Road, just north of Five Points Road. This early mill operation outlasted most other mills in the northern part of the county. Isaac and Emalia Osbun, from Washington County, Pennsylvania, purchased a land track in Weller Township in 1814. Because of the "unsettled condition of the time," they did not relocate to Ohio until 1816, when they settled in Mansfield. They remained there until the fall of 1821, when they moved to their farm in Weller Township. Isaac built the first frame house in what was then the village of Mansfield. He built a gristmill and sawmill soon after he settled in the area. Isaac added a valuable gristmill to the property in 1835, and he held several offices in the township and the county. In 1821, he was appointed Associate Judge; a position he held for fourteen years.

Isaac and Emalia's son, Charles, was born in Mansfield on December 25, 1821. He lived with his parents until he married in 1843. He and his wife settled on part of the family homestead and farm, where they raised seven children.

Figure 106. The Osbun Grist and Saw Mills are in the valley near the center of this 1885 photograph. A portion of the mill dam can be seen. The miller's home and farm building are at the top of the hill in this picturesque scene.

Isaac and Emalia's second son, Alfred, was also born in Richland County. He lived with his parents for 35 years before marrying and settling with his wife on a farm about three miles from his parents. By 1880, the gristmill built by Isaac had been abandoned, but the sawmill was still in operation. Alfred was a boy in 1834 or 1835 when the gristmill was built.[58]

Garber interviewed Isaac's great-grandson, Hugh Osbun in 1950. He was the 4th generation of his family to own the farm. Hugh confirmed that Isaac was probably the individual who built the mills, although Graham's *History of Richland County* makes it clear that it was Isaac Osbun who built the mills.

Hugh described the mill as being about 30 x 40 feet and was 1 ½ stories above the basement, and used one pair of 45-inch French buhrs. At the time these buhrs still lay on the bank of the old tailrace. The dam was five-feet high and afforded a seven-foot head of water at the wheel. He described both the grist and sawmills as tub mills with the tub wheel for the gristmill 48 to 60 inches in diameter, and that for the sawmill 42 inches in diameter. These wheels were used until 1898, when a turbine was installed that generated 4 horse power. In addition to the operation of the mill, the power was used to produce electricity and lights on the farm – the first in the section to have such lighting.[59]

Hugh recalled that a bolting system was used in the mill, but in his memory the mill never made flour. It was used for custom grinding until 1913, when a flood washed out the dam. The mill ceased to operate and deteriorated until its final collapse on April 29, 1923.

The county road crossed the Brubaker Creek bottom at the mill dam. A bridge afforded crossing for the millrace immediately above the mill, but a ford was used for crossing the creek at the dam's edge. The county road was abandoned as a through highway about 1902; but the west end continued as an access road to the mill.

During winter when water was ample, the sawmill ran continuously. However, in summer months when the water in the race was exhausted, considerable delay and interruption of operation resulted. After the sawmill ceased operation, the equipment was sold. Later it was donated to the Richland Rural Life Center where it is to be used in getting out material for buildings projected for that activity.[60]

Isaac's son Alfred operated the mill after his father died. In turn, Alfred's son Jacob succeeded him in ownership and ran it until 1913, when the mill ceased to operate. He died on Labor Day, 1945.

The Charles-Linn Grist and Saw Mills

The Charles-Linn mills were located at the present day junction of Mansfield-Adario and Adams Roads southwest of Olivesburg. The mills were southeast of the junction at a loop in the stream where a dam and headrace cut across to provide the necessary fall of water. Today there is a large swamp or backwater on the north side of Adam's Road and it is easy to understand how that area would flood.

In 1818, Elijah Charles built a sawmill on what became known as the Charles Millsite. In 1835, Elijah Charles died and his son Isaac Charles erected a gristmill. For a quarter century Isaac ran both grist and sawmills successfully, notwithstanding the litigation of the courts. Isaac had more than his share of problems with his neighbors. The dam for his mills was not far from where the Mansfield-Olivesburg Road crossed the Black Fork . There was insufficient fall to provide the necessary power needed to operate the mill. As a result, the dam that Elijah and Isaac built would often back up as far as three miles, causing the stream to overflow into the lowlands and marshes.[61]

A Mr. Lee brought a lawsuit against Isaac Charles that went on for several years. He sought to have the dam removed, arguing that the overflowing water into the marshes caused a "miasmatic" (noxious) condition, which was unhealthy. Ultimately Lee won his litigation and Isaac Charles was required to lower the dam by one foot. Isaac Charles had a son also named Isaac. In 1868, Isaac Sr. moved to Bluffton, in Allen County, where he lived several years. He was murdered by his son, Isaac, for reasons unknown. The son was found guilty of the murder and sentenced to spend the rest of his life in prison.[62]

David Linn also had an interesting background. He was born in 1811. His grandfather was David Rowlands, a staff officer under George Washington during the Revolutionary War. David moved to Ohio in 1835 and settled in Weller Township.[63] Tracy Pittenger, a neighbor of David Linn, knew him well. He told Garber that Linn was "very conscientious, too good for his own good."[64]

Linn was also deeply religious. On January 22, 1894, he wrote in his journal, "I seen in a dream or a vision on this night, Dorcas my wife and Elvira my daughter standing by me dressed in brilliant white. They looked very beautiful and brilliant." Dorcas was David's first wife who died at the age of nineteen, eight days after giving birth to a son, Corneliaus. Elvira, their daughter, died at the age of two. The grief at the loss of his wife and child was with him always.[65] David and his brother Jacob purchased the Charles Mill shortly after the end of the Civil War. As a result of the ongoing litigation that Lee brought against Isaac Charles, the mills were in poor condition and required repairs and refitting. David and Jacob operated under the name D. Linn & Co. They employed Levi L. Bowers, an experience miller, to help them.[66]

David was considered a competent miller. If he had a flaw, it was his gullibility and a willingness to blindly trust people. Because of this, David all too often found himself in situations leading to litigation. David chose to ignore claims for reinforcement, causing the men whom he had trusted and who owed him money to avoid him. David turned to his journal to express his frustrations. He wrote:

> The following is some of the trouble and experience I had while living at the Charles Mills. It appeared as though all the Charles were corrupt and sought every means with others to defraud me and when I had the most trouble I prayed most earnestly to be delivered out of the hands of my enemies. Just at that time I heard a voice nearby me say that my enemies shall come to naught. This was a very short time before William Lynn and Mary Clingen was married. The Rev. Mr. Ball married them. He was a splendid Bible scholar. I told Mr. Ball what I had heard when I was alone. Mr. Ball said there is evidence in the Bible of many cases where men in trouble was delivered out of the hands of their oppressors and comforted when in trouble.
>
> I will now give the names of all the persons that I lost money by (who) was living when I had the vision:
>
> L. G. Matson. Now dead.
>
> G. W. Cantiwell. Now dead.
>
> I. Charles Sr. Now dead.
>
> I. Charles Jr.
>
> Judith Williams. Now dead.
>
> Charley Williams. Now dead.
>
> James Horton.
>
> R. D. Horton. Now dead.
>
> Jo. Evens. Now dead."[67]

With the notation, "Now dead," David must have come to terms with the fact that the debt was closed. His relationship with his brother Jacob, who lived in Ashland, also suffered. David wrote, "In regard to the sale of the mills, you, (Jacob) promised to divide the money with us and give us enough to buy a new home. Did you keep your word – no, you took all the money and got mad when I told you to do as you had promised."

According to Mrs. Charles (Norma Tingley Linn) Dorman, her grandfather David operated the Charles Mill for many years. In an interview with Garber in 1951, she recalled trips to Mansfield where he sold the flour he made. She said that David operated the mill until shortly before he went to Kansas in 1898 or 1899. Sometime later, he returned and purchased The Charles Mills that were long known as the Linn Mills."[68]

The following article appeared in the *Butler Enterprise* on August 6, 1903.

> East of Olivesburg, in Ashland County, "sick wheat" was often produced in the early settlement of the county. This condition could not be accounted for. The grain would look as plump and perfect as the best quality ever grown and the flour made from the same would be as white and nice as any ever bolted, and when made into bread , it would be palatable, except the bread would have a sweetish taste. But whenever eaten by man or beast, a distressing sickness would follow. The cause of "sick wheat" was never ascertained.

Nothing in the article indicates that the "sick wheat" described above came from the Charles-Linn Mills; but neither does it eliminate the Charles-Linn Mills.

Harvey Imhoff was born a short distance from the millsite. When Garber interviewed him in 1951, he then owned the land where the Linn Mills had stood. At the age of 81, he remembered the mill well and described it to Garber as follows:

> 40 x 60 feet, 1 ½ story above the ground level, slant roof, not hip, 2 sets of buhrs, overshot wheel, 10 to 12 feet in diameter, (?) 2 to 2 ½ feet wide. A large saw mill was operated in connection – an up and down mill. Linn would put a log on to be sawed into a plank or board and leave it, return to the grist mill and tend to work at that place for about 15 minutes and return to the saw mill in time to take care of the log as it was sawed through.[69]

The mill was torn down perhaps about 1900, sometime before the Taggert Woolen Mill which he (Imhoff) helped tear down in 1904. The dam was immediately on the opposite side of the bridge, upstream from the mill, which stood in the angle of the road and creek on the southeast side. The sawmill was on the north side of the creek and the same side of the road as the gristmill.

Mr. Imhoff told Garber that a "man named of Dickson bought the mill of David Linn and run it a while, but let it go down."

Dickson & Taggart Carding Mill

This mill was in the northeast quarter of section 30 in Weller Township, which today is northeast of Epworth on the east side of 545 near the junction of Charles Road. It was an early carding mill. The following advertisement appeared in *The Western Sentinel* on June 8, 1831:

> Wool Carding
>
> The Subscriber informs the public that he is prepared to card wool, at the new mill, known as the Dickson & Taggart's Mill, one mile south of Charles Mill, on the Black Fork – which will be done at the customary prices. He has engaged an experienced hand to attend the machine, and work will be done in the best manner. He will take wheat, rye, corn, beeswax, tallow, or good wool in fleece that has been washed on the sheep's back, in payment.
>
> Wm. Taggart, June 6, 1831[70]

Many of the early families were linked through marriage. John Dickson arrived in Weller Township in 1815 and purchased the quarter section of land adjoining Elijah Charles. In 1818 he married the oldest Charles daughter. In 1830, he formed a partnership with William Taggart, who had married the third daughter of Elija Charles. They were brothers-in-law, and together they built a gristmill on a spring rising out of the Big Hill side. Two years later, they built another gristmill about 40 rods below the other on the same stream.[71]

Taggart was described as a man of great physical strength and endurance, an excellent workman and hunter. He had very black hair and black eyes, and his face and chest were covered with such thick hair that his skin could not be seen. He was described as "generous in his impulses, honest in his dealings and an accommodating neighbor."[72]

In his *History of Richland County*, Graham wrote that Taggart: "In days of 'corn husking' he was first choice in a race; he would become so excited sometimes in an exciting race as to leave marks of blood on the corn husks from his lacerated fingers. These simple facts are given simply to exhibit faithfully the spirits of the times a half century ago, and the habits of our fathers."[73]

Apparently in his later years Taggart had marital problems. Graham was not specific in his *History of Richland County*, but their differences were probably much like those encountered by married couples today, although a divorce was less likely to be a solution for them. Graham wrote,

"A dark shadow had fallen over the threshold of his domestic relations, and the cloud never lifted from his brow, or the load from his heart. He became a wreck, mentally and physically, and never did the weary heart look forward with deeper longings for the grave that should cover it, or the spirit with earnest yearnings for the brighter and better land, than did his."[74]

Because Garber was part of that generation that bridged the end of water-powered mills, he was fortunate to have access to those who witnessed the ending of the old sawmills, gristmills, the carding mills, and the others that were so crucial to the building of America. Tracy Pittinger was 75 when he was interviewed by Garber. He owned the farm where the Taggart factory had stood. His father owned the property when the mill was torn down in 1904.[75] According to Pittinger "the old Taggart Mill stood on the creek side of the road, not too far upstream from the cross roads towards the Charles Mill. A house and barn stood a little beyond and on the opposite or hill side of the road from the old mill." He went on to say that woolen yarn was made at the mill and described the mill as being:

> about 30 x 40 feet, 1 ½ story above the ground level, with an overshot wheel about 10 feet and about 2 feet wide. The mill was fed by water from numerous fine springs on the hill above the mill. Three especially were used being large. The water was diverted from them by ditches or small races into a community pond where the water was impounded and fed to the mill by a flume. In his time the flume was iron pipe from the pond to the penstock.[76]

Pittinger said that Amos Jump was the last person to operate the mill. Jump was married to a woman named Della. Pittinger further stated that there was a mortgage on the mill while Amos operated it.[77] Today it is almost impossible to pinpoint the exact mill location, but just east of 545 on Charles Road,

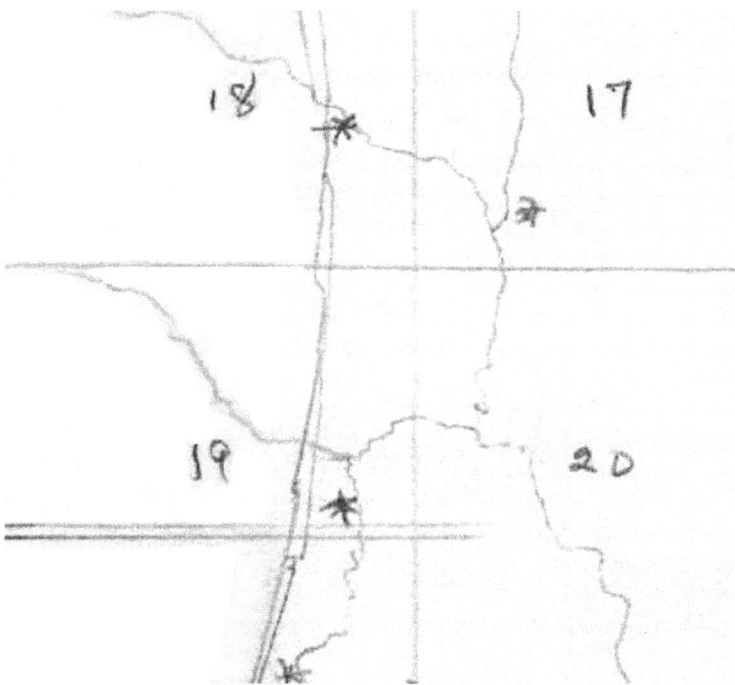

As pictured in the Andreas Atlas of Richland Co. 1873. The Black Fork of Mohican meanders from the NW corner of Sec. 18, Weller township and in the east middle of this Sec. 18, the Charles-Linn Mills were located. The Black Fork goes through the SW¼ of Sec. 17 and is joined by the Whetstone Creek running in through Sec 17 from the north. The stream continues south through Sec. 20 and the "Spring Run", coming off of Big Hill and joins the Black Fork in the NW¼ of Sec. 20. In the NE¼ of Sec. 19 two small spring fed runs join and meander east to their junction with the Black Fork in Sec. 20. One of these "Spring Runs" coming from the south, furnished the water power for the Dickson-Taggert carding mill in the NE¼ of Sec 19. The mill was located just south of the junction of the two spring runs.

The John Sherman Map of Richland Co. 1840. Shows a grist mill in the SW¼ of Section 17 on Whetstone creek just before it joins with the Black Fork.

A grist mill is also shown on this map in the SE¼ of Sec. 19 on a small spring run running from west to east. These two grist mills are not otherwise identified.

Figure 107. Hand drawn map by Garber.

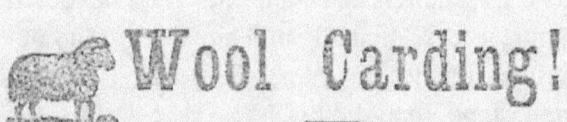

there are two beautiful spring-fed ponds on the north side of the road. Traces of early hillside water channels are evident in the woodland on the south side. This was perhaps the site of the old Dickson & Taggart Mill.

The Montgomery Grist Mill

The Montgomery Grist Mill was located at the south side of Olivesburg on the east side of the Whetstone Creek near the park. The stream crosses route 545 below the millsite and is quite small. The first gristmill in the township was built by Benjamin Montgomery on the Whetstone at Olivesburg in 1817.[78]

Graham, in his *History of Richland County*, adds that Montgomery was "among the first settlers of Weller Township."[79] It was Montgomery who laid out the town of Olivesburg in 1816 and named it after his daughter Olive.

Figure 108. Advertisement for Dickson-Taggert Woolen Mill.

Figure 109 An illustration of a side shoot or tub mill waterwheel as they were called. These were generally used on sawmill return carriages in conjunction with a vertical waterwheel. The Osbun Mill may not have had sufficient fall of water and volume to support vertical wheels.

Drawing by Architect Paul Shuler, Lexington, Ohio.

He was respected in this new community, and in that same year, he was elected Justice of the Peace. Montgomery first settled in what was originally Milton Township, which later became a part of Weller Township. By 1881, Benjamin Montgomery was well established. Montgomery kept a tavern, Abel Montgomery had a black smith shop, and Jonathan Montgomery operated a one-horse mill and water mill.[80]

Figure 110. Montgomery Mill. According to Lona and Abigail Swineford, the spring in the roadside park, not far from the mill, was where General Beall stopped with his troops during the War of 1812. They stayed overnight and perhaps longer...Chris Fike is on the loading platform and William Earick is standing on the ground to the left.

The following advertisement appeared in the *Mansfield Gazette & Richland Farmer:*

Sale of Lots

On the 13th day of August 1830 there will be offered at Public Sale a number of town lots in Olivesburg, on liberal and accommodating terms...It is situate in a fertile country abounding with water privileges. The State roads from Loudenville to Lower Sandusky and from Wooster to Upper Sandusky intersect at this place. There is a grist mill and saw mill in operation and other sites unimproved near town. There is a Store and Post Office.[81]

John B. Mohn, originally form Dauphin County, Pennsylvania, moved to Richland County with his parents. His father taught him the millwright trade. He married Elizabeth S. Miller, who also moved to Ohio from Lancaster County, Pennsylvania. John purchased the Olivesburg gristmills and operated them for nearly 18 years. Subsequently, he sold the mills because of bad health. He invested in a small track of ten acres near Shiloh, in Richland County. John served with Company B, 161st Ohio Volunteer Infantry and marched with Sherman to the sea. He died on July 25, 1905.[82]

Figure 111. Olivesburg Mill taken from the rear shortly before it was torn down.

Garber interviewed two of John Mohn's nieces, Miss Lona L. Swineford and her sister Abigail. Lona and Abigail's mother was a sister to John Mohn. They told Garber that the mill was sold to John Mohn and Jake White. In 1872 White sold his interest to Leonard Mohn, John's father. The sisters' story is somewhat different than the previous sources cited. They stressed that John and his father Leonard operated the mill until 1884 when the mill was sold to Christian Fike. According to the sisters, "Levi Nelson bought it from Fike and was probably the last owner. Fike moved to Lucas where he was probably involved in the old Rummel Mill. William Earick was a fireman in the Olivesburg Mill during the time Fike operated it, indicating that steam power was probably added to the mill at this time.[83]

Less than a month after the interview with Garber, Miss Swineford wrote to him saying that she made a further inquiry about the old mill and learned that it was sold by Christian Fike to Levi Nelson. This accounted for the neglect and ruin because he wanted the land and other buildings only. Conrad Wolfe, one of the villagers, tore it down in 1918 and sawed it up for firewood. In her letter, she wrote that some of the machinery had already been taken out. Traces of the old water millrace could still be seen along the east side of the old bridge which crosses the Whetstone on 603 at Olivesburg.[84]

Israel Dille Grist and Saw Mills

The Israel Dille Grist and Saw Mills were located in eastern Weller Township on the east side of Brubaker Creek Road near a point where the road turns straight north. Brubaker runs north off of Five Points East Road. No signs of the millsite are visible today, but the *Sherman Map of 1830* shows a Staat's Mill, a gristmill, on the southwest ¼ of section 14 in Weller Township. At that time Franklin Township embraced two tiers of sections on the east that were later cut off and made part of Weller Township, Weller being composed of parts of Milton and Franklin.

Israel Dille was a respected member of the community and a Civil War veteran who had achieved the rank of Captain. The *Mansfield Gazette*, when reporting on the "festivities and ceremonies to the celebration of the 4th of July" commented on Captain Dille as follows: "Captain with his rifle company attended and assisted in performing the usual ceremonies. Appropriate music accompanied the procession, and gave zest to the toasts." According to Garber's notes, "The committee on arrangements returns their thanks to Capt. Dille, his officers, non commissioned officers, musicians & privates for their attendance in their military capacity in the celebration of the day."[85]

After Israel Dille died, an executors sale was held. The property listed did not include the mills which presumably were left to his son, also named Israel:

Executors Sale

There will be offered for sale on the premises on Thursday the 12th day of June next, by the subscribers, executors of the estate of Israel Dille deceased, late of Franklin Township, the following property, viz:

One young mare, Wagon, Gears, Harness, Ploughs, Wind Mill, with other implements of husbandry too numerous to mention; Also a number of Cows, Sheep, and Hogs. Sale will commence at 10 o'clock, when terms of the sale will be made known and due attendance given.

Thomas Clark, Israel Dille Jun. Exr., Franklin, May 20, 1828.[86]

Three years later the son advertised the property, including the mills, for sale:

Valuable property for Sale

Consisting of a lot of land containing 24 acres handsomely situated in Franklin Township, Richland Co. 7 miles north of Mansfield. On the premises are a grist mill and saw mills in complete operation, a new frame dwelling house 30 x 23 feet and other out buildings, all of which will be sold low. Enquire of the subscriber on the premises.

Israel Dille, Franklin, March 14, 1831.[87]

In May, 1830, Andrew Oswalt placed an article in the *Mansfield Gazette* about a "large and well built mare colt" of his that had strayed. The article identified Oswalt as the subscriber "who lived one half mile north of Israel Dille's Mill." From this additional information Garber concluded that Staat's Mill and the Dille Mill were one and the same.[88]

Williamson Distillery

The distillery was located a few yards from where Windsor Station stood in 1880. Deacon Williamson, who came from Jefferson County, Ohio, in 1817, ran the mill. The good Deacon must have been quite a character. Graham, in his *History of Richland County*, wrote, "The good Deacon, who was indeed a worthy man, would, after putting his buzzing, seething, enginery in operation, take a seat at the place the precious fluid made its exit, rubbing his hands together, would begin to sing—' Come, thou fount of every blessing.'"[89]

The Fleming Grist Mill

Located in the gorge below Fleming Falls on Fleming Falls Road east of U. S. Route 42 northeast of Mansfield was the Fleming Grist Mill. Camp Mowana now owns the land where the falls are located, and a lower road in the camp passes the deep gorge. The mill was located in or near this flood-prone stream before it enters the flat swampy valley. In 1898 A. J. Baughman, in an article for the *Mansfield News*, wrote, in part: "The first gristmill in Mifflin Township was built at the falls by John Fleming and was operated by him for a number of years, and the gudgeon holes can still be seen in the rocks where the waterwheel was placed. But the floods came and, although the mill was built on rocks, the superstructure was washed away."[90]

Baughman also pointed out that William Fleming, John's brother, was a blacksmith, and had a smithy between the falls and the Mansfield road, and he operated a trip hammer and ran a grind stone by water power. He was a genius in his line, as well as a skilled workman, and among his output were tuning-forks for "singing masters."[91]

John Sherman, an American Republican representative and senator from Ohio during the Civil War, had fond memories of Flemings Ravine. He wrote in his memoirs that the Fleming Ravine was:

> … about five miles from Mansfield, was the gathering place for young and old. A small stream had cut a deep ravine with rocky banks on either side. An old mill with an overshot wheel spanned the ravine and filled it with a noisy rattle. The adjacent woods, where a fire was lit and coffee made, and the farm lands stretching beyond, made a picturesque scene often described and often admired. Here we had dances, frolics, speeches and fun, with healthy exercise in the open air. These frolics were often made the subject of description in newspapers.[92]

Garber located additional information on the Fleming's Mill (also known as the Fleming's Falls Mill) at the Ohio State Museum Library. William Reynolds was running the "grist mill in Mifflin Township (afterwards washed away) known as Fleming's Mill, six miles west of Mansfield." The Mill was located on Reynolds Run, or Williams Run, which emptied into the Black Fork. Reynolds hired Joe Smiley to tend the gristmill. Smiley was born in Clarendon, Vermont, but immigrated to Richland County in April, 1817, from Rutland, Jefferson County, New York. "While tending the mill, a nephew of John Wiler of Mansfield, called for flour, Mr. Smiley took his watch for security. In after life Mr. Smiley asked old Uncle Wiler where he got his first start in life. He replied, "With an old watch probably worth 2 or 3 dollars."[93]

The Fleming Grist Mill was listed in 1846 as owned by the heirs of David Fleming. The date of the flood that destroyed the mill is unknown, but speculation is that it happened in the 1883 flood.

The Kohler Grist Mill

Downstream of the Fleming Mill was the Kohler Grist Mill. It may have been near the bottom of the hill just before entering the flat ground of the valley, but floods have erased any traces of it.

The Kohler Mill was built by Daniel Kohler about one-half mile below the falls. Daniel was primarily a farmer, but he became familiar with the sawmill business through his father-in-law when he married Nancy Brubaker. Nancy's father operated a gristmill in addition to his sawmill. Daniel later operated a mill on his own, but continued farming as well. Amos Kohler, Daniel's son, was born in Fleming's Falls, Richland County, on January 15, 1847. He married Alice A. Cotter, daughter of William Cotter, in 1871. He and his wife moved to a farm in Ashland County, near the Black Fork that was owned by his father-in-law. After about three years, Amos and Alice returned to Richland County where they purchased land about four miles from Mansfield. He farmed, but also operated a grist and sawmill in partnership with two other men. That partnership lasted for about three years before Amos sold his interest in the mills and returned to farming.[94] In 1902 the gristmill building was still standing, but the buhrs and hoppers were gone.[95]

A. J. Baughman submitted an article to *The Butler Enterprise* on Friday, October 31, 1902. He described the Kohler Mill as follows: "A gristmill was built about half a mile below the falls by Daniel Kohler, and was known as Kohler's Mills. The building is still standing, but is buhrless and hopperless now."

The John Buler Saw Mill

Records indicate that The John Buler Saw Mill was located at the same place as the Kohler Mill; and it is possible that the two mills were one and the same. These mills often went through partnerships and different owners, making it difficult to sort out the details of who sold it when. Buler was evidently associated with the Kohler's at one time, and the mill was recorded as the Kohler Mill.

The Hershey-Staman Grist Mill

This is another one of those mills with a convoluted history that Garber researched. One of the problems he encountered was the spelling of the name. Baughman, in his *History of Ashland County*, pointed out that the name "Staman" was originally spelled "Stenmann." A number of families who immigrated to the United States were Swiss Mennonites and included the Staman, Kauffman, Graybill, Hershey, Musser, and Brunaker families. Once in America the Staman name underwent changes that included Staman, Stamen, and Stemen. A brief summary of the Staman family may help the reader.

Jacob and Barbara (Hershey) Staman were living in Lancaster County, Pennsylvania, where Jacob, with his brother-in-law, Jacob Musser, built a mill. During the War of 1812 prices for wheat rose to $3.60 a bushel; but when the war ended, prices plunged to sixty cents a bushel, and they suffered heavy loses. Their business failed, and they eventually migrated to Ashland County, Ohio, around 1820. Jacob and Barbara Staman were the paternal grandparents of John Kauffman Staman.[96] Benjamin Staman, their son, moved with them to Ashland County. Ana Kauffman, who eventually became his wife, moved to Ashland County with her parents who were also from Lancaster County, Pennsylvania. They married in 1827 and spent the rest of their lives in Mifflin Township. Their son, John Kauffman Staman, was born on March 8, 1833. As a child and young man he worked on the family farm and in his father's sawmill. He worked at the sawmill for 49 years. During those years the mill was repaired and added to several times.

The Hershey-Staman Grist Mill was located in Mifflin Township, Ashland County, along the east side of the Black Fork on Route 603, about two and a half miles north of downtown Mifflin. The mill was a few hundred feet north of the I-71 overpass where an old abandoned truss bridge can be seen, with difficulty, through the forest of trees. It is quite likely that the mill was just upstream of the iron bridge, which replaced an earlier bridge at the millsite. A tree line along the field below the roadway still marks the path of the headrace for the mill.

Knapp in his *History of Ashland County* wrote about the Hershey-Staman mill:

> Benjamin Henshey (Hershey) emigrated from Lancaster Co., Pa. in October 1825, and settled on the south-west quarter of Section 31, Montgomery Township, being land he had purchased the year previous. A year or two subsequent he purchased, of Andrew Newman, the mill property on

the Black Fork, in Mifflin Township, which he subsequently sold to the present owners, the Messrs. Stayman.[97]

Graham in his *History of Richland* County added to the story when he wrote:

> In 1819 a grist mill and sawmill were erected near each other on the Black Fork, about a mile above Petersburg (Mifflin) on Section 10. The grist mill was the second built in the township, and still is in operation. [as of 1880] Several dwelling houses have gathered around it, and a tan yard is in operation, owned by Mr. Augustine of Mansfield, but the place is yet nameless.

Garber noted, "This is the Clapboard town of Jay Middletown."

Graham's account continued:

> The mill has changed hands many times. It was built by Andrew Newman, and run by him until 1825, when it was sold to Jacob Staman, who, in 1828, transferred it to Benjamin Hershey. This gentleman tore down the log structure and built the mill in its present form, afterward sold it to Jacob Staman & Bothers. It was at different times transferred successively to Benjamin Staman, Joseph Gouwger and in 1871, to John Zehner, its present owner. It has long been known as the Staman Mill.[98]

There is a discrepancy between Knapp and Graham as to who purchased the property from Newman. Knapp's account indicates that he sold it to Benjamin Henshey, who then sold it to the Messrs. Staman. Graham's later account indicates that in 1825 Newman sold it to Jacob Staman first, who then, in 1828, transferred it to Benjamin Hershey. Graham's account provided the additional information that it was Hershey who sold it to Jacob Staman & Brothers.

Garber interviewed Jay Middleton in 1948 when Middleton was 87 years old. He told Garber that the Staman Mill in Mifflin was a three-story mill with 2 runs of burrs. Middleton said that the Staman who owned the mill was a brother of Benjamin Stamen, who built the mill in Mifflin, and a great uncle of Willard G. Staman. A covered bridge stood immediately at the mill, the mill being on the right bank, just above the bridge. A considerable community existed at the place at one time and the settlement was called Clapboard Town. There were "6 houses, 1 gristmill, 1 sawmill connected with the same water power but a short distance upstream from the gristmill, 1 tannery run by a man named Parks, and 1 shoemaker's shop run by Parks who prepared his own leather."[99] In March 1948, Garber noted that 1 log house, 1 brick house, and the miller's house still stood on the site.

"The mill never ground flour but was used for other farm grinding. There was also a saw-mill in connection with this establishment." According to Mr. Middleton, "the last owner and operator was John Staman. Previously it had been run by his father, Ben Staman. The Staman Mill was torn down about 15 years ago." (c. 1933)[100]

Guy A. Kister, a third generation millwright from Millbrook, Wayne County, was a long time friend to Garber. Kister operated Kisters Mill, a combination water-powered gristmill, planing mill, sawmill, cider press and machine shop, all in one building. The Kister Mill is still standing intact and operable, an Ohio treasure. Guy Kister had many of his father's and grandfather's millwright records. One of the documents was a letter Jacob Manner, who lived in Newville, wrote to George C. Kister. Manner wrote:

> Perrysville, O., Sept 13, 1870.
>
> Sir; Yours rec'd. Your answer is not altogether satisfactory as I intend to propose to Stamens start up a mill for so much and I necessarily will have to know somewhat near what it will cost to tear down and put it up again. So that I will know how to make my proposition to Stamens &c

please tell me by return mail somewhere what it will be worth, you can by making a calculation, say for taring (sic) down and building up again considering that it will do again to go up just as it is with the addition of one new run of buhrs.

Make a careful calculation and tell me immediately.

Respectfully Yours
Jacob Manner[101]

Garber's research made it clear that Manner was not a millwright himself, but he was credited with having erected three mills and repairing a fourth. There is reason to believe that it was Jacob Manner, through a contract with George C. Kister, who rebuilt the Staman Mill in 1870-71. The mill passed out of the Staman hands in 1871 and John Zehner acquired it and was operating it in 1880. Garber was unable to locate a response from Kister to Manner. It was not unusual for an old mill to literally shake itself to pieces from machinery vibrations and rotting foundation timbers. The mills were then often rebuilt on the old foundations and much of the old equipment was reused.

The Benjamin Staman Grist Mill

The Benjamin Staman Grist Mill was located about a half mile directly north of Mifflin on present day Township Road 1215 along Ruffner Run. The millsite is shown on the *1874 Ashland County Atlas*. Floods and modern construction have erased all traces of it; although a deep ravine for a small feeder stream may well have been an additional water source. A home and buildings below the road now occupy the millsite. When the mill was built or how long it was in operation has not been determined.

The Staman "Ruffner" Saw Mill

The Staman "Ruffner" Saw Mill was located about a mile and a half south of Mifflin east of Route 603 on Seymore Run along present day Township Road T 1095. Records are not clear, but a gristmill was built in that location in 1820 by James Neely. With passing time and the falling water table, it is likely that there was only enough water for a sawmill. A gristmill owned by W. W. Matthews is shown in the *1874 Ashland County Atlas*. Staman may have been the later owner who described it in the following 1902 *The Butler Enterprise* story by A. J. Baughman titled, "A trip to Staman's Mill."

> This locality was once quite a business place, a grist mill and tannery having been operated here in the past for many years.
>
> Cross the river on a high iron bridge, then turn to the right and after a short distance the road bears to the left and as you cross the upland the site of the Ruffner cabin is to the right. A short drive further and you will be at John Staman's where you will want to stop and take dinner for Staman's dinners are in high refute with Mansfield people.
>
> This Staman farm is frequently called "The Ruffner Place," but Ruffner's cabin stood on another quarter of the same section. From the fact that the Ruffner Run (error – Seymore Run) furnishes waterpower for Staman's chip and saw mills and the historical associations of the locality, Staman's is called the Ruffner place.[102]

The Martin Ruffner cabin south of Mifflin was the site of one of two Indian massacres during the War of 1812. The Indians were thought to have retaliated against the burning of their nearby

Figure 112. The Copus monument is along Ashland County Township Road 1224, a small gravel road.

village, Greentown. A monument, a short distance off the road on private land along the east side of Route 603, marks the site of the Ruffner cabin. No road sign indicates there is a monument, but it is on the right of the private drive, back a hundred feet or so. The land owner has thoughtfully kept the area around the monument mowed. In turn, visitors are asked to respect the owner's rights by walking in from the road rather than driving in as there is no place to turn around.

John Gongawan Distillery

The John Gongawan Distillery was in operation in the early 1830s and is shown on the 1832 through 1840 tax records.[103] The distillery was located in the northeast part of Mifflin Township, Ashland County, along what is now road T-1335. No other information has been found, but its location puts it near the Hershey-Staman gristmill. The services of the gristmill would have been needed. Old John must have produced some pretty good liquor, but he moved on in the early 1840s. Perhaps he saw the temperance movement was about to begin, or his still was not profitable because of competition.

Figure 113. The 1812 Ruffner massacre monument is on private property.

The Yeaman Grist and Saw Mills

Along present day Harlan Road south of 430 is a small spring-fed stream that crosses Harlan. This is the general area where the Yeaman Grist and Saw Mills were located. The roads in this area were recognizable on the 1856 or 1873 Atlas maps. The mill locations shown on both early maps are now under water, and the shoreline is a wilderness, except in those areas where homes have been built.

John Yeaman Sr. was born in Washington County, Pennsylvania, in December 1779. In 1807 he married Ann McCready, and they moved to Mifflin Township in 1814, where he purchased three quarter sections of land. A carpenter by trade, Yeaman built a small, twelve-foot square cabin with a clapboard roof and an earthen floor. He built a sawmill in 1830, and a flour-mill in 1832, the first built in his part of the county. The original buhrs used were nigger-heads. The first miller was a man named Cotter, who was then followed by John Stafford. Because of the reputation of the mill, people traveled great distances to have their produce ground.[104]

Life in the early 1800s was not easy and often dangerous. Neighbors in those days were usually several miles away. Yeaman, at one time, spent a number of nights at the home of the Zimmer family, who were his neighbors. One lonely night, the Zimmer family was murdered by Indians.

John Yeaman Jr. was born in Mifflin Township on February 13, 1818. He was born crippled, and according to Graham in *History of Richland County*, because of his handicap he received a "liberal" education. "He began teaching school at the age of 19 and taught for thirteen terms. At some point, his father gave him a farm where Nicholas Henry now lives. John Yeaman, Jr. still owns a small farm with a steam sawmill. He was known as a 'sawyer.'"[105] The timeframe referred to by Graham would be about 1880, when he wrote the book.

The sequence of owners of the Yeaman mills is not clear at this point. A miller, T. G. Wolf, came to Ohio in the fall of 1878. He worked for Snyder Mill as a practical mechanic, and he was a first class miller. Graham wrote that the Snyder Mill was the mill that Yeaman built in 1832. At the time Graham's *History of Richland County* was published, the mill was still considered one of the best mills in the county. The owners had continued expanding the mill, adding a sawmill

Figure 114. The Yeaman Mill.

using a circular saw manufactured by the Mansfield Machine Company. Graham pointed out that the mill was doing "a very extensive business in sawing and lumber of every dimension for building purposes.[106]

Mrs. John D. Harlan was living on the mill property in 1949 when Garber interviewed her. She said that the mill was a 2 ½ story structure above the ground level. It had a millrace about a half mile long that began at the "Cole" place and gathered water from other springs along the way to a two-acre millpond adjacent to the mill. The foundation of the mill is now under the water of the Charles Mill Lake, and only a portion of the penstock shows.[107]

John D. Harlan put in a turbine and did custom grinding of corn meal, buckwheat, feed, etc., but no flour, since he did not replace or repair the bolting system. He also used water power for running a cider press. John C. Snider owned and operated the mill in the 1880s, and apparently he became financially involved with a man named Tandy. As a result, the mill was sold at a Sheriff's sale by L. Tressel, Sheriff of Ashland County, on January 16, 1890. James Dickson bought the mill at that time. He owned it for 28 years, until January 16, 1918, when he and his sister Lillian R. Dickson jointly deeded it to John D. Harlan. It was known in years past as the Snyder Mill. James Dickson never operated the mill as a mill. He had a cheese factory not associated with the mill property. The mill was about 30 x 50 feet and was torn down when sold to the Conservancy District about 1930.

According to Garber's notes about the Yeaman Mill:

> The mill was located on the west bank (probably a small run or springs near the creek) of the Black Fork, and the remains of the mill are located perhaps a half a mile south of Route 30 on the road to Charles Mill. A pair of French buhrs from this mill lay on the bank, by the side of the road, above the millsite. This was an over shot mill with a

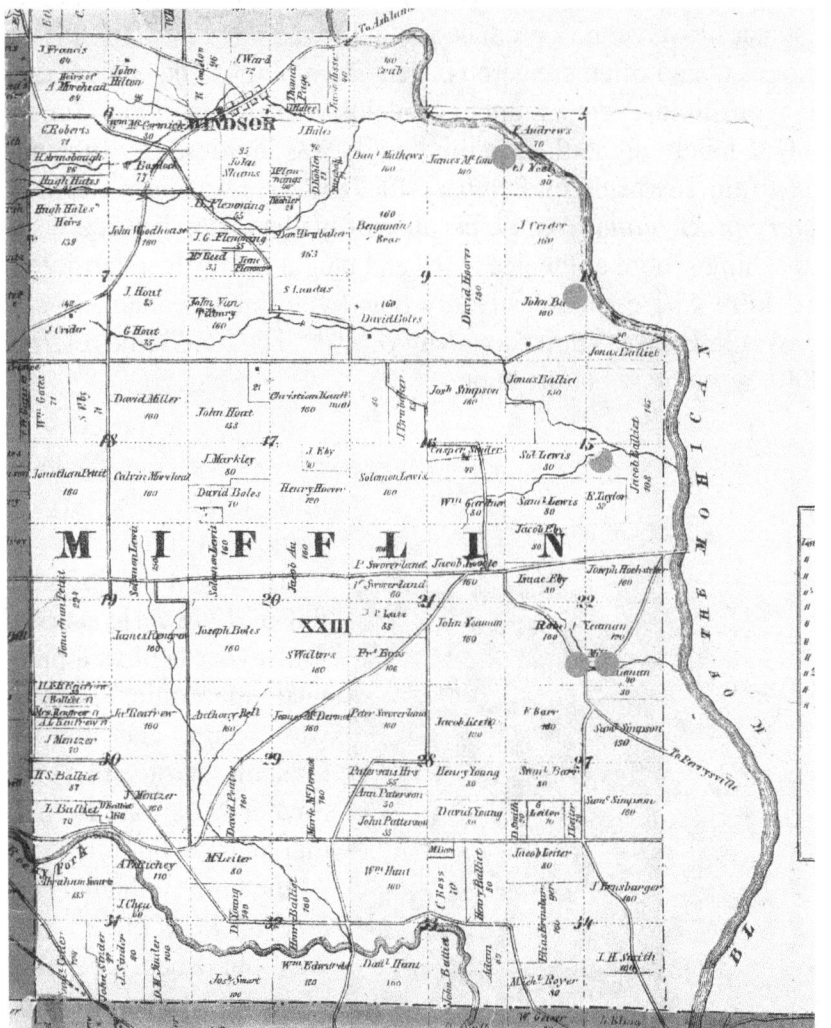

Figure 115. Mifflin Township was organized in 1814. The Black Fork of the Mohican forms a boundary on portions of the north and northeast, and the Rocky Fork flows through the southeastern portion, so that the township was furnished with abundant water and mill privileges. In 1817 the population of the township was 901.[108]

long flume and large wheel similar to the Springville mill (Wayne Co) and the Wolf Mill. C.M. Switzer, aged Mayor of Mifflin, a former miller, rebuilt the flume at one time and stated that it was 16 feet high and 4 feet square. About 1925-30, a turbine was installed as the operating power.

Os (probably Oswalt) Harlan lives or lived at the house, which he built on the hill where the buhrs from the mill are located.[109]

The Eby Mill

The Eby Mill was located near where Crider Road crosses a small spring-fed stream near the intersection of Laver Road. This early mill did not last long due to a diminishing water supply as the water table dropped. The stream that provided water was near the Madison–Mifflin Township border. Garber quoted the history of the Eby Mill from the book *The Swiss Eby Family – Pioneer Millwrights and Millers* as follows:

> While he was yet living in Lancaster County, this Benjamin Eby (1767–1850) and his wife Sarah (Baer) had a son they named Benjamin Eby, (1801–1867) married a Scotch Lassie, Rachel, the daughter of Sarah Jane (Alexander) on May 30, 1821. Having learned the milling business from his father, Benjamin Eby, (1795–1882) young Benjamin Eby (1801–1867) contacted the western fever even as his father before him and in 1829 over the mountains he went, with his young Scotch wife and his babies, to Mifflin Township, Richland County Ohio. Quickly written and easily said, but oh what a journey in those days! On April 9, 1830, a son was born to Benjamin and Rachel (Elder) Eby. Having named a previous son, Elder Eby, after his mother's family, the Elder family of Path Valley, Franklin Co. Pa., they named their new son Alexander Eby after his grandfather's family in Path Valley.
>
> Benjamin Eby (1801–1867) built and operated a merchant mill in Richland County from 1829 to 1838. He also anglicized his name in Ohio from Eby to Aby, and again western fever raged in his veins. Loading all his earthly possessions in a prairie schooner for a second time, he journeyed in 1839 from Mifflin Township, Richland Co., to Millbrook Township, Peoria Co., Illinois. He assisted Charles Whitcomb Stanton to maintain and operate the Stanton Mill on Spoon River, Millbrook Township, Peoria Ill.[110]

The Lewis Grist Mill

The mill stood very near the western edge of the district on the east side of Koogle Road, near the junction of dead end Township Road 294. Its water source was derived from a spring-fed stream. The site is now part of the Charles Mill Lake Conservancy District.

When Garber interviewed John Vail in 1948, Vail told him that the Lewis Grist Mill stood below the hill from the Koogle School house. The large overshot wheel was powered with a flume. The mill was similar to the Wolf Mill at Loudonville. The Lewis Mill was owned and last operated by Solomon Vail, grandfather of John Vail. It was a 1 ½ story building with a 48-inch nigger-head buhr. In 1948 the buhr was still at the millsite and to the right of the road opposite the house.[111]

There are five acres of land in the present property, which is part of the Muskingum Conservancy District, with headquarters at New Philadelphia, Ohio. The occupants of the old house in 1948 rented from the District.[112]

The Samuel Lattimore Grist Mill and Saw Mill

The Samuel Lattimore Grist Mill and Saw Mill were located on Seymore Run, along the east side of present day T 1095, just west of 603 in Ashland County. This was an early sawmill with a gristmill built later, typical of the pattern followed by the early settlers who built water-fed mills. Little information on its operation or how long it operated is available. It was shown on the *1873 Ashland County Atlas,* and at that time it was owned by W.W. Matthews.

The Archer Saw Mill

The Archer Saw Mill was located in the southeast corner of Mifflin Township, Ashland County, fed by a small feeder stream that ran in a westerly direction along Charles Mill Road C-2256. The mill was located on the north side. The side road that led up to the mill no longer exists. The mill was listed in 1832, but was gone by 1839.

The John Stafford Grist Mill

The John Stafford Grist Mill was on the upper reaches of the spring-fed Seymore Run. It was somewhere along the stream south of old Route 30A and southbound C-1095. There is little information on the Staffords. The family was listed as farmers with no mention of the mill. Because the mill was so far upstream, it is doubtful that it lasted much beyond 1840.

The Charles Mill

The Charles Mill is one of those special mills that Garber enjoyed researching. Between the Charles Mill and the Charles Lynn Mill, Garber filled fourteen pages with notes transcribed from various county histories or interviews. The name Charles Mill has a special ring to it. A flood control dam was named after it, the Charles Mill Lake, which is part of the Muskingum Watershed Conservancy. The original Charles Mill was located very near the junction of Charles Mill Road, C-2256, and State Route 603. The mill went through a series of owners.

Silas Longworthy built a small water-powered mill three miles southwest of the village of Mifflin, on the Black Fork in 1825. He sold his mill to John Hershey, who then sold it to Charles Lewis, and finally to Daniel Kauffman, who operated the mill. Kauffman was a skilled millwright. He tore his mill down in 1845 and erected an updated mill that he sold to John Charles. The new mill, propelled exclusively by water, at the time was regarded as one of the best in the county. A sawmill was also attached to it. After Kauffman sold his mill, he turned his attention to farming.[113]

Baughman, in his *History of Ashland County,* stated that Kaughman traded, not sold, his mill property in 1849 for homestead (farming) property that consisted of one hundred and sixty acres comprising the northwest quarter of section 14 on the Black Fork, a mile north of Mifflin on the Black Fork road.[114]

Whether traded or sold, John Charles took possession of the Kauffman Mill. John Charles was born in Lancaster County, Pennsylvania, on July 13, 1802. The youngest of a family of three children, at age 24 he moved to Ohio. He married Maria Huber, also of Lancaster County, on March 9, 1826. They reared a family of six children. For some years Charles engaged in farming. He purchased one of the finest tracts of land in this section. His property was close to the farm where James Copus, Martin Ruffner, and others were massacred by Indians in September 1812. At a sheriff's sale, he purchased 160 acres from Ruffner for $650. He cleared 100 acres and sold it for $8,000, before purchasing the site and mill property on the Black Fork in Mifflin Township. His mills were constantly in operation, "conducted by first-class hands giving universal satisfaction."[115]

E. H. Charles came with his parents in 1859 and made his home on the Black Fork on Section 35, Mifflin Township, where he remained for half a century. He and his father, John, owned the gristmill and sawmill for forty years. Charles managed it himself for thirty-two years. He left the mill in 1882, and when his father died, the property was sold. Charles gave his attention to general farming afterward.[116]

Figure 116. This rare early picture of the 1845 Charles Mill shows the water-powered mill on the left when a shaft ran under the road to power the sawmill on the right. Difficult to see is a bridge over the headrace in the foreground.

In 1862, Charles married Fannie Kauffman, who was born in Mifflin Township, Richland County, five miles east of Mansfield, on November 18, 1838. Her parents were Christian and Anna (Staman) Kauffman.[117] Communities were much smaller in the early 1800s. It was not unusual for close, friendly associations to be developed with one another despite competition between businesses, such as between the millwrights and mill owners. Inter-marriage was not unusual from time to time. Millwrights often relied on one another for assistance, and as families became acquainted, they became friends and occasionally spouses.

C. M. Switzer, the Mayor of Mifflin and a former owner of the Kauffman Mill, was 82 when Garber interviewed him.[118] Switzer indicated that it was Manuel Charles, one of the sons of John Charles, who bought the mill from Kauffman and ran it for nearly forty years. Hill's *History of Ashland County* indicated that it was John Charles who purchased this mill from Kauffman and operated it with his son E. H. Charles. It is possible that Manuel Charles was a son of John Charles and participated in the operation of the former Kauffman Mill. Although somewhat confusing, Switzer went on to say that the mill was eventually sold to John B. Neal and his wife Anna. This Neal was long associated with Elam A. Plank. The two operated the Plank and Neal Mill on the Clear Fork, near Mansfield. The mill was sold to his sister Mary Ann Weaver for $3,000 in 1891. Manuel Charles died in May 1928 at the age of 93.

In December 1898, C.M. Switzer and an uncle, John Miller, jointly operated the mill. Chris Miller and John Miller, brothers, were in fact, real millers who were good at what they did. They taught Switzer the mill business. He continued to work for them or with them until his marriage in 1902. Some time before this he bought the entire interest in the mill, and after his marriage he ran it himself as owner and operator.

"Snow Flake" was the patent name of the flour Switzer made and sold. It was widely used and had an excellent reputation, as shown by numerous entries in his ledger of accounts while at the mill.[119] His father-in-law, Melvin Vail (father of H. John Vail), ran the mill for a couple of years before Switzer sold it in 1915 to Elza G. Sheets, John's father-in-law. John learned the milling business by working at the Charles Mill in 1901 and 1902 while it was owned by his brother-in-law—Switzer was married to Vail's sister.

Vail then worked elsewhere at different trades until 1918 when he returned to work at the Charles Mill. In 1919 he tore the mill down because of the loss of water power. He moved it to Lucas where he rebuilt it. The mill's appearance was the same as when it originally stood on the Black Fork. Melvin Vail ran the mill for some time for both Sheets and Switzer.

Potential flooding was always a concern. After the flood of 1904, when the water came up to the mill about eighteen inches, Switzer raised the mill about three feet on its foundation, believing that it would be safe from flooding for all time. The flood of March 1913 proved Switzer wrong. Flood waters exceeded all previous records. The water was so high it reached above the window

Figure 117. What was known as the The Charles Mill was built in 1845 by Daniel Kauffman, a skilled millwright. He then sold the mill to John Charles, and it was always known as the Charles Mill even after ownership changed. It was damaged in the 1904 flood.

Figure 118. The Charles Mill as it appeared just before it was dismantled and moved to Lucas. Low water, the flood of 1913, and the advantage of electricity coming to Lucas in 1920 no doubt prompted the move. Notice the higher foundation.

sills on the first floor, but it was not high enough to get into the roller system. Much work was required to clean up and dry out the mill floor and the bottoms of the elevators.

A steam-powered sawmill operated in connection with the mill, but was not connected to the mill for that purpose during the time Switzer owned it. Switzer's father had a farm a quarter mile downstream, with a huge sycamore tree standing on the place. It was the largest tree he ever sawed, measuring 33 feet around the stump and about ten or twelve feet above the ground before it branched. Switzer put up a scaffold, and with difficulty, sawed it down with a cross-cut saw. The log was over six feet, taller than a man, and when finally hauled to the mill, it could barely be managed for sawing.

Switzer told Garber of two incidents that occurred at the mill during his ownership. The first incident in 1905 or 1906 was nearly a tragedy. A mill shaft extended up to the comb or top floor of the building with a set screw projecting from it a half or three quarters of an inch. Little was thought of it since it was so small and its location seldom visited. Willie Wilson, Switzer's nephew, was visiting the mill. He loved to explore, and one day the mill suddenly stopped. Switzer knew at once that something was wrong, and he ran from one floor to another, trying to locate the source of the problem.

Willie had been playing in the area of the extended screw, and his clothing somehow got entangled in the set screw and the revolving shaft. All of his clothing was twisted and torn off

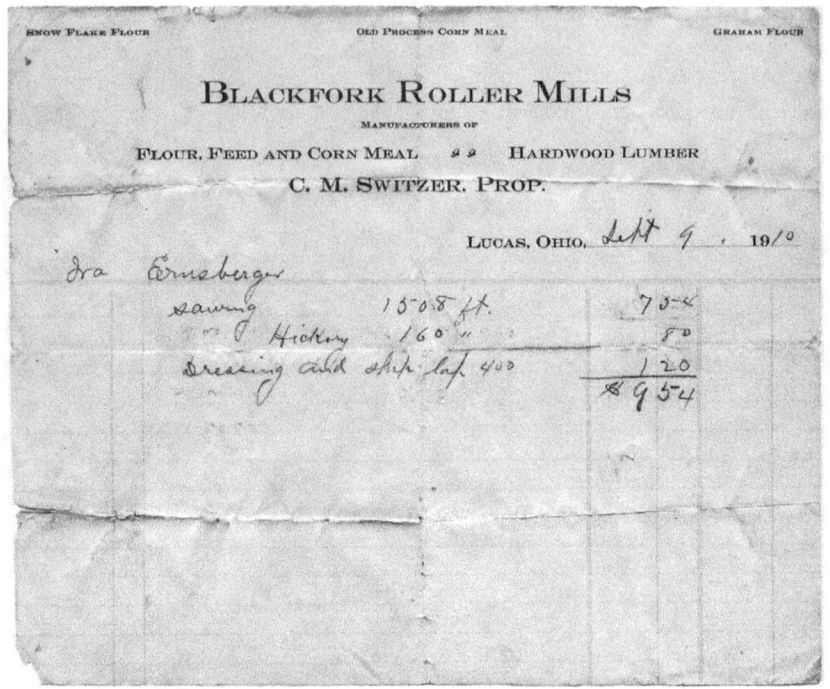

Figure 119. A surviving bill for sawmill work done by Ira Ernsberg while C.M. Switzer ran the mill in 1910.

except a small garment on his chest. John Laughlin, an assistant at the mill, arrived at the scene and saved Willie's life by throwing off the belt and stopping the mill. Willie was bruised and burned on one side, but otherwise safe.

On another occasion, in 1901, two young men arrived from Loudonville in a horse-drawn buggy. They had come to Mifflin to see a girl. Because it was an exceptionally dark night on their return trip to Loudonville, they borrowed a lantern from George J. Mowery to help them on their way. Switzer was visiting his girl friend, who was living with her parents in the old miller's house. Suddenly he heard someone yell, and he rushed out to see what the trouble was. It was very dark, and as he listened to the cries for help, Switzer became confused. He missed the path and found himself in the millrace.

The two young men, trusting the better eyesight of their horses, suddenly found that the horses had missed the path. The buggy, the horses, and the young men also ended up in the millrace. The buggy was on its side, but the boys managed to escape drowning. The horses were retrieved, the men were taken in, dried out, and put up for the night. The buggy was completely under water, but they salvaged it the next morning. Some ten years later, while Switzer drained the race to clean it out, he found the lantern that the two young men borrowed, as well as a pint of whiskey that they lost in their struggles in the water.

After John Vail moved the mill to Lucas, he rebuilt it and ran it for a cooperative for 14 years. It was then sold to George Smith, who apparently did not have sufficient capital or backing, and the mill ceased to run for two or three years. It was run by electric power at this location.[120] In an interview with Earnest W. Stafford of Widowville, Ashland County, in May 1959, Garber learned that a line shaft for the original mill ran under the road from the gristmill to the sawmill, protected in a boxlike structure. Stafford also gave Garber a photograph of the Charles Mill taken about one week before it was torn down—about 1920 or the early 1920s.[121] On Wednesday, July 31, 1957 an article "Landmark Destroyed" appeared in *The Mansfield News Journal*. The article read in part:

> A Lucas land mark. The Lucas Mill, once known as the Charles Mill was destroyed by fire at 7 p.m. last night. Firemen from Mansfield and Perrysville helped battle the blaze at the corner of First Avenue and Bond Street.
>
> The fire apparently started in bales of straw stored outside the 100 x 60 foot building under an overhanging roof. Lucas Fire Chief Clayton Heimberger said the building owned by William Sweezie had been used for storage in recent years. The larger part of the structure was once the

Charles Mill located on the site of the present Charles Mill Lake dam. A former Lucas School building which once stood on the site of the present Lucas Post Office was combined with the Charles Mill to make the Lucas Mill 39 years ago."[122]

Figure 120. The Charles Mill dam on the Black Fork was to give its name to the present flood control dam. Its construction erased all traces of the mill.

John Woodhouse Oil Mill

The John Woodhouse Oil Mill was located a mile south of Windsor on the north side of Fleming Falls Road, east of Windsor Road. The mill was located near the slight jog in the Fleming Falls Road, in the very southeast corner of section 6. An oil mill was a rare sight in early Richland County. Flax seeds were ground, and oil was pressed out, producing linseed oil, the base of early paint and varnish, and it could also be used as a dryer. After extracting the oil, the leftover cakes of seed were used as animal feed. The fiber of the plant straw was sometimes used in linen cloth or paper making, but there is no record of such an undertaking in Richland County.

A. J. Baughman described John Woodhouse's operation in 1898.[123] He used the water from the north branch of Fleming Run to operate the oil mill where flax seed was ground into meal and the oil pressed out—making two marketable commodities, oil and meal-cake. The mill dam was used as an ice pond in the winter. Ice was taken and stored until the next summer when he hauled it to Mansfield for sale. Woodhouse was a pioneer in the ice business in the area.

The Woodhouse oil mill was in operation in the 1830s, but it closed by 1849. The land was still in the family into the 1870s. It is not known how long the mill was in operation, but because it was on a feeder stream nearly three miles upstream from the Black Fork, it would not have lasted many years. No other information about John Woodhouse was uncovered other than that in 1880 he lived in the township's oldest brick house.

The Braden Saw Mill

The Braden Saw Mill was located on a small stream about a mile southeast of Mifflin, in Ashland County, where the stream crosses C 1095. It began operation in 1836, but was out of business by 1840. Lack of water may have been the culprit. Today one can easily step across some of these streams that once supported a mill. With modern farming, tiled fields, and land clearing for increased crops, some waterways have almost disappeared.

Mifflin Oil Mill.

JOHN WOODHOUSE would respectfully announce that he still continues to manufacture and keep on hand the best qualities of

LINSEED OIL

at his Oil Mill, four miles north east of Mansfield, and nearly half a mile south-east of Windsor.

He *warrants* his oil to be a *pure article* of the best quality, and feels a confidence in recommending it to the public, as his mill is old and well established; its reputation is surpassed by none in the State.

Mifflin tp. May 5, 1852—6m.

CABINET WARE,
AT THE
MIFFLIN OIL WORKS.

Mr. John Woodhouse also manufactures and keeps constantly on hand every variety of

Tables, Bureaus, Center Tables, Bedsteads

and all other articles usually called for in that line, which he warrants to be made of the best materials and in the most workmanlike manner.

N. B. Coffins made on the shortest notice.

Mifflin tp., May 5, 1852—6m

Figure 121. An 1852 newspaper ad for the John Woodhouse flax seed oil mill indicates linseed oil was not his only endeavor. All types of household furniture and coffins on short order were available. There were very few flax mills in Richland County.

Monroe Township

The Black Fork enters Monroe Township near the northeast boundary, travels south a little over two miles where it is joined by the Rocky Fork, then turns east unto Green Township in Ashland County. This area is rugged and heavily wooded even today, and surprisingly no mills are recorded on this section of the Black Fork. The east-west path of the Rocky Fork is a different story. Its nearly five-mile path across the township is dotted with mills. These will be covered in the last section of this book. The mills on the southern tributaries of the Clear Fork were covered in the first section.

Green Township

Green Township is in Ashland County, and its rugged hilly terrain supported many mills and distilleries. The *1832 Auditor's records* shed some light on the latter. Thirty-four full-time distilleries

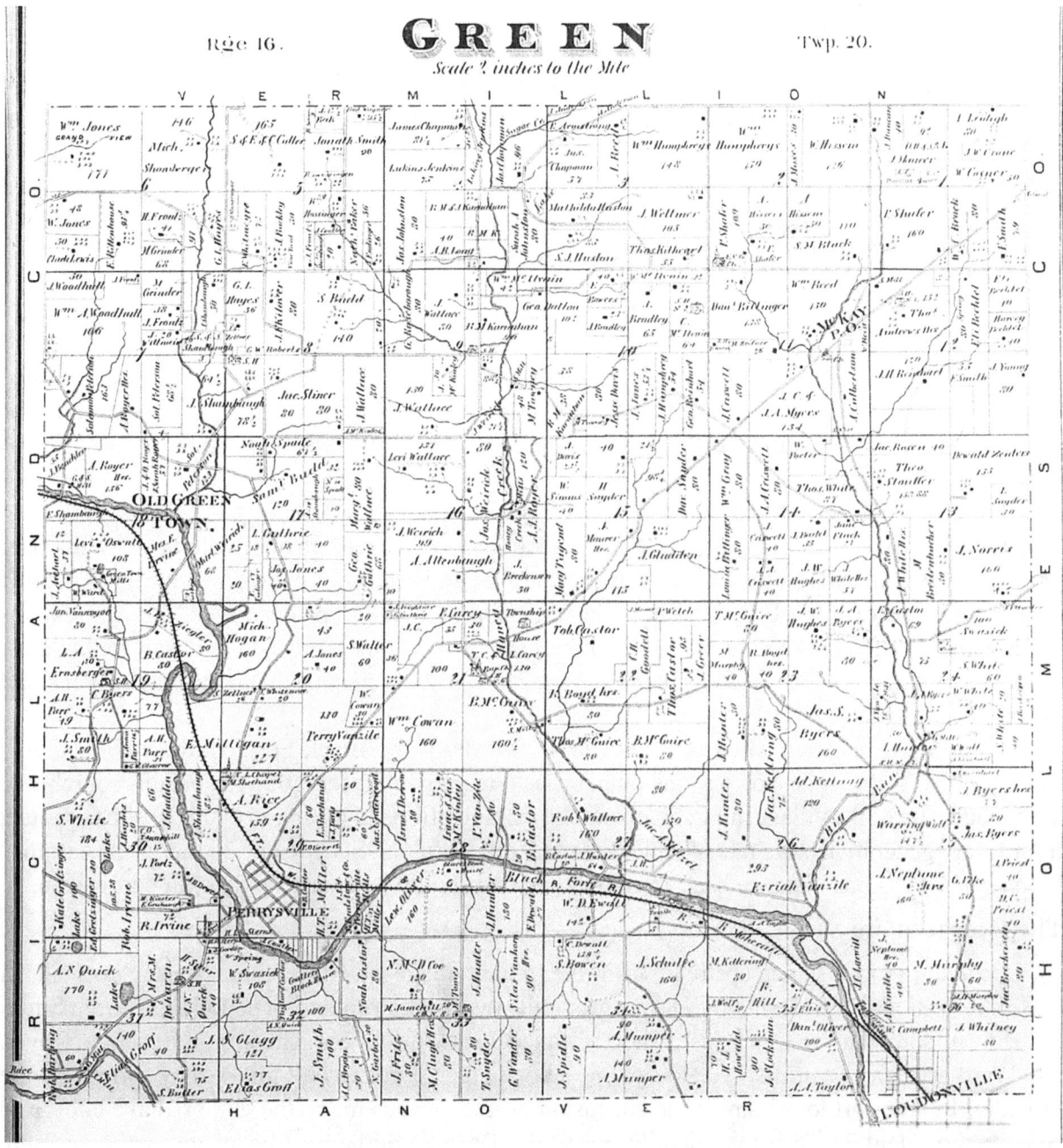

Figure 122. 1874 Map of Green Township.[124]

were in operation in Richland County that year, and only those full-time operations were taxed and recorded. Numerous small stills were known to exist, but because they served a family or limited clientele, they were not taxed. Green Township had six full-time distilleries, the most of any other township in the county. Evidently, there was a good deal of illness and snake bites. Whisky was the cure all, and of course, it was the favorite choice after a hard day's work or social event.

Numerous mills, distilleries, and tanneries are listed in the old Auditor's Records but no locations are given. In Green Township, section 16 was set aside for school lands. The land was rented with the money going to support schools; however, the recording problem in Green stems from the fact that the whole southwest corner of the township (9 sections—each a mile square) was also rented or leased. Taxes of seven percent were based on land improvements, but exact property locations were not listed. Eventually the land was sold, often to the renters, but a gap in historical records exists.

In 1985 the *Ashland County Genealogical Society* published an excellently researched book on the Green Township records and villages. *Green Township* is a source that goes beyond the writers' records and is recommended to those who might be interested.

Greentown Spring Mills

The Greentown Mills were located in the southwest corner of section 18 on the south side of the Black Fork, on the east side of County Highway 1075 about a tenth of a mile south of State Route 39. The spring-fed mills gained their name from the Greentown Indian Village, that was once located a short distance to the north. The *1874 Ashland County Atlas* shows the mills as owned by Levi Oswalt.

The Indian village was settled by mostly Delaware and Mingo Indians in 1782. It grew to an estimated 150 dwellings. The Indians were peaceful, and early settlers often interacted with them. During the War of 1812, however, they were removed to Piqua by American Militia, who feared they would side with the British. The village was burned and crops destroyed after the Indians grudgingly left after being assured they could return after the war. This action is believed to have led to the massacre at the Ruffner and Copus cabins, a dark chapter in the history of Richland County.

The upper Greentown Mills were on the north side of the Black Fork. In the *1874 Ashland County Atlas* A. Royer is shown as the owner. The Greentown Preservation Association purchased the 52-acre site of the village, and volunteers are making efforts to clear and open the site to protect it for future generations. A State of Ohio historical marker along State Route 39 marks the entrance to the site. It is some distance back from the road and should be entered only with permission.

The George Smith Saw Mill

Located a short distance upstream from the Indian village was the George Smith Saw Mill. It was in operation by 1835, and by 1839 a gristmill was up and running. His father, George Smith Sr. had a gristmill and distillery just a short distance further upstream. The Smith, Beachler, Royer, and Ward grist and sawmills were located near each other, evidently all four fed by springs on the hillside. In an effort to minimize the confusion on the various mills, the authors have chosen to refer, to the extent possible, to each mill separately. Because of the frequent changes of ownership that took place, it is difficult to get a clear understanding of the history of these mills. The Smiths, however, were gone by 1841.

Baughman, in his *History of Ashland County*, wrote about the early settlers in Green Township:

> The Black Fork of the Mohican enters the township from its western borders and flows in a southeasterly course until it reaches Loudenville, in Hanover Township, a distance of about ten miles. The low banks and sluggish current of this stream renders its water privileges of little value. There are however, two dams in Green Township. One of these runs two pair of buhrs and one saw was formerly owned by Mr. Beachley, and the other known as the Stringer Mill, but is now owned by A. A. Taylor and has three pair of buhrs. The valley of this stream is generally broad, and its fertility is not excelled elsewhere in Ohio.[125]

Baughman used Knapp's *History of Ashland County*, published in 1863, as at least one of his sources in describing the mill activity in Ashland County. Baughman's verbiage above is almost word-for-word as in Knapp's account.

Graham states in his *History of Richland County* that: "The mill now owned by William Ward two and a half miles from Perrysville, is located on a large spring. The first mill in this place was erected by William Clemmens. It was subsequently taken down and the present one erected by Nicholas Swearengen.[126] In the *Records of Township Trustees of Green Township, 1819-1832*, the 1827 list of householders in Green Township show William Clemens living in the southwest ¼, section 18.[127]

Knapp's account in the following paragraphs was also used by Baughman with minor changes:

> Upon the Clear Fork, which only runs about a mile through the southwest corner of Green Township, there is one dam, furnishing power for running a grist-mill with three pairs of burrs, and a saw-mill with one saw. These mills are now the property of Thomas W. Calhoun.
>
> Honey Creek originates in the Quaker Springs, near the southeast line of Vermillion Township, and pursues a southwardly course through Green, a distance of about five miles, and terminates in the Black Fork, upon the land recently owned by the late Abraham Dehaven. Upon this stream there are six saw-mills and one grist-mill.[128]

Knapp also provides a delightful description of distiller mills in Green Township; a description that seems appropriate here. He wrote:

> In the early days, among the sylvan shades of wild and beautiful Green Township, were no less than eight distilleries. A staunch, buzzing, seething, chattering, peerless one, was that which stood on the green slope just a few rods above Greentown meeting-house: old settlers will tell you now, with a sneaking, fun-loving twinkle in the half averted eye, "it made most delicious whisky." ... Another distillery was near where Warring Wolf now lives, a mile or so below McKay; another on the Van Horn estate; one on the Vanscoyoe farm; another on Richard Guthrie's; another on Jesse Parr's; and the last one we can remember, near the old Manner Mill, on the Clear Fork.
>
> Thank God! they are all gone now.[129]

In January 1955, Garber bought a 1837 volume from Earnest J. Wesson, a well-known Ohio book dealer that contained the following advertisement:

Valuable Mill Property A Bargain Offered

> The subscribers offer for sale 80 acres of first rate land in Green Township, Richland County, Ohio, on the Black Fork of the Mohican, one mile below the mouth of the Rocky Fork, which makes it a never failing stream. There is now in operation a first rate SAW MILL, CARDING MACHINE & FULLING MILL, on said premises with all the necessary articles required for such machineries. There is also on said premises a good site for a grist mill with eight feet of head and fall without being encumbered by any adjoining farms. Said establishment is situated in the heart of a Richly Settled Country, to wit 6 miles from Petersburg, 7 miles from Hayesville, & 9 miles from Loudenville. There is also on the said premises a good dwelling house. Any person wishing

to purchase such property will do well by calling on the subscribers living on the premises. - Terms will be made accommodating by: James Royer & Ephraim Royer, June 13, 1837.[130]

Between 1948 and 1950, Garber interviewed several individuals on the topic of the Beacheler Mill including Weldon Fightner, Gar Beachler, and Mrs Tom Byers. In 1948 Fightner resided on the Greenwood Mill property. He pointed out to Garber the location where the mill stood, and he recalled that it was a three-story mill. The remains of the dam were not far upstream from the mill seat and according to him the millrace could still be seen. He also stated that there was a sawmill connected with Beachler Mill.

Fightner was the owner of the Greentown property when Garber interviewed him in June 1949. He recalled that both the Ward (Greentown) Mill and the Beachler Mill were but a short distance from his property. Garber noted that The Greentown Mills' names were not known locally by the people interviewed, but they did recognize the Ward Mill by name. Even Beachler, 44 year-old son of John Beachler who had owned both properties, recognized the Ward Mill name.[131]

It is not quite clear when Ward took possession of the Ward (Greentown) mill, but he had his share of problems. A brief announcement in *The Richland Star* in December 1850 reported that "Some Rascals raised the head gates of Mr. Ward's mill, which is situated on the Black Fork above Perrysville, late at night, and before the mill could be stopped considerable damage was done. He caused some parties to be arrested but they were released for want of evidence."[132]

Gar Beachler was born on the Greentown home site. He told Garber that the Greentown Mill was three stories and that it had two runs of stone. He recalled his father, John Beachler, who died in 1924, describing the mill to him. Gar was 13 or 14 years old when his father passed away. He stated that his father told him that the source of water for the mill were large springs that were located across the road from the millsite and some distance up the low ground.[133]

Fightner told Garber that some evidence of the millrace could still be seen, but most evidence of the mill disappeared with time and cultivation. There may have been a source from springs and a millpond above the mill on the same side of the road. It is possible there was another millpond as well.[134]

Mrs. Tom Byers, also interviewed by Garber, said Tom Beachler sold his property to her husband in 1918 or 1919. She said they had lived on the property ten years when they rented the mill as tenant property to a man named Ott Evans. The county took thirty acres of the property for road construction. She said that the top of the mill was missing when they lived there, and the old structure was used for stock and storage.

A man named Olney purchased the mill after Evans had lived there for some time. The Olney family finally tore down the remains of the old mill structure between 1933-1936. Gar Beachler stated that French buhrs were used, and he thought the Onley descendants might throw light on the disposition of the remaining mill equipment.

Garber interviewed O.D. Culler in July 1949. Culler told him that William Ward was killed by a Pennsylvania Railroad train at a crossing near his home. He was driving a gray horse with a spring wagon toward Mansfield. Ward made an extra fine corn meal that sold well in Mansfield, and to meet the demand he made about three trips a week to Mansfield with his horse and wagon. Culler identified the remains after the accident, because he was near the crossing at the time.[135]

In May 1950 Garber interviewed John K. Cowan, from Perrysville. He told Garber that on one Halloween Willis (Wilson) Peterson and a number of other boys sawed a plank used for crossing the pond to the mill at Wards. It was only partially sawed through so that it was weakened. They then slipped into the mill and started it running. Mr. Ward heard it and rushed over to shut it down. As he started across the plank, it broke under his weight, and he was thrown into the water. The pranksters had to fish him out to keep him from drowning because he could not swim.[136]

Nathan DeHaven Saw Mill

The Nathan DeHaven Saw Mill was located on the northeast quarter of section 27 near the mouth of Honey Creek. The Black Fork would have required a larger dam and there was little fall of water at that point. The DeHaven family arrived in 1839, and then purchased the site to build a mill for $50.00. The sawmill was in operation the next year. John Chapman (Johnny Appleseed) leased a parcel of land for 40 years just to the south to DeHaven along the Black Fork.

The present day location of the mill is near County Road 775, near the intersection of Township Road 2724. In early days a bridge crossed the Black Fork near the millsite. Baughman noted in his *History of Ashland County* that the source of Honey Creek was in Quaker springs in Vermillion Township and pursued a southwesterly course through Green, a distance of about five miles, and emptied into the Black Fork at the farm once owned by the late Abraham DeHaven. Several sawmills and one gristmill were located on this stream.[137]

Graham's *History of Richland County* adds additional information on the original mills in Green Township. He wrote:

> Several mills have been erected, from time to time, in the township. The settlers first went to Mount Vernon for their grinding, and later to the mill at Newville. The "Darling" mill on the Clearfork, was erected probably as early as 1818 or 1820. The "Stringer" mill was erected in 1842, on the Black Fork, one mile below Perrysville. One of the early mills was erected by Isaac Meanner in the northeast corner of the township; it is now operated by a Mr. Wolf. One of the early mills was also located on Honey Creek, three miles northeast of Perrysville; it was erected by Jesse Vanzile – now owned by A. J. Royer. The mill now owned by William Ward, two and a half miles west of Perrysville, is located on a large spring. The first mill in this place was erected by Nicholas Swearengen.[138]

Garber found evidence of a mill of substantial proportions located on the west side of Honey Creek, close by the confluence of the Honey Creek stream and the Black Fork of the Mohican. The mill stood in the angle of the Honey Creek Road, with Honey Creek to the right driving toward Loudonville. An old road led to the Black Fork, no more than 50 yards long, and it crossed the Black Fork over the old DeHaven covered bridge. The old bridge, built by Van Zile, the father or grandfather of Orland Van Zile of Watts Mill at Newville, was washed out in the 1913 flood.

Figure 123. Sections 9 and 16 of Green Township.

Honey Creek Mills

Several mills were located on the upper reaches of Honey Creek. One mill was on the southeast quarter of section nine east of present day County Highway 775, on Township Road 2475, just on the east side of Honey Creek. The 1874 *Ashland County Atlas* shows the headrace and mill location of the Weirich Saw Mill.[139] It is located in Section 9, in the southeast corner. Three quarters of a mile south of the Weirch Mill are the Royer Mills. They were located near Township Road 827, east of where it crosses Honey Creek (Section 16, upper corner, east side). This is about three miles east of Perrysville. Today it is easier to find by going north off State Route 95 on County Highway 775. The first two roads to the right go to the millsites.

Karnahan-Jennings Mill

One of these early mills along Honey Creek was erected by Jessie Vanzile. Royer Vanzile was listed as owner as late as 1845, and in 1880 was owned by A. J. Royal.

Garber interviewed Edna and Lena Jennings who were living on the old Karnahan-Jennings property. The old mill was about 30 x 40 feet and 2 ½ stories tall as they recalled it. It had one run of buhrs and did custom grinding, but it never had a bolting system, and flour was never manufactured. They said that Robert Karnahan acquired the property in 1863 and ran the mill for 20 years, until his death in 1883. Joseph D. Jennings, who married Robert's daughter, Theresa J. Karnahan, learned the milling business from Karnahan and continued to operate it until 1890.

The sisters also told Garber that a millwright named Kister, of Millbrook in Wayne County, came to dress the stones and make necessary repairs. Garber knew both Guy Kister and Hen (Henry) Basore, both millwrights who had worked at the Honey Creek mill at various times. Kister came until Jennings learned to dress them himself. Miss Jennings stated that the corn meal, made from the first two or three grists of the stones was of a fine texture and had a slightly burned or scorched taste that they relished.

Garber noted that apparently the sawmill was much older than the gristmill, but it does not appear on the *1874 Ashland County Atlas*.[140]

When Garber interviewed William Simms in 1950, Simms told him that he helped his father, Shannon Simms, erect the Karnahan Mill about 1885. He recalled the building well, and his statements are doubtless accurate. He did not infer that his father did the millwright work. He did say that Kister put in all the mill machinery and that there was a turbine for both the saw and gristmill. Simms said that no grinding was done after 1920.[141]

Figure 124. Robert Karnahan.

Weirich Mill

The Weirich Mill was downstream from the Karnahan Mill. When interviewed by Garber in 1950, C. E. Weirich said that his wife was born and lived on the farm adjacent to the mill property on land then owned by his brother. According to him the mill was 3 ½ stories above the basement and about 40 x 50 feet, with an overshot about 15 feet in diameter and 2 ½ feet or more wide. The one-acre millpond was located ¼ mile above the mill. Two sets of buhrs, one of these a niggerhead buhr, could be found in his brother's barn at that time. The mill always operated by water power with a wheel; it never had a turbine.

According to Weirich, Jack Royer owned and operated the mill. The sawmill was in active operation during his time. Next to own and operate the mill was Levi Zimmerman, and he was the last man to operate it. The mill was always a buhr mill and never had a roller system. Godfrey Shawecker owned and occupied the property after Zimmerman, but he never operated it. By the time Shannon Simms acquired the mill from Shawecker, it was badly deteriorated and no longer of value as a mill. Shannon Simms and his son John Simms dismantled it and tore it down.[142] John

Figure 125. The possible remains of the Weirich Grist Mill on Honey Creek are difficult to pinpoint. Road improvements and farm pond grading may have erased headrace remains but what appear to be foundation stones remain. It is very difficult to locate millsites that vanished over a century ago.

Simms provided the timeframe that the mill came down—in 1915-1916. Afterward it was used for farm purposes for many years. John was 75 years old when Garber interviewed him and his wife in 1950. Garber noted that Simms and his wife were "both bright with clear memory."[143]

The Simms confirmed the size of the mill and added that the two sets of both nigger-head and French buhrs were 48-inch buhrs. Most of the buhrs were buried under the ruins of the filled-in foundation. The last buhrs used were French buhrs. Simms was positive that the metal waterwheel was 22 feet in diameter and about 4 to 5 feet wide. No turbine was ever used. The one-acre millpond was about 8 or 9 feet deep. The mill used a bolting system and made flour.

They confirmed that Zimmerman was the last to operate the gristmill. Jack Royer apparently followed Zimmerman, and Royer continued the operation of the sawmill and the cider press. John's father Shannon Simms purchased the mill property about 1900. He was born November 20, 1842 and died on November 13, 1927.

Honey Creek Mill

John Simms' brother William, who provided information about the Karnahan Mill, was also familiar with the Honey Creek Mill. He said the mill was about 40 x 60 feet and had 3 sets of buhrs, one for feed and chop and two sets for flour. This mill had a turbine, and two ponds provided water to the mill, a one-acre pond and a larger two-acre pond located about ¼ to ½ miles above. William was the first to plow the property after the pond was drained and mill operation discontinued. Silt had so enriched the land that he said it was the finest and best piece of land he ever worked.

William Taylor Grist and Saw Mill

Located east of State Route 95 near the junction of County Highway 775 junction with 2654 was the William Taylor Grist and Saw Mill. Both mills were listed in the mid-1830s, but in 1839 only the sawmill was registered. The 1861 Atlas map shows the sawmill only owned by George Cake, and the 1874 map lists B. McGuire as owner with the mill still in operation. No other information has been found. The mill must have been a successful operation and was well built or rebuilt over the years.

Records of Trustees of Green Township, 1819-1832 show that the Thomas Taylor gristmill appraised at $1,200 in 1829; the sawmill appraised at $400. Garber noted that on the *John Sherman map of 1830*, a gristmill is shown on the southwest ¼ of section 22, close to the section line with section 21, immediately to the west. This mill may well be identified as the Taylor-Martin Mill.

Warren Jennings, in his 1841 edition of *The Ohio Gazetteer and Travelers Guide*, wrote: "Martins Mill, the name of the post office in Green Township is about 13 miles southeast of Mansfield and 75 miles north east of Columbus.[144]

When Garber interviewed John K. Cowan in 1950, Cowan told him:

> The Martin Mill is believed to have been located near the Honey Creek crossing – east of Perrysville. It is also believed to have been the Taylor Mill. The 1836 election was at the Taylor Mill on Section 21 (or 22) as shown on the Sherman map. This mill was known as a saw mill by the Cowan Family and was located in what was known as the "mill corner" of the field below the barn on the property.[145]

John K. Cowan's father purchased the property at a Sheriffs sale, but the former owner did not relinquish the old deeds. So there are no old records available except at the courthouse. Garber noted that a nigger-head buhr from the old mill was located in the front wall of the barn on the William Cowan farm. William was John's brother and served as Postmaster at Loudonville. The old buhr was 34 inches in diameter and 12 inches thick when Garber measured it. It was built into the foundation when the barn was built in 1872.

Simon Rowland Saw Mill

The mill was located somewhere north of Township Road 2404. This road runs east from State Route 60 and ends near the majestic crossroads village of McKay. It was located on a small stream that flowed in a westerly direction into Honey Creek. Being on a small spring-fed stream, the Simon Rowland mill was doubtlessly left high and dry as the water tables dropped. Today it is hard to believe the remains of the water course once supported a sawmill. Little is known of Simon Rowland or the mill he operated from 1837 through 1845. It is believed it was his father, James Rowland, who bought the land from the government in 1831.

Big Run Mills in Green Township

The "Big Run" has its start in the northeastern corner of Green Township and runs in a wiggling fashion south, until it empties into the Black Fork a mile or so above Loudenville. Not as big as Honey Creek, it nevertheless supported a number of mills.

Thomas Andrews Saw Mill

This mill is shown on the *1874 Ashland County Atlas* but not on the 1861 map. It may have been water powered but there is the possibility it was steam. After the Civil War steam-powered circular saws gained favor, because they could be moved as demand required. Once much of the timber around a mill was consumed, moving closer to a new source was easier than moving logs a great distance to the saw.

Joseph Rinehart Saw Mill

The Joseph Rinehart Saw Mill was located on a small stream that fed into Big Run about a mile south of McKay along Township Road 2474, which follows the stream. In operation in the late 1830s, it was gone by 1845, evidently because it lost its water supply. Rinehart was then listed in the census as a farmer.

Isaac Menor (Meanor, Mennor) Grist Mill, Saw Mill & Carding Machine

In public records the Menor name is spelled several ways. Isaac Menor built a carding mill on the east side of Big Run near the junction of State Route 60 and Township Road 2724. It was quite an undertaking in the late 1830s, because, as shown on the 1874 Atlas, it required digging nearly a mile-long headrace. In 1831 the gristmill and sawmill were in operation, and by 1838 Menor had built a carding mill. The carding mill was probably in a separate building to keep wool fibers from drifting into the flour of the gristmill. The expense or failure of the latter may have caused financial trouble for the Menor family as seen in the following article:

Sheriffs Sale

By the Court of Common Pleas of Richland County I will expose at public sale at the house of John Wiler, in the town of Mansfield, on the 3d day of February 1844, between the hours of 10 o'clock and 4 P. M., one shearing machine, one horse buggy, one set of single harness, one black mare, one ten plate stove and one cow, seized and taken as the property of John C. Meanor and Armstrong Meanor, at the suit of William McMillen and William Irish.

Sheriff's Office, William Kerr, Sheriff, December 25, 1843.[146]

A second advertisement added something that Sheriff Kerr missed—one carding machine. Perhaps the carding mill was a financial failure, or they were unable to pay for the machines or millwright services.

The Green Township Trustees list of householders includes Isaac Meanor in 1827, and it mentions a mill in 1828. No other mention has been found except that the *1840 Richland County Auditors Records* do list Joseph Mannor as owner of one gristmill and sawmill. No location is given. Perhaps these were on leased school lands. In 1845, Armstrong Menor owned the original grist and sawmill in Section 24, while John Menor owned the carding mill nearby. In 1874 only the gristmill remained, and it was owned by a man named Hunter.

The Wolf Grist Mill.

John Wolf arrived in 1815 for assignee Isaac Wolf who was to settle on the northwest ¼ of section 25 in Green Township. The hillside spring may have been an appealing source of water power but dates of ownership are vague. Isaac Meanor built a mill at this location in 1831. It was subsequently rebuilt and is the present mill building moved to Mohican Park. The mill property

Figure 126. The rebuilt and relocated Wolf Mill near Loudenville and Mohican National Forest is the finest example of a mill in old Richland County. The mill is open on weekends in summer and has a good collection of original milling equipment and gearing. It is well worth a visit.

eventually passed to his son Warren Wolf in the 1840s. One source states that the mill was in operation until the 1920s. The Wolf Mill is the only remaining example of the many water powered gristmills that once dotted old Richland County.

The following was copied by Miss Virginia Wolf from *Early Homes of Ohio* by L. T. Frary:

> Although out of place in this discussion I cannot resist introducing an illustration of the great overshot wheel formerly at Wolf's Mill near Loudonville. It is difficult to realize that within memories of living persons such wheels constituted practically the only source of power, excepting the horse that was utilized in this country. This mill is particularly interesting because of the fact that all the water required for its operation flowed directly from springs through a flume, in sufficient volume to turn the wheel without necessity for impounding it in a mill pond. The spring still yields the same abundance of pure water but the machinery lies unused almost intact within the mill. It is to be hoped that this will be preserved as an historic monument to illustrate the vast strides that have been made in industrial development from this simple power house to the great plants of Cleveland, Youngstown, Warren, Lorain and other industrial cities that have given northern Ohio the name "Rhur of America."[147]

Not long after this was written, the machinery was stripped from the mill and sold. Then it was remodeled into a tea room. The great wheel fell to pieces and robbed posterity of still another relic of the past. Much has changed since Garber completed his research; but fortunately for mill enthusiasts today, the Wolf Mill still stands, although in a different location. It was dismantled in 1972-73 and moved to a new site. In the past State Route 60 north of Loudonville made a jog around the old mill. When the State Highway Department straightened the road, the mill had to go. It did go, thanks to Edward and Lavern Pennell.

Figure 127. This shows the south side of the mill and stone foundation showing the size and construction of these buildings.

Pennell hired help to number and dismantle the timbers of the old mill and moved it to the edge of Mohican State Park. There it was re-erected, with a new flume along with a 16-foot overshot waterwheel, and the remodeling transformed the tea room into an ice cream parlor that was opened inside.

Renamed the Wolf Creek/Pine Run Grist Mill, the venture was partially successful. It was open only in summer, with the waterwheel, bull gear inside, and center vertical power shaft the only moving atttractions in the mill. Little in the way of milling equipment was left. After Pennell passed away unexpectedly in March 1983, the building sat unused. The State of Ohio bought the property and planned to make it into a tourist attraction. The plans never materialized. In 2000 the Wolf Creek/Pine Run Grist Mill, with broken windows and leaking roof, was again slated for demolition.

A professional building restorer, Mark J. Smith, stepped in at the last minute and organized a nonprofit "Friends of the Mill" group. With a lot of persuasion, donated funds, volunteers, and donated material, his group leased about 50 acres of the park and rebuilt and repaired the mill.

Milling equipment from the crumbling Rummel Mill near Butler was donated and moved inside, and millstones from the old A. A. Taylor Mill at Loudonville also found a new home.

Today the Wolf Creek/Pine Run Grist Mill is a welcomed tourist attraction, well worth a summer weekend visit for anyone wanting to see an old mill and milling equipment. It is the only waterwheel turning mill left in what was old Richland County, a county that in 1840, likely had as many as 190 such mills. Volunteers are invited to become students of the milling craft at the Wolf Creek/Pine Run Grist Mill. Additional information on the mill and volunteering is located at: http://oldmills.scificincinnati.com/ohio_mills_ashland_wolf_creek_history_page.html.

Figure 128. The hillside spring that was the source of water for the Wolf Mill made a beautiful photograph. The area is now grown over with trees and brush.

Figure 129. The 18-foot waterwheel and flume were still standing but showing the deterioration from the ravages of time and weather. This picture shows the construction and support needed for both the wheel and the flume.

Figure 130. A pipe from the spring to a fountain was for drinking water for both man and beast. In winter it led to this spectacular scene.

Figure 131. There are three sets of millstones in the Wolf Mill. The grain was put in the hopper (top) which is supported by the hopper rest. The grain was fed from the hopper to a lightly vibrating shoe (center) and from there it fell to the center of the millstone and ground. A wooden hood (bottom) surrounds the millstones to prevent milled grain from scattering and to guide it to a conveyer below and on to the bolting system.

Figure 132. Top to bottom, a hopper for holding grain, the hopper rest with feed shoe and the millstone hood are over and around the millstones. All can be lifted away when the millstones need to be dressed and balanced.

Figure 133. The waterwheel shaft turns the cast iron bull wheel (or master wheel) inside the mill which meshes with wooden gearing to turn the millstones and vertical shaft to power equipment on upper floors.

Figure 134. This 1930 post card picture shows the aging mill and the highway that went around it. The structure was almost lost when the State Highway Department planned to straighten the road. The mill still stands in a new location.

The Stringer Grist Mills

Located on the north side of the Black Fork, not quite a mile downstream from Perrysville, were the Stringer Grist Mills. Today a canoe livery operates across from the millsite. The history of Stringer and his mills is quite interesting, and it can be pieced together from three sources, Knapp's *1863 History of Ashland County*, Hill's *1880 History of Ashland County*, and Graham's *1880 History of Richland County*. Knapp, in his 1863 history, wrote that the mill was then owned by Augustus A. Taylor, and described that the mill operated "with three pairs of buhrs and one saw."[148]

Hill wrote, "Thomas Stringer erected a large gristmill, on the Black Fork, about a mile below Perrysville, in 1839. He owned it but a short time. It has had a stirring career, and has passed through many hands. It is a valuable property, and capable of doing a large business."[149]

Graham, whose history was published in 1880—the same year as Hill's, wrote that the Stringer Mill was erected in 1842, three years later than Hill's account. According to Graham, William Endslow owned the mill at that time (about 1880). The *1874 Ashland County Atlas* shows the location of the mill and lists J. Endslow & Co. as the owner of the Perrysville Mill.

Nathaniel McDowell Coe purchased the Perrysville Mills in 1888 and operated them until 1894. Coe was born on May 26, 1834, near Dalton, Wayne County, Ohio. He had been a farmer for most of his life before purchasing the mill.

The Stringer Mystery

Thomas Stringer, the son of Joseph and Mary Dawson Stringer, was born in Trumbul County, Ohio, on November 4, 1811. Stringer married Harriett Potts on April 12, 1836, and they remained in Ashland County, Ohio. After their marriage they lived at Ashland, Loudonville, and Hayesville. He owned a mill in Perrysville and mercantile businesses in Loudonville and Ashland. His mercantile businesses failed, and in 1849 he went with Paul Oliver of Loudonville[150] and others (John and Allen Oliver, Curtis Drake) to California.[151] On the way out he became ill, but the others could not leave without him since he owned the equipment. Stringer recovered enough to complete the trip to California, where he accumulated some wealth, despite continued illness. Among his interests were a sawmill, a ranch, or perhaps two, as well as property he leased to tenants. In February 1854, he wrote to his son-in-law, Lewis Armstrong, saying that he was purchasing the leases and selling out his interests so he could "come home, money or no money."[152]

Four months later on June 8th, 1854, Stringer was making arrangements for his return to Ohio when he was killed by a tenant named Kize. Kize, who had been sued for breach of contract, laid in wait for Stringer and shot him as he was driving to his sawmill. Kize fled the scene, and Stringer's body was not found until two days later. Stringer was buried at night in the Masonic Cemetery, on land he had given for the cemetery, in Sonora, California.[153]

At least this was what his family back east was told. Twenty years later, more of the story was revealed. In 1875, Tom's son, Elza, a businessman in Ashland, was told that his father was living in southwest Missouri. Elza went there to see if this was his father. The man later visited Ashland. Quite a number of those who knew him when he lived in Perrysville believed that this was the Tom Stringer they had known, but Elza later stated that the Missouri Stringer was not his father.[154] The man acknowledged that he once had a mill but that it was on the Eel River in Indiana. He was very familiar with the Perrysville region, and he knew some people there.

According to a 1956 letter that Garber uncovered in his research, several articles in February and March 1875 appeared in the *Ashland Times* about the Stringer

VALUABLE PROPERTY FOR SALE.

THE proprietor having purchased from Thomas Coulter the farm immediately adjoining his mill property, now offers for sale the whole premises comprising one hundred and seventy acres of land, about ninety acres of which is well improved and in a good state of cultivation. The mill is entirely new, being built in 1839 and completed in every particular; consisting in part of three pair French Bur mill stones, three bolts, screen, smut machine, grain and meal Elevators, packing room, packing machine, &c. comprising all the machinery necessary for the manufacture of good work, and the saving of labor.

There is also on the premises a good orchard, a comfortable brick house, 20 by 30 feet, two stories high, well finished, together with a kitchen and a good log barn (being about forty rods from the mill) also a new frame house, 17 by 23 feet and one story high about to be completed, adjoining the mill, also on the farm a new log house.—The above property is situated in Richland county, Ohio, near Perrysville, on the black fork of Mohican one of the largest and most durable streams in the quarter of the State through which it passes, and on the road leading from Mansfield to Loudonville.— The location is one desirable, being in the midst of a rich and fertile country, well accommodated with roads from every direction. The property itself is most beautifully situated, and for pleasantness is perhaps seldom surpassed.

Men of capital wishing to make investments and having in view health, wealth and comfort, would do well to call & examine the property, as nothing is better calculated to recommend, than an actual examination. The water power will yet warrant much additional machinery, at least an additional run of mill stones & a saw mill. Persons living at a distance, and wishing any additional information relative to the property can no doubt obtain it through any friends they may have residing in either Richland or Wayne county, as the property is generally known. For cash in hand it will be sold extremely low, or for a portion in hand and the balance in payments. All those who may wish to purchase, will make application in all cases to the proprietor at the establishment.

T. STRINGER.
Richland Mills, Nov 8, 1840 44tf.

Figure 135. John Stringer was a miller and a salesman. He advertised manufactured waterwheels of an unknown design, and the question is was it a wheel or an early turbine.

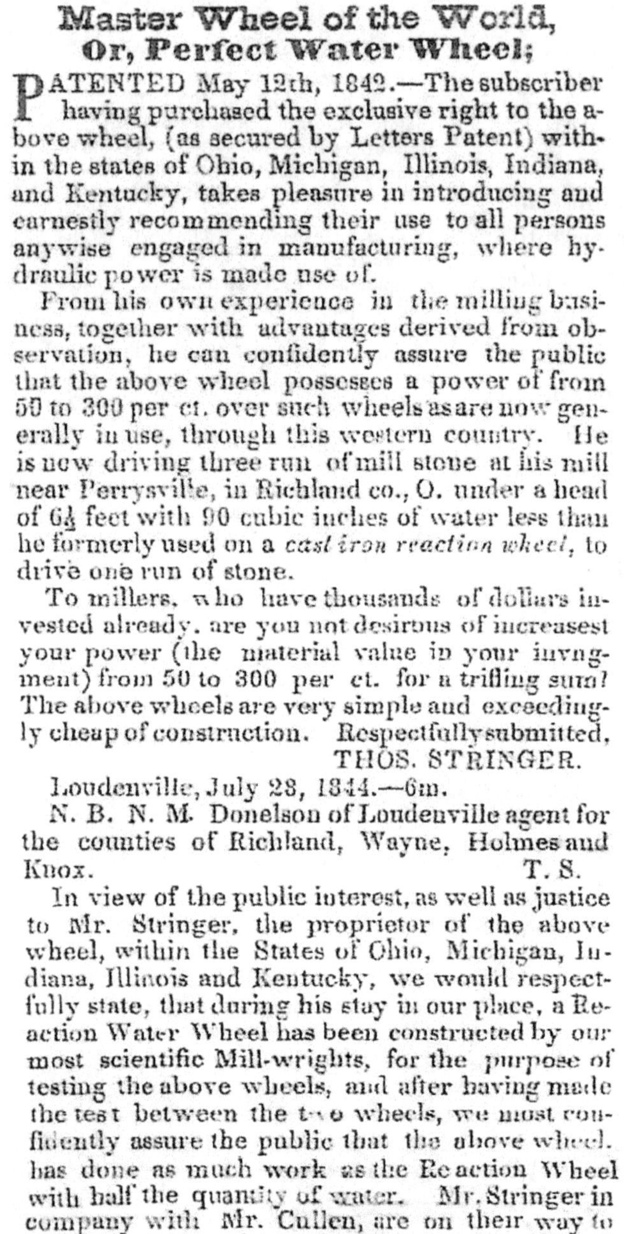

Master Wheel of the World, Or, Perfect Water Wheel;

PATENTED May 12th, 1842.—The subscriber having purchased the exclusive right to the above wheel, (as secured by Letters Patent) within the states of Ohio, Michigan, Illinois, Indiana, and Kentucky, takes pleasure in introducing and earnestly recommending their use to all persons anywise engaged in manufacturing, where hydraulic power is made use of.

From his own experience in the milling business, together with advantages derived from observation, he can confidently assure the public that the above wheel possesses a power of from 50 to 300 per ct. over such wheels as are now generally in use, through this western country. He is now driving three run of mill stone at his mill near Perrysville, in Richland co., O. under a head of 6¼ feet with 90 cubic inches of water less than he formerly used on a *cast iron reaction wheel*, to drive one run of stone.

To millers, who have thousands of dollars invested already, are you not desirous of increasest your power (the material value in your invngment) from 50 to 300 per ct. for a trifling sum? The above wheels are very simple and exceedingly cheap of construction. Respectfully submitted,
THOS. STRINGER.

Loudenville, July 28, 1844.—6m.

N. B. N. M. Donelson of Loudenville agent for the counties of Richland, Wayne, Holmes and Knox.   T. S.

In view of the public interest, as well as justice to Mr. Stringer, the proprietor of the above wheel, within the States of Ohio, Michigan, Indiana, Illinois and Kentucky, we would respectfully state, that during his stay in our place, a Reaction Water Wheel has been constructed by our most scientific Mill-wrights, for the purpose of testing the above wheels, and after having made the test between the two wheels, we most confidently assure the public that the above wheel has done as much work as the Reaction Wheel with half the quantity of water. Mr. Stringer in company with Mr. Cullen, are on their way to the south-west, we hope they may meet with good success in introducing his wheel into gengeneral use, and the public thereby be highly benefitted.   JOHN HOLLINGSWORTH.
W. BEAUMONT.
M. LOWDAN,
J. D. DUNLAP,
R. B. GREEN,
JOSIAH SPAULDING.

Zanesville, May 7th, 1846.

N. B. Persons desirious of purchasing individual rights or right of territory, will address T. Stringer, Loudenville, Ashland county, Ohio.

Figure 136. 1842 Article.

mystery. One reported that because Tom Stringer was in debt, he put clothes easily recognizable as his own on a corpse that he found. When a friend of his discovered the body wearing Stringer's clothes, he told the authorities that Stringer had been murdered.[155]

The Loudonville Mills

The Loudonville Mills have operated under various owners and survived many changes since its beginnings in1819. The present mill still operates today, shipping flour by semi or railroad car. One of the first mills on the Black Fork, the Loudonville Mills' history is fascinating.

The A-frame mill was small, with two runs of buhrs and a bolting system for making flour. It was built in 1818 by Alexander Skinner, and Caleb Chapel was the carpenter as well as the first miller. When Skinner died in 1821, T. J. Bull became owner of the mill. He sold it to Thomas Carlisle. Ownership passed to Gray & Freeman of Cleveland in 1835, and they ran the mill for ten years. In 1845 James Christmas and John C. Larwell assumed ownship. In 1861, A. A. Taylor erected a new mill, run principally by steam with nine runs of stones. Seventy-five barrels of flour were manufactured daily.[156]

The mill, erected on the old Indian portage route at Loudonville, was constructed with a lock allowing all watercraft and rafts passage in either direction because the Mohican and Black Fork were navigable then. Skinner was authorized by the General Assembly of Ohio on January 22, 1819 to build the dam. It also specified the size of the lock and condition for its use. The lock was to be 18 feet wide and 80 feet long. The miller was required to keep the lock in good repair. The lock was to be opened without delay when requested, and such persons were to pass free of expense.[157]

No evidence has been found to show that Skinner was a miller. He employed Caleb

Chapel to operate the mill after it was completed. In either case, the requirement to provide free maintenance for the lock was a burden, and it may be the reason he sold the property to his son-in-law, Nathaniel Haskell, just two years later.

Figure 137. The smokestack was for steam power which supplemented water power as the mill grew. This photograph was taken before 1912 and shows a few adjoining buildings, one that would have been the coopers shop. The tailrace can also be seen.

It is likely that flat boats were built in the slack water above the dam. Once loaded with flour and produce, they passed through the lock to descend the rivers to New Orleans. There both boats and cargo were sold. In 1836, the Canal Commission decided not to extend a canal up the Black Fork and Rocky Fork to Mansfield. It was just not feasible. On March 14th of that year, authorization for the construction of the Walhonding Canal was granted. Gray & Freeman, owners of the mill at that time, no doubt were quick to eliminate their biggest headache, the lock.[158]

Carding and fulling mills were added by Haskell, but they were not in operation for any length of time. Millers were baffled in their attempts to combine grist and woolen mills. Despite efforts to prevent it, wool fat and lanolin eventually contaminated the flour, and the housewives rejected it.

Although A. A. Taylor rebuilt the mill when he bought it in 1861, the advent of the Civil War stimulated demand; he rebuilt both the mill and the dam completely. His new enterprise flourished.

Figure 138. The mill dam at Taylor Mill.

In 1876 at the Centennial Exposition at Philadelphia, Loudonville flour received national attention when it was awarded the first prize and a gold medal. Jacob A. Stitzel Sr, a Bavarian-born miller employed by Taylor, was responsible for the recognition. Stitzel developed a secret process for manufacturing patent flour with buhrs. He personally supervised a demonstration at the Exposition where bread was baked from new flour each day. The Loudonville mill sold for a dollar more a barrel than other brands, and the mill was unable to meet the demand.[159]

Garber interviewed H. J. Bebout, a resident of Loudonville in 1952. He provided Garber with a great deal of information about the Loudonville mills. The smokestack was built in 1876 and

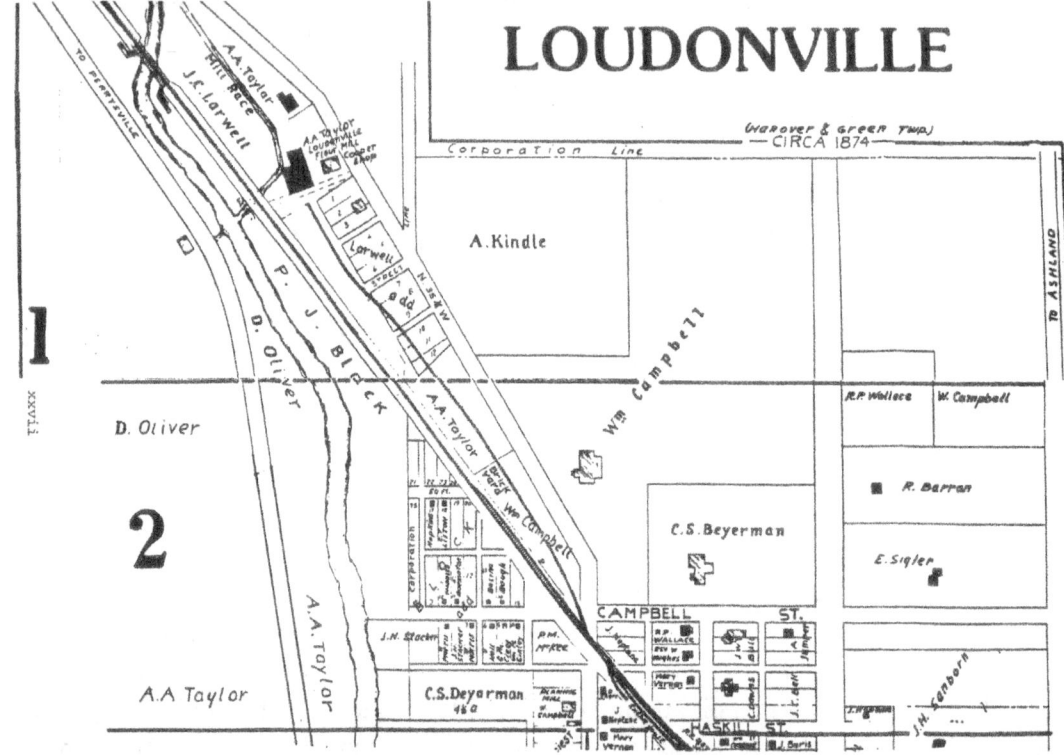

Figure 139. This is a partial map of Loudenville showing the Taylor mill and millrace in the upper left corner. The headrace is still there although overgrown with brush and trees.

steam was added to the mill. The date the mill was built was marked on the stack. Before the water-powered mill abandoned water as its source of power in 1909, the dam was downstream just below a bridge that was once halfway between Perrysville and Loudonville—upstream from the mill. Once water power was discontinued at the mill, the dam became a subject of controversy. One farmer whose land adjoined the area protested, saying his land was affected by the change in the course of the stream caused by the dam. He felt removing the dam would correct his problem.

The officials at the mill were reluctant to do this, because they were not sure whether water power would be needed in the future. The matter was resolved one night; however, when "person or persons unknown" dynamited the dam. The flood of 1913 completed its destruction. Flood water reached upper levels in the mill, covering the lower part where 1000 barrels of flour were stored.

Bebout worked in the Mt. Vernon mill of the Northwestern Elevator and Milling Company where he started at the bottom as a sweep to learn the milling business. He progressed rapidly, and in 1908 he took over the Loudenville Mill that included 54 acres of property. Prior to its destruction by fire in 1922, the water-powered mill was about 40 x 60 feet, with 3 ½ stories above the basement floor, and was equipped with a Bernard & Lee system.

The mill contained a cooper shop employing 8 coopers. At that time the mill capacity was about 350 to 360 barrels a day. Bebout arranged for timber men to obtain desirable hoop material from down the narrows of the Mohican River and ship it to the mill on the old Walhonding Railroad.

Then known as the Taylor Mill, part of the Northwest Elevator and Milling Company, flour was distributed widely under two brand names, "Mimosa" and "Perola." Much of the Perola, a soft, winter wheat flour, was shipped to the Argentine. Argentina is now one of the primary grain-producing countries in South America. When Bebout assumed management of the mill in 1908, a large number of

Figure 140. An advertisement from 1884 showing prices then.

expensive flour sacks, of a canvas-like material bearing the Taylor brand names and stencils, were in the mill.

In 1912, the Taylor family decided to consolidate their interests at Toledo and Mt. Vernon, apparently because of over extension of expansion and building programs. A stone archway at Mt. Vernon was just one example of expensive developments. When they expressed a desire to sell the mill at Loudonville, Bebout owned some stock in the mill. When it was offered for sale and no interest was shown by possible buyers, Bebout discussed possible options with local businesses and friends, resulting in him organizing the Loudonville Mill & Grain Company in September 1912. Bebout was named the vice president of the $80,000 business when it was taken over from the Northwestern Elevator and Mill Company. Under the new management, the mill was expanded, and it prospered until it was destroyed by fire on October 30, 1922.[160]

Figure 141. The old mill burned in a disastrous 1922 fire and was rebuilt, with part being the present 5-story complex.

The mill complex was rebuilt with increased capacity and larger storage, capable of producing 1,200 barrels a day. It was rated fourth in the state. Sunshine Biscuits Inc. purchased it in 1953 to produce flour for its bakeries. ConAgra bought the mill in July 1985. The mill ran 24 hours a day, seven days a week, shipping up to 8 to 9 semi tankers of flour daily all across the country. The railroad siding was always busy with incoming carloads of wheat, and outgoing rail cars carrying up to 225,000 pounds of flour. It is now owned by Ardent Mills LLC.

Figure 142. Most of the flour today is shipped in 8 to 9 trucks daily.

Figure 143. The Con Agra flour mill received grain by rail car and had the ability to ship flour the same way in a rail car that can hold 225,000 pounds.

Figure 144. A 54-inch Stout & Temple turbine that powered the Loudenville mill until 1909 was salvaged and rests at the entrance to Ardent Mills on Mill Road at the edge of town.

A century and a half or more ago, in the days of water-powered buhr-stone mills, this level of production was unimaginable. The flour mills are a part of Loudonville's rich heritage. The dam is long gone from where it stood two hundred feet or so below where Big Run joined the Black Fork.

On the west side of Mill Road, down over the hill, a section of the headrace for the old mill can still be seen, although now heavily overgrown. At the entrance to the Ardent Mills complex rests the 54-inch Stout, Mills & Temple turbine that powered the mill until 1909. Manufactured in Dayton, it is the largest turbine to be found in old Richland County.[161]

Green Township Distilleries

George Smith had a distillery near the lower spring-fed Oswalt Greentown Mills in the late 1830s (39) while Jonathan Grubaugh was busy two and a half miles north on section 5 doing the same thing. John Guthrie's still was on the south side of the Black Fork, possibly near a spring along Township Road near T 749.

Thomas Calhoun, Joseph Grove, and Ortho and William Conine also had distilleries going full blast but records do not give a location. They were no doubt on the rented or leased school lands.

More full-time distilleries were located in Green Township than any other township in the county. In 1832 there were 34 in old Richland County. Madison, Washington, Jefferson, Troy and Orange had three or four each but Green topped them all with six. All were dependent on water-powered gristmills.

In 1820, according to historian Rosella Rice, Judge Thomas Coulter constructed a flatboat capable of carrying three or four hundred barrels at the dam in Loudonville and began a new trade route via the Mohican to New Orleans. One such boat included a shipment of "whisky pickles." The pickles—or cucumbers—were raised by Jedediah Strong Smith, packed in barrels, and covered with whisky. Smith went to New Orleans with his cargo, and he sold at a handsome profit.

He sent the money home to Perrysville, and with the experience gained from the trip, began his career as one of the greatest mountain men, fur traders, and western explorers. His career was launched with thirty barrels of whisky pickles from Green Township. Whisky and flour were common shipments south rather than bulkier grain or produce. This new market kept the flour mills and distilleries busy bringing much-needed hard currency back into the local economy.

Mills in Hanover Township

According to Garber's research, no mills were found on the Black Fork in Hanover Township below Loudonville, because the river is rather wide and prone to flooding.

Section 3

Water-Powered Mills on the Rocky Fork of the Mohican River

For if the flour be fresh and sound, Who careth in what mill 'twas ground? -

Henry Wadsworth Longfellow

Water-Powered Mills on the Rocky Fork of the Mohican River

The Rocky Fork begins at the big springs in northeastern Springfield Township and flows east into Madison Township, descending rapidly to the valley below. In less than a tenth of a mile it drops nearly 90 feet to the twisting rocky bottom of the stream, then drops another 106 feet in elevation before reaching Mansfield. It then meanders southeast through Lucas, dropping another 110 feet before it joins the Black Fork near the Richland-Ashland County line. Today the flow pattern of the stream is different in some places, especially in the Mansfield industrial area, but the overall flow of water made it a desirable water source for mill building.

Springfield Township

Spring Mills

Spring Mill was located on Gfrer Road, just east of the State Route 39 and Lexington-Springmill Road intersection. Gfrer Road is hardly used today. It dead-ends north of Route 39, stopping at the railroad crossing. At one time, the old mill still stood alone; one of the oldest, free-standing mills known to exist in old Richland County. Today it is a beautiful private residence. A former owner bricked the south side and the front of the old landmark. A flume from the spring-fed millpond once fed a good-sized waterwheel inside the mill.

Garber was intrigued with Spring Mill. His research covers nearly four pages of notes and is more or less organized chronologically. The mill was converted into an elegant private home not open to the public; but driving by, one can imagine the sound of the waterwheel turning as the water from the streams runs over it and of the grinding of the wheat or corn.

The work of historians A. J. Baughman and A. A. Graham are critical to any understanding of the history of Richland County. To a great extent, their work is the foundation upon which today's historians build. Graham wrote in his *History of Richland County* that Springfield was formed in 1818 when Madison Township was split in half. The first mill in Springfield was a sawmill built in 1817 by Condon & Welch on the northwest quarter of section 1. A gristmill later followed.

In the ensuing years, the mills became known as the Spring Mills. As often happened in that era, mills were destroyed by fire, floods, or torn down and rebuilt many times, and mill ownership often changed. Welch ran his mill for several years until he sold it to Mordecai Bartley, who was well known in the surrounding area. A lawyer, Bartley served in the War of 1812. He was elected to Congress and served from 1823 to 1831. In 1844, he was elected Governor of Ohio.[1]

Baughman, in his *History of Richland County*, cites a 1902 article by William Walters, in the *Mansfield News*. Walters wrote, "About four miles northwest of the courthouse was a beautiful spring of clear water – the source of the Rocky Fork branch of the Mohican river. To utilize the sparkling water of this beautiful spring, a Mr. 'Eleck' Welch built a flouring mill there, known as 'Welch's Mill,' or the 'spring mills.'"[2]

One of the most memorable historical events involving Richland County took place in 1782 when Colonel William Crawford was placed in command of nearly 500 volunteer militia, most coming from Pennsylvania. Their mission was to destroy the Indian towns along the Sandusky River. Crawford's goal was to conduct a surprise attack to destroy the villages and to kill as many Indians as possible; but from the time the mission began, the British and their Indians were well prepared for Crawford's arrival.[3]

Crawford and his troops traveled northwesterly from the Muskingum River to the Killbuck River. Their encampment was ten miles south of Wooster. One man died where the force encamped. His name was cut into the nearest tree to mark the spot. The following day they passed near Mansfield and encamped that evening, June first, "at the place which is now known as Spring Mills Station, on the Pittsburg, Fort Wayne, and Chicago Railroad. The following morning, June 2, they moved out for the Sandusky River."[4]

Somewhere between 200 and 500 Delaware, Mingo, and Wyandot Indians, along with British reinforcements, were waiting for Crawford and his men. The battle began on June 4, 1782. That first day the Americans lost 5 men, and 19 were wounded. British casualties were estimated at 5 killed and 11 wounded. On June 5, an estimated 100 British rangers and an additional 110 Shawnees provided reinforcements for the Indians. The Americans were surrounded.

On the evening of June 5th, the Americans attempted to withdraw; but the Indians heard them pulling back and attacked. Crawford's men became confused, and many were separated from one another. When Crawford held back looking for his son and son-in-law from whom he had been separated, he and several others were captured by the Indians. They were taken to Chief Wingenund's camp on June 7, and on June 11 they were taken to the village of Half-King. Along the route Crawford passed the bodies of a number of prisoners who had been scalped. Most of the prisoners were killed and scalped. Only a few managed to escape. Crawford alone was brutally tortured and burned at the stake.[5] For over a hundred years, his death at the stake became a rallying call for the torture and murder of Indians, until they were ultimately forced onto reservations.

Garber spent considerable time researching Spring Mills; however, ownership of the mills is not entirely clear. His notes do not specify the date when Joseph Welch purchased Spring Mills back from Mordecai Bartley; but family records indicate that the mill remained with a branch of the family for the next sixty years. A. C. Welch, Joseph's son, took over the operation from his father. Among his employees was Peter Wentz who had been employed by his father. Wentz worked at Spring Mills for two years. In November 1854, Wentz married Margaret Benton Welch, granddaughter of John Welch. Wentz and his wife moved to Pennsylvania, but returned to Springfield Township in 1882 and purchased Spring Mill. It is not clear how long they lived in Springfield.

By 1900 the village reached its greatest prosperity. The success was largely due to the arrival of the railroad. The Sandusky, Mansfield & Newark (later the B & O) had a station in the village. They built a boarding house below the mill for the track crews and agents. Trains stopped in Springfield to take on wood and water. The early railroad builders followed the Rocky Fork south into Mansfield.

The relationship between Peter Wentz and other mills is not clear. An article appeared in the *Richland Shield & Banner* in 1856 that indicated at least one relationship between Peter Wentz and other mills may have existed. It read: "Walter Gledhill who operated the Union Woolen Factory in Monroe Township advertised for wool under the above date, 'Wool to be delivered to, among others, Mr. George Owings, (Miller) at the Spring Mill.'"[6] Other industries may have worked in conjunction with Spring Mill; but no others could be found in Garber's notes.

In the early years, a number of roads converged at the mill. The Lexington Springmill Road, Plymouth Springmill Road, Springmill Road West, and Springmill East (known as Cairns Road), and Springmill Street in Mansfield became State Route 39. In 1905, at the bottom of the hill below the mill, vehicles and pedestrians had four railroad tracks to cross, the B & O, two for the Pennsylvania, plus an interurban track.

The roads to the mill were always busy, and unfortunately there were a number of accidents. Because of the frequency of these accidents, around 1930 the state changed the road. Spring Mills was bypassed, and a bridge was built over the railroad tracks. With passenger trains reaching speeds as high as seventy miles per hour, these changes were inevitable.

A brief announcement appeared in the June 1938 edition of the *American Miller* stating that "L. J. Coulson, formerly of Shelby, early in May purchased the Spring Mill Flour Mills, Rt. 1 from Mansfield, and is now operating the plant." According to Garber, Coulson did not remain in business for very long. Garber identified John Gfrer as the last owner of the mill to "actively operate it."[7] Gfrer died in either 1948 or 1949. Two World War II veterans, William J. Breitinger and Robert Blackledge, both from Mansfield, sought to get the old mill up and running.

An article in the *Mansfield News-Journal* in December 1946 describes the activities of these two veterans. It reads in part:

> The ancient machinery of the old Spring Mill that ground the corn meal for Richland County 131 years ago is back on the job again. Of course not all the old machinery is in working order now, Breitnger said. But we are using some of it, including the old French buhr we found in the place.
>
> However, the new proprietors had to buy a gasoline engine to turn the milling machinery, instead of the old mill wheel. Altho (sic) the wheel remains in good condition, the two mill ponds are out of repair and do not hold enough water to operate the mill.
>
> When children, they lived in the neighborhood and worked the mill when it was operated by John Gfrer. Gfrer, now retired, owns the old landmark and leases it to the veterans. He still lived near the mill.
>
> Although the old mill has been reinforced with brick and mortar, the beams and one side of the building remain just as they were 131 years ago. In some parts of the building square nails and wooden pegs, construction aids of the period, still can be seen...[8]

Garber never had the opportunity to interview John Gfrer. His notes reveal that he spent some time on June 15, 1951 exploring the grounds where Spring Mill stood. He loved exploring old mill grounds, and Spring Mill was no exception. He estimated the size of the mill as 30 x 50 feet, adding that it was a pretty "close approximation." The millpond, spring-fed, was about two acres. All mill machinery had been removed, and the building in 1951 was used largely as a storage place for miscellaneous "junk." It was inhabited by an old man of 76 who had no knowledge or interest in the background of the mill. That man and another old man with him voiced the opinion that the two young men, who operated it briefly after returning from the service, wished to run a "sneak still" in connection with the mill.[9]

Figure 145. The old Spring Mill as it appeared sometime around 1910. The miller is evidently feeding the ducks seen in the lower left on the millpond. The building possibly dates from the 1860s or 1870s.

Figure 146. A turn of the century view of the two-acre millpond. The second pond is still there but the springs that fed it are greatly diminished. The mill is in the background.

Figure 147. Garber took this photograph in June 1951 after all mill machinery had been removed and the store closed. Two old men were living in the junk-filled building.

Figure 148. The Spring Mill has now been converted to a private residence not open to the public, but it is well worth a trip to drive by to see it and the millpond. It is one of only three mill buildings left in Richland County that at one time numbered 190.

Madison Township

The Keith Mills

The Keith Mills were located just below where the Rocky Fork crosses the Bowman Street Bridge south of Cairns Road. The mill was on the northeast side of the old B & O (now the Ashland Railroad). Industry, road, bridge, and stream alignment have erased the mill location. Little is known about the Keith Mills except what is found in Baughman's *History of Richland County*.

Baughman wrote: "...the Keith Mills [were] erected by the father of Judge H. D. Keith. The location of this mill was near the junction of the Rocky Run with the Spring mills, or main branch of the Rocky fork."[10]

Laird & Bender Carding and Fulling Mill

This mill was located just north of the U.S. Route 30 overpass, where it is joined by another stream, the Rocky Run. The latter originates from the Mansfield Correctional Institution property and crosses State Route 13 just a short distance north of Longview Avenue. Baughman wrote that "Jacob Bender, the grandfather of Jacob Laird, had a carding mill on the new state road, propelled by the water of the Laird spring, now known as the upper reservoir. The spring had an output of four hundred gallons a minute."[11] Garber was an excellent researcher who kept meticulous notes, but all too often he failed to cite either the source of his information or the date it was recorded. This is true here regarding the information he had pertaining to the Laird & Bender Mill. Garber wrote:

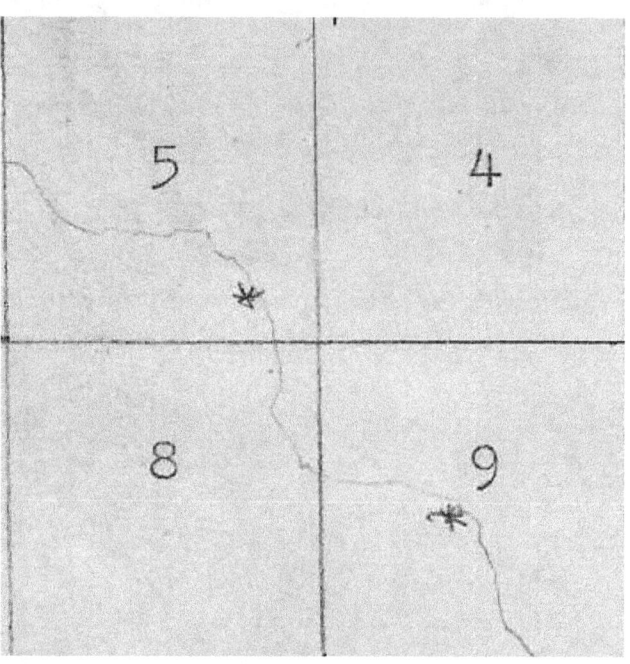

Figure 149. Hand drawn map by Garber copied from the Recorders Office, Deed Records.[12] Section 9: Laird and Bender Carding & Fulling Mill. Section 5: Keith-Weaver Grist Mill.

William B. Laird and Jacob Bender were partners in the mill firm of Laird & Bender. Laird was the husband of Jacob Bender's daughter, Mary. Early records show that Jacob Bender was known as "Bender" at the time the business was established with his son-in-law. In ensuing years the name appears as Bender, Penter and eventually Painter. All three names were used but probably with a common pronunciation. Bender eventually became Painter and his estate was settled (1850) under the name Jacob Painter. However, records signed by his children in the name of Jane Bender, John Painter and Andrew Painter. Jane consistently signed her name as Bender. Christenia, the widow, signed with a mark that is quite distinctive, signed as both Bender and Painter.[13]

Jacob Bender died apparently early in July 1845. The will is recorded in Vol. 5, page 216 of the administration records.

A double carding machine, a shearing machine and a set of shearing blades were unsold at the sale, no bid being received. They were described as "old and out of date &c.,...and were left on the place."[14]

Garber located the Laird-Bender Mill in section 9 of Madison Township, probably in the southwest quarter; since the taxes paid by Bender's executor covered the southwest quarter of section 9, and part of the southeast quarter of the same section. The portion of the southeast quarter was traversed by a small stream (Rocky Run), doubtlessly fed by the springs that were the source of water power for the mill. The 1845 taxes for "SW ¼ Sec., 9" valued at $766 were $13.02 and $3.40 for a Carding Machine valued at $200.

The mill operation was evidenced by a few of the following accounts found:

    Daniel Marks, 1835, to weaving 16 ½ yards $1.48

    1839, to weaving 27 ¾ yards, Jan. 3, $4.16

    1844, to weaving 34 ¾ yards, Jan. 27, $3.82

    1845, to weaving 23 ¾ yards, Feb. 14, $2.58

    James McRay, 1838, for weaving, $32.45.

    Thomas Rutlege, 1838, to spinning 5 dog and 8 cuts of yarn, $.96.

John Crooks Saw Mill

This unrecorded sawmill was located in the northwest quarter of section 7. The mill is mentioned only once in 1839 in the Auditors records and was located on the small stream that runs through the present day Ohio State University campus between Lexington-Springmill Road and State Route 39. No other information has been found.

Jacob Gates Saw Mill

In 1839 Gates had a sawmill on the property of the Ferson-Baird woolen mill just east of the old reformatory. Information on this mill is included with the Ferson-Baird mill history on pages 165-166.

James McCoy Saw Mill

The McCoy sawmill was located in present day Mansfield, just north of Park Avenue West and east of Trimble Road along the stream the bike trail follows, probably over the hill from the Kingwood Center. The mill operated from the late 1830s through 1848. It was another mystery mill, that like most sawmills, did not last long.

Figure 150. Sawmills were in great demand and were more easily constructed than a gristmill. A single up-and-down blade supported by a moving wooden "sash" powered by a waterwheel cut at a slow but reliable rate of one half to one inch per stroke depending on timber size and hardness. This mill is in Nova Scotia. In the late 1800s a few of these mills were converted to more efficient circular saws.

Mendenhall's Improved Patent Grist Mill

Figure 151. Overall Rendering of Water-Powered Sawmill (exterior siding and roofing not shown).
Drawing by Paul Shuler, Lexington, Ohio.

Figure 152. Back movement of the saw carriage. 1. Near the end of the saw cut, a trip closes the sluice gate to the flutter wheel. 2. The mill operator opens the small sluice gate to the tubwheel rotating the cog wheel. 3. The cog wheel engages the ragwheel, pulling the carriage back for the next saw cut.
Drawing by Paul Shuler, Lexington, Ohio.

Figure 153. Operation of the saw cut. Flutter wheel, 1) drives crank 2) operating arm, 3) which causes up and down movement of saw gate, 4) which frames the saw. The down movement of the saw causes arm, 5) to pivot at rigid ell, 6) pulling arm, 7) into the ragwheel teeth. The rotating ragwheel shaft has rounds embedded at the carriage frame which mesh with cogs in the carriage frame, moving the carriage and log into the saw.

Drawing by Paul Shuler, Lexington, Ohio.

An advertisement Garber found in an unnamed local newspaper may have been a new idea that did not work out.

MENDENHALL'S IMPROVED PATENT

GRIST MILL.

A MILL on the above construction may be seen in operation for a few days, at the factory of Carr & Smith, 2 miles North of this place. This improvement of the Grist Mill, on account of the economy of the construction and power, merits the particular attention of Farmers, Distillers, &c.

Persons wishing to purchase individual or township rights will apply to DE LORMA BROOKS, at Mr. *Kelley's* Tavern in this town, or at the factory aforesaid during the stay of the mill there.

DE LORMA BROOKS,
WM. HILLERMAN, } *Proprietors.*
JONATHAN PIERCE.

Mansfield, February 19th 1899

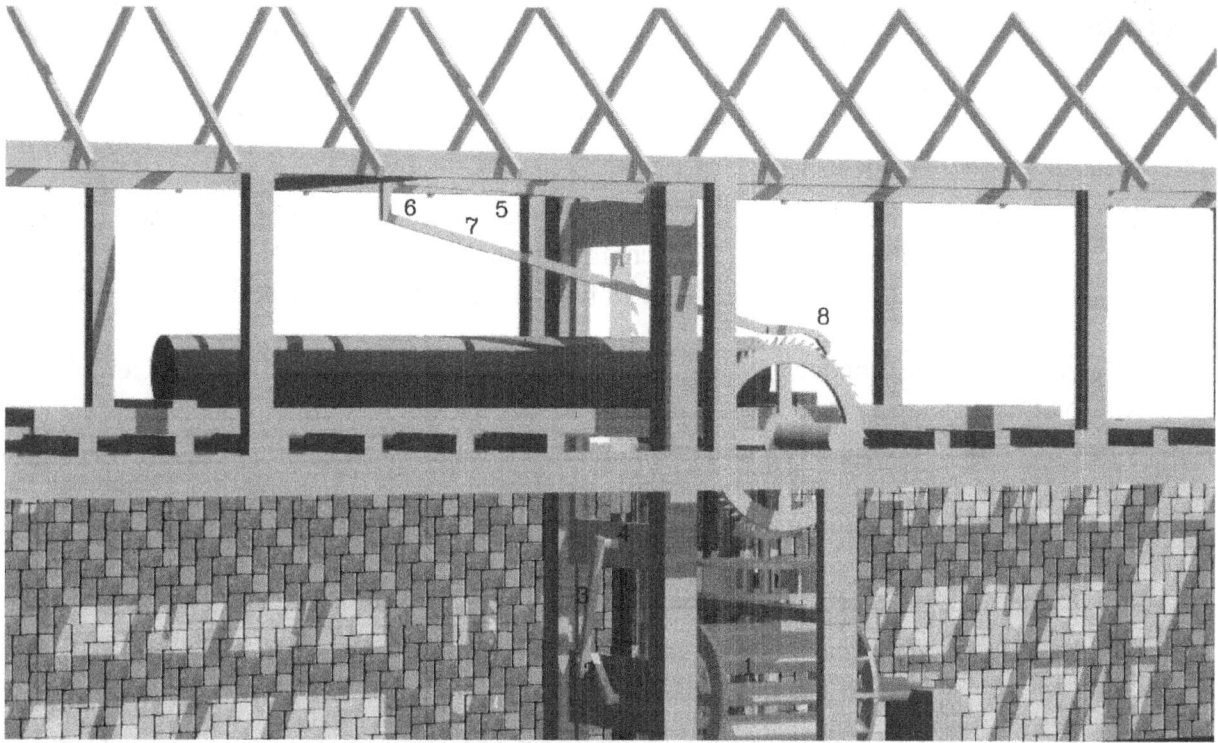

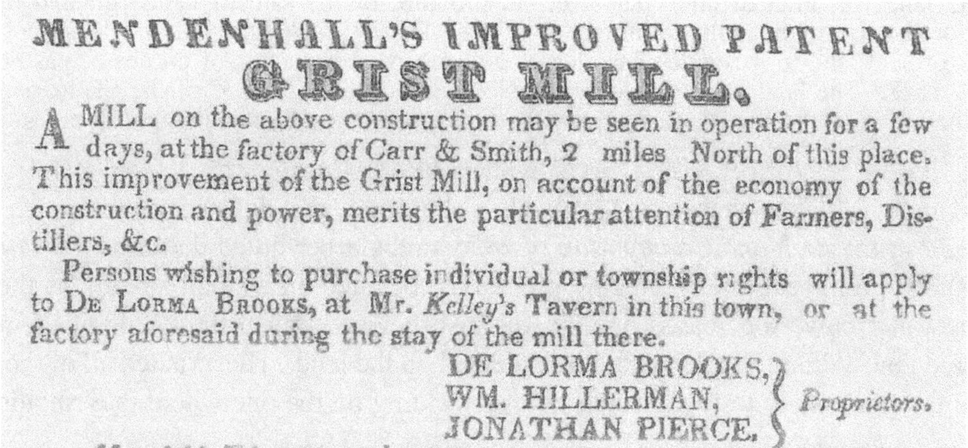

Figure 154. Mendenhall Mill. Sometimes little can be found on the history of early mills. The Mendenall Mill is an example. Two miles north of town would have been in the valley around Longview Avenue and the Rocky Fork.

The only Smith that owned land "2 miles north of Mansfield" was associated with the Tingley Woolen Mill south of State Route 545, east of the Mansfield Correctional Institution. This was likely a traveling example of a "horse mill" or woolen machine for salesman purposes only. The meeting at Kelley's Tavern may have helped increase the number of sales orders.

The William Tingley Woolen Mill

This mill was located on the east side of the Ashland Railroad on what is now the Mansfield Correctional Institution property. The mill went through a series of partnerships and is not shown on any maps. No doubt it did not last very long as the timber was rapidly cleared for farmland, and the water table dropped.

In March 1951 Garber conducted a lengthy interview with Mrs. Charles Dorman. Her maiden name was Norma Tingley Linn. She explained her family's history. William Tingley, the pioneer settler, was the father of Thomas Tingley, born on October 21, 1822, and died on September 10, 1904. His wife's name was Mary, who was born on September 10, 1823 and died December 24, 1892. Mary Catherine Tingley was married to Cornelius Linn, and they were Mrs. Dorman's parents.

Mrs. Dorman told Garber that the brick house north of the reformatory is the old Tingley homestead, part of the original Tingley property that had never been out of the family. The old Tingley Mill building was used as an ice house when she was a girl. Ice was cut from a millpond adjacent to the old mill. The mill stood "across the railroad," on the small stream across from the homestead.[15]

Garber's research indicated that the Tingley land was not that of William Tingley, the pioneer settler; but rather his son, Thomas Tingley. The Tingley land was originally part of the Virginia Military lands that had been set aside for school purposes. It was patented or deeded to Thomas Tingley on December 31, 1855, and not to his father William. Garber pointed out that William Tingley may well have occupied the land for many years under a purchase agreement before the patent was issued. Land records indicate that:

> The land was granted under an "Act" to provide for the sale of lands, granted by Congress for the use of Schools within the Virginia Military Land District, and to authorize the lessees of said land to surrender their leases and receive certificates of purchase, passed January 28, 1828. The land is described as the North ½ and the South ½ of the SE ¼, and the E ½ of the SE ¼ of the SE ¼ of Section 10, Twp. 21, Range 18, containing 120 acres of land.

/s/ William Medill, Governor[16]

The Tingley Mill's existence was probably a short one, as it does not appear on the *Sherman Map of 1830* or the *Richland County Map of 1856*, and Garber noted that the *1873 Andres Atlas* does not show a mill seat on the Tingley property. Located on a small stream, as the land was cleared the water power decreased until it was insufficient to meet the needs of the mill. Mrs. Dorman said that William Tingley and family settled on the land. They visited all of the numerous springs on the property to taste the water before deciding on the one where they should build the house.

Garber's research indicated it was "quite possible" that the mill was not actually located on Tingley land. A tax receipt from 1845 that he found, showed it was located on the east part of the southeast quarter of section 10. A quit claim deed by John and Mary Harmon, dated May 13, 1835, containing 80 perches, was located in the southeast quarter of section 10, "Beginning at the SE corner at a stake between Tingley & Freeson & Tingley, from thence north 8 perches along the road from William's to Wooster, etc."

Figure 155. Tingley Dam & Springs. The dam for the Tingley Woolen Mill was one of the most substantial built in Richland County. A stone quarry that furnished sandstone building blocks for homes and commercial buildings in Mansfield was just over the hill. The dam can easily be seen from Crawford Street just south of the old Mansfield Reformatory.

Figure 156. The Tingley dam leaks, but a pool of water and a pond where ice was once cut for delivery still remains. No trace of the millsite or headrace could be found due to recent land grading.

A recent search to find the old Tingley brick house was a puzzle to be solved. A total of ten two-story brick houses on State Route 545 (Mansfield Olivesburg Rd.) are located across the road from the old prison. All are of the same size and architectural design. This may have been Tingley property at one time; and the houses, built reasonably close together, were no doubt built to rent or sell to prison personnel. They appear to have been built at the same period by the same builder with the same materials.

Crawford is a street west along the south side of the old prison (the entrance) and then turns south to a dead end. On the left, after

Figure 157. A second hillside spring still feeds the pond in front of the old reformatory building. When the prison was built, a streetcar line went there. It was a popular spot for picnics. Prisoners kept the lawn and flower beds carefully tended. They were not invited to dine.

the bend in the street and back some distance, is an arched dam made of heavy sandstone blocks. At an earlier time a good-sized stone quarry was just up the hill above the dam. There are two springs on the hillside, one above the dam, and the other still feeds a good-sized pond in front of the old prison. One or both of these may have fed the millpond and dam for the Tingley-Ferson Mills.

The old Reformatory was built between 1886 and 1910, after the mills ceased operation. The dam was of no use to the prison operation; therefore, it must have been constructed for the mill. The mills would have been near the east side of the Ashland Railroad. Recent storm-water grading has erased any trace of a headrace; but the pond below the dam is very scenic.

Carr-Ferson (Tingley) Carding Mill

Ownership and names of mills often changed; sometimes resulting in a convoluted effort to find out who, what, and when. Garber's research did not stipulate when the Carr and Ferson Carding Mill was founded. He did find an 1828 announcement in the *Mansfield Gazette* and *Richland Farmer* that read:

Wool Carding

The subscribers respectfully inform the public that they have got new cards for their machines and by the 20th of this month will be ready to card wool in the best manner and without delay at the old stand of Tingley & Carr two miles North East of Mansfield. Persons who bring wool from a distance may at all times get their rolls with them by staying one night.

Grain and other kinds of country produce will be received for cardings, and 4 ½ cents per pound will be given for good rags.

The fulling, dying, etc. is carried on as usual.

Solomon M. Carr
Daniel Ferson[17]

Tingley and Ferson Carding Mill

It is not clear when Solomon M. Carr died, but probably between May 1828 and May 1829. The Tingley & Ferson firm is introduced in the May 13, 1829 issue of the *Mansfield Gazette and Farmer*. The article reads:

> The subscribers take this method of informing the public that they have just received a set of new cards from Philadelphia, and by the 1st of this month we will have them in complete operation. We will now be able to card wool in the best manner and on the shortest notice. All those who live at a distance, may during the summer season, get their wool carded by staying one night with us and will be accommodated with good pasture for their horses free of expense. And we particularly desire the public to understand that the business (since the death of Mr. Carr) will be carried on under the firm of Tingley & Ferson, in the same manner for that it has been heretofore without any variation whatever. We have the same workman both in Fulling and Carding that we have had for four years past and will continue to have the work done in the same manner. We will receive all kinds of country produce for old debts and carding and fulling. 5 cents will be given for old rags and we will card for 5 cents a pound in cash.[18]

Garber's notes, carefully studied, are a great source in following the trail of who owned what and when regarding mills in Richland County. This is especially true in tracking the changes in ownership and partnerships in the mills previously discussed. His research inevitably leads to the Ferson & Baird Mill. He wrote: "Solomon Carr and a man named Smith owned and operated the Ferson & Baird Mill in February 1828. By May of that year, the ownership had changed again and the mill was run as the Tingley & Carr factory. In May 1829, the mill appears as the William Tingley and Daniel Ferson Mill."[19]

Ferson & Baird Fulling Mill

An advertisement placed by Thomas Baird in the *Mansfield Gazette* shows him to be an experienced miller. Baird announced that he would continue to do business at his old stand in "New Lexington." The advertisement continues:

> From his long experience in the business of his profession he flatters himself that he will be able to give general satisfaction. The following articles of trade will be received in payment: Corn, rye, wheat, flax seed, beeswax, deer skins and rags, delivered when the work is done. (Rye and corn will be received at William Bulls) cloth will be received and when dressed returned at and to the following places: C. & I. Hazlett's store in Mansfield, and at M. Kelley's on the Delaware Road.[20]

Garber located the Ferson & Baird Fulling Mill and Carding machine on 40 acres of land in the east part of the southeast quarter of section 10 in Madison Township. In 1845, the assessed value of the land was $380 on the mill property. By 1851, the value of the property had increased to $970. Located at the mill seat, the dwelling house where Tom Baird lived was valued at $100 at the time of his death.[21]

The advertisement above demonstrated Baird's willingness to use agents to expand his business. Owners of mills like the Ferson & Baird Mill often had agents throughout the area who could receive wool to be carded, cloth to be fulled, or wool to be weaved. When the work was completed, the mill returned it to the local agent who delivered it to the customers and received payment. One such agent who worked for Ferson and Baird was Jacob Armentrout. In a letter to Mr. Armentrout, Baird wrote: "Mr. J. Armentrout. Sir Pleas to pay Jacob Leedy two dollars & twenty three cents when you collect money for me and oblige. Thos. Baird &c. April 2d, 1842."[22]

Records show that a sawmill was built in connection with the Ferson & Baird Fulling Mill.

Jacob Gates, a sawyer by trade, owned the sawmill. Records show that he did work for Thomas Baird on a regular basis. For example, on April 21, 1842 he produced "340 ft 3 x 5 scantling at 50 cts. - $.1.70"[23]

The Newman-Beam-Rogers-Campbell Grist and Saw Mills

The Newman-Beam-Rogers-Campbell Grist & Saw Mills were located on the Rocky Fork below Mansfield near the Mount Zion Road and State Route 39 intersection. This may be where the Newman-Beam's Mill, the first mill in Madison Township, was built. The beginning of the settlement of Madison and Richland County began in 1807.

In the spring of 1807, Jacob Newman moved to Ohio where he built his first cabin, with the help of brothers Isaac, Jacob, and John Brubaker and their sister, Catharine. All of these individuals lived in this small cabin as they cleared the land. The following spring of 1808, Michael Newman and his wife joined the others and, at this point, all of these early pioneers shared this small cabin. In the fall of 1808, Jacob went to Canton and brought his son Henry back to his new home. Jacob, lonely for a wife, went back to Pennsylvania and found one whom he brought back to Ohio before the end of the year.

More and more settlers arrived. Newman saw the need for a sawmill, but it would not be built until the spring of 1809. Once completed, the Newman sawmill became the first mill of any kind to be built in Richland County.[24] About that same time, Newman began construction on a gristmill. Newman was related to General James Hedges who had been sent west to survey part of the territory acquired by the new America following the Revolution. When General Hedges surveyed the land where Mansfield was laid out, Newman realized that Mansfield was to be the center of the new county. Hedges was one of three men who laid out the city. Newman sold his home, the sawmill, and the not-yet-completed gristmill to Michael Beam.[25]

Beam finished building the gristmill, and it quickly became known as "Beam's Mill." The *Mansfield Saving Bank & Trust Company Almanac*, 1928, described Michael Beam, his wife, and his mill as follows:

> …Michael Beam, who being a practical miller, added two sets of wheat grinding stones, built a block house, which was located on the hill just north of the present mill. This block house was a shelter in time of war and was also used by the settlers while waiting their term at the mill. His wife was known as Mother Beam, was largely instrumental in bringing customers to the mill. Settlers were often compelled to wait several days for their grinding, meantime boarding with Mother Beam, who was noted for the excellence of her corn cakes, corn dodgers, and her general superiority as a cook. After Beam's death the mill was passed to a man by the name of Campbell, then to the Amsbaugh family. The present mill was built in the early 1840s and stands on part of the original foundation of the Newman Mill. For many years it was known as Campbell's Mill.[26]

Beam's block house not only protected the settlers during Indian threats; but during the War of 1812-13, it was also a military post. Thirteen soldiers died in the area while posted to Beam's block house. The cause of death was not known for certain, but apparently they died of an unknown illness or from natural causes. Baughman wrote in his *History of Richland County*, that those soldiers who died were "buried on a beautiful knoll on the bank of the Rocky Fork, a half mile below the mill."[27]

Beam owned the mill through 1828, when it was sold to John Rogers—Rogers appears to be the next owner, but he died a short time later. In 1832, the mill was listed as owned by "the heirs of John Rogers;" however, John Rogers was still listed as the owner through 1839. John Campbell was listed as owner through 1856, and the mill is shown on the *1873 Richland County Atlas* as being owned by John Mentzer.

At a later date, H. L. Goudy purchased the mill, and it became known as Goudy's Mill. In 1882 Goudy and other mill owners sued the city of Mansfield because of loss of water in the Rocky Fork. The results and cause of their case appeared in a March 1884 edition of *The Bellville Star*. The article read as follows:

> The case of H L. Goudy vs. the City of Mansfield, continuing ten days ended Saturday in a verdict for the defense. When the city established its system of water works twelve years ago it made use of springs and a creek in the vicinity of the city which furnished water power for the grist mill of the plaintiff, there by diminishing the capacity of the mill for grinding. A large number of other property owner's claim to have sustained damages through changing of the water course, and a number of damage cases against the city are pending.[28]

In 1948 Garber interviewed the mother of Richard Hunt, who resided on the farm adjacent to the old Campbell Mill property. The mill was located on the west side of the bridge and faced north. A millpond immediately upstream was used for both the grist and sawmills. According to Mrs. Hunt the Campbell Mill was last owned and operated by a miller named Riley Amsbaugh. She confirmed that the mill was about the size of Darling Mill after examining a photo for comparison. In later years when the water power was no longer sufficient, Amsbaugh supplemented the power with a gasoline engine. He did not operate the mill for sometime after it came into his possession. It was never reconditioned as a flour mill because of the deterioration resulting from neglect. Replacing bolting cloths and repairing flour milling machinery would have been too costly. Amsbaugh operated the mill only for farm grinding, chop, corn meal, buckwheat, etc., that did not require bolting cloths and other refinements of finer grinding. The mill was torn down after it fell into disuse.[29]

In March 1952, the old Campbell Mill site on State Route 39, the first settlement in Richland County, faded into history with the property sale that took place on March 15th. The headline of the article in *The Mansfield News Journal* read "Early Land Site Sold." The article read:

> Mrs. M. E. Chatlin, Mansfield R.D. 4, purchased the property which lies along Rocky Creek adjacent to Route 39 east of Mansfield near the Richland Hospital for $3,750. Nearly 50 people attended the auction which was conducted by Neil Robinson, Mansfield, a representative of the Ohio Legislature, and real estate dealer.[30]

When parts of State Route 39, including the bridge, were rebuilt in 1934-35, the bricks from the old roadbed were thrown into the old millrace for fill. Evidently, a portion of the stream was deepened or cleaned with heavy equipment years ago. No trace of the mill remains.

The Andrew Painter Woolen Mill

The Andrew Painter Woolen Mill was one of the longest lasting of the woolen mills and factories in old Richland County. This mill was located on Grace Street at the bottom of the hill across from Liberty Park. The millpond was located where the park is today and was fed by the Painter or Bender springs. The mill was south of Grace in the valley between 7th and 8th streets at Ashland Road. It is shown on the *1873 Richland County Atlas*.

According to Harry Painter who was interviewed by Garber in 1950, the mill was built by Andrew Painter, his father. It was a woolen mill as well as a carding and fulling mill. The mill was about 50 x 60 feet and 2 ½ stories above the basement with a very large overshot wheel that was nearly 45 feet in diameter and about 5 feet wide. The main shaft was 24 inches in diameter and 25 to 30 feet long; the bull wheel was about 12 feet in diameter. The millpond, now in Liberty Park, covered about three acres. There was never a dam, and no gristmill, sawmill, or cider press were ever located there. A church now stands on the old millsite.

Andrew Painter was probably a millwright since he built the mill and maintained it through the years that he operated it, and he lived to see it torn down.[31] He operated the mill from the beginning but his sons and grandsons assumed active responsibility at various periods of its life. Andrew made much of the wooden machinery. He learned the latest on weaving, carding, and fulling as well as dyeing in England.

Andrew Painter was a very large man, weighing about 350 pounds. A metal chair he used had ropes attached overhead to assist in pulling him up out of the chair. When the factory was going full force, as many as 30 people ate at the family table. Andrew insisted that those working there stay and eat. Food was prepared in a separate kitchen with an enormous fireplace across one end with high copper kettles and pots. The food was carried to the 20-foot-long table in the old long house.

Figure 158. A monument to the Painter's graves stands on the corner of Grace and Sixth Avenue not far from Liberty Park on the northeast side of Mansfield.

The basement of the mill was taken up with the master wheel, fulling mill, etc. Carding machines and "Mules" for weaving occupied the 50-foot-long first floor. Other mill equipment occupied the second floor. Wool was stored in the half floor at the top. Barns and other available space were also used for storage. Andrew bought and stored wool so that the mill's operation could be extended over a greater period of time, rather than just being seasonal.

One large dyeing vat of gleaming copper, about 12 feet in diameter and 5 feet deep, was erected on a base in the back yard so that it could be fired from beneath. Dye materials were bought from

Europe. After each batch of dyeing, the vat would be scoured for the next one. Satinette, flannel, linen, blankets, and yarns, etc. were all made at the mill.

Two large ice houses on the property were filled each winter, and ice was sold in Mansfield during the following season. The millrace, and sometimes the wheel, froze as early as November or December, forcing the mill to close until spring thaws released the ice bond. The mill building itself was unheated.

About 1875, Harry's brother, Henry Painter, built a steam gristmill across the road from the woolen mill. He ran it for about ten years then it was abandoned. He then operated a tile and brick yard. The brick for the Memorial Building and much of the street paving brick came from Painter's tile and brick yard.[32]

A monument erected to Andrew Painter and his two wives stands on the intersection of Orange and 6th Avenue, a block from Liberty Park in Mansfield and near the site of the pond and mill that he built and operated. The following inscriptions, each on separate sides, reads:

    Andrew Painter, Born April 4, 1804, Died December 23, 1878.

    Catherine Painter, Born Sept. 13, 1803, Died January 8, 1845.

    Mary Painter, Born April 10, 1817, Died January 25, 1878.

Painter's pond and the hillsides were favorite spots where youngsters skated and sledded in winter, and the pond was an attraction in summer long before building a future park was considered.

Figure 159. What is now the Liberty Park lake once served as the millpond for the Painter Woolen Mill that was located south of Orange Street in the valley.

Figure 160. An ancient "picker" combed and cleaned wool as a first step before it went to a carding machine for further processing into wool bats for spinning and weaving. This picker is the first process to start pulling the wool fibers. The picker attempts to straighten the wool and starts to fluff out the wool. It also picks out bits of remaining burrs and waste.

Figure 161. A carding machine had a revolving drum equipped with rotating rolls with nail-like projections that combed and straightened the wood that could then be used as batts or spun into yarn for weaving cloth by hand or on looms. One of the very last of these machines in Ohio sold for $5.00 at an auction near Millersburg, Ohio, a few years ago.

The Pollock Carding Mills

These mills really do not belong in this book of water-powered mills. They were oxen-powered mills located in the downtown Mansfield area. Such mills were unusual and did not last long; but they are interesting, and because they were in downtown Mansfield, they are included here.

Baughman wrote in his *History of Richland County* that:

> The first mill in Mansfield was located where the jail now stands (today where the courthouse stands). It was built by Clement Pollock. It was a tread mill, operated by three yoke of oxen. The mill was duplex – it ground corn and sawed wood.
>
> Robert Pollock erected and operated a carding mill on East Fourth Street near Adams. It was propelled by horse power, and simply made rolls, prepared wool for the spinning wheel.

There was a brief announcement in *The Mansfield Gazette* that read "Stephen Lindley takes over management of the Robert Pollock carding machine in Mansfield."[33] Almost three years later, in June 1827, Samuel and Michael Douglas announced that they had purchased the "stand" where Robert Pollock's mill was located. The announcement reads in part:

> The subscribers having purchased the stand lately occupied by Robert Pollock in Mansfield intend to carry on the business of wool carding. They have the machines in complete order, they have also employed an experienced hand to attend said machines; work will be done in good order on reasonable terms. Most kinds of produce will be taken as payment, such as flax-seed, flax, tallow, bees wax, oats, rye, wheat etc.[34]

Smart Mill and Distillery

Not much is known about the Smart Mill and Distillery. It was located about a quarter mile north of Liberty Park in the valley along the east side of 5th Avenue. A spring-fed stream feeds the pond at the park. By May 1831, James Smart the owner, decided to get out of the business. He placed the following advertisement in *The Western Sentinal* on May 13th:

Figure 162. Staley Distillery. Pictured is the rebuilt Staley Distillery in Miami County which turns out some pretty good rye whisky. The Staley farm has never been out of the family and uses an original 1820-era copper still. Open on weekends for tours, the legally operating distillery sits next to an 1818 gristmill with all the original wood gearing and equipment.

> The subscriber [James Smart] wishes to sell his Distillery and Mill, situated one mile from Mansfield, with eighty acres of land, or any less quantity of land can be had with the mill and distillery down to thirty acres. There are fifteen acres cleared on the premises, with a young orchard of 160 trees of grafted fruit; two cabins, and three first rate springs of water. The mill is small situated on a spring, just calculated to grind for the distillery, the works of which are copper, and in reasonable good order for business.[35]

The mill and distillery did not sell right away. James Smart added the following lines to an advertisement that he placed in the *The Western Sentinal* on August 24th: "If not sold soon, the subscriber will rent it, put it out on shares, or hire a capable person to carry on the distillery."[36]

The Clark Saw Mill

The Clark Saw Mill was built on Toby Run, west of Bowman and south of the railroad tracks where the stream runs along the north side of the Gorman Rupp property. The stream has been altered according to maps; but the mill was evidently somewhere along the Gorman Rupp property. No trace of the mill dam or millrace remains. Ownership information remains sketchy.

Both Baughman and Graham wrote little about the Clark Saw Mill in their histories of Richland County. Baughman wrote "Thomas Clark built a sawmill on Toby's Run, west of the Baltimore & Ohio depot."[37] It was sometime in the late 1820s or early 1830s that "the Tom Clark Mill was built a little west of town on Toby's Run."[38]

Mansfield North Lake Park Mills

The Jacob Bell Grist Mill

The *1843 Tax Records* indicate that Jacob Bell had a sawmill in the valley that now encompasses North Lake Park. Today, a poured-concrete dam is located in the stream on the west side of the park, in the area that once was an amusement park. A roller coaster, swimming pool, dance

Figure 163. This dam on Toby Run at the west end of Mansfield North Lake Park is constructed with poured concrete indicating it may have been built for the Luna Amusement park that was there from the turn of the century until before World War II. It may have been for a swimming pond but now has silted in and may have replaced an earlier mill dam. No records have been found.

The picture above, taken around 1894, shows the western end of the park valley where the ice barn can be seen in the distance.

After the lake was no longer used for ice harvest, the ice barn was remodeled into the theater and amusement complex known as The Casino.

Figure 164. The building in the far left was quite possibly the old sawmill. Later it was used as an ice barn when ice was cut from the upper ponds. Fed by Toby's Run, a good fall of water ran through all three ponds or lakes. In 1924 the stream was rerouted around the lakes. Floods, possibly the flood of 1913, had filled the upper or western lake with gravel.

Photo courtesy of Timothy Brian McKee.

Figure 165. Constant flooding was a problem for the mill and later park.

Photo courtesy of Timothy McKee.

hall, and an array of amusements were located there in the early 1900s. Below the dam, in the stream bed, are an assortment of good-sized sandstone rocks that may have been part of an earlier dam. Because of a good fall of water in the stream bed and the location this would have been an ideal place to build a sawmill. This is just speculation as no other record has been found of this mill. The concrete structure might have been for the amusement park and perhaps replaced an earlier dam. This is another mystery mill.

Garber's records mention but do not confirm the location of another mill just below or downstream from the park lake. Toby Run does not feed the lake but bypasses it, and there is evidence that the stream bed was altered. The North Lake is fed from a small spring-fed stream that begins just south of South Park and passes down through both South and Middle Parks to feed North Lake which joins Toby Run below the lake dam. Jacob Bell is listed as the owner of a sawmill in 1856, evidently on land that passed to him by 1843. Bell at that time owned 157 acres that encompassed all of present day North Park and part of Middle Park. The sawmill did not endure long. The lack of water in summer or flash floods on Toby Run, which to this day still floods the north end of Mansfield along Sixth Street, may have destroyed it.

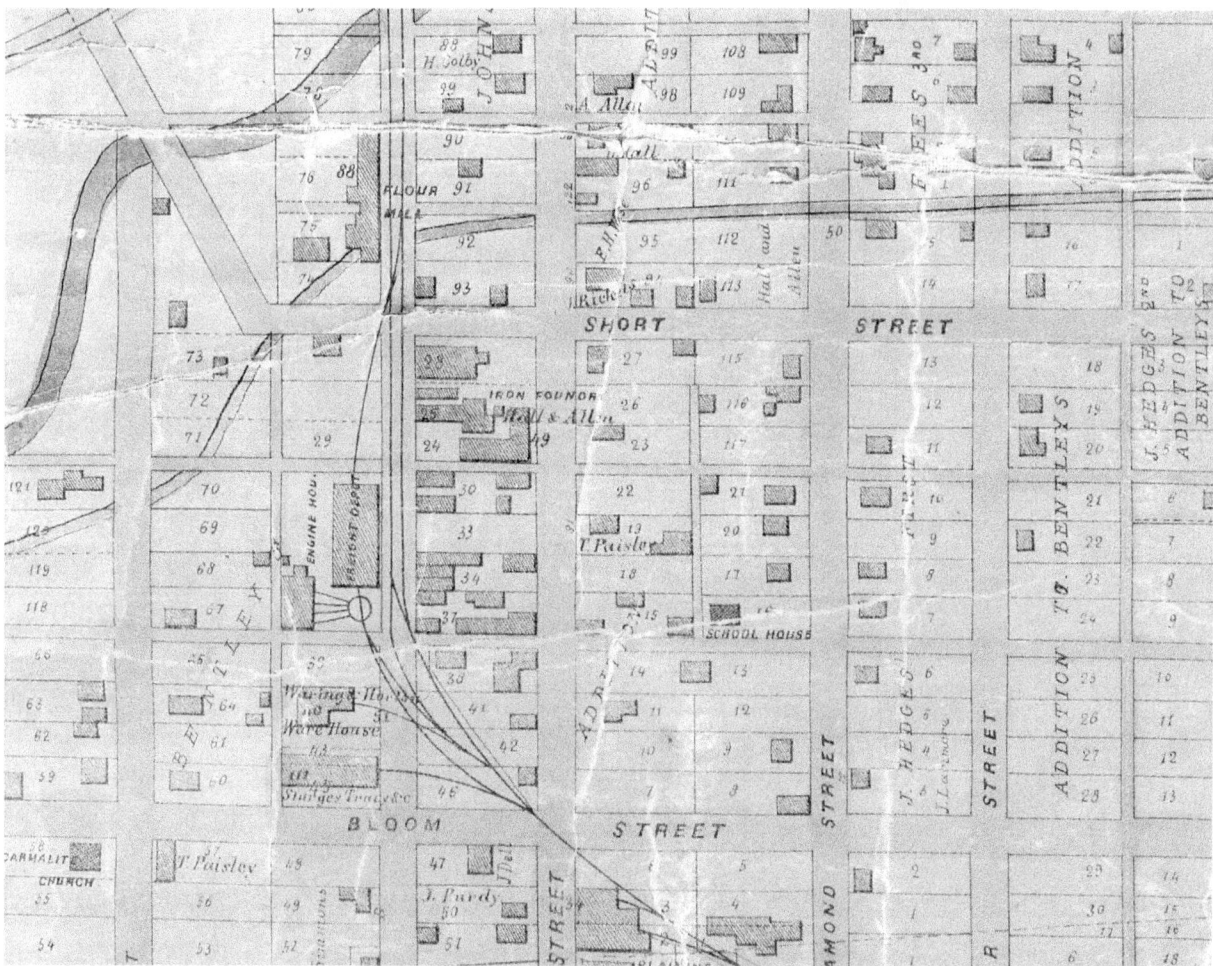

Figure 166. This 1853 map of the north end of Mansfield shows Toby Run, the wide stream in the upper left. The smaller stream is the headrace and tailrace for the flour mill. Short Street is now named Sixth Street. The mill was on North Main Street.

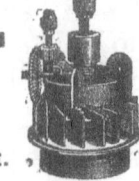

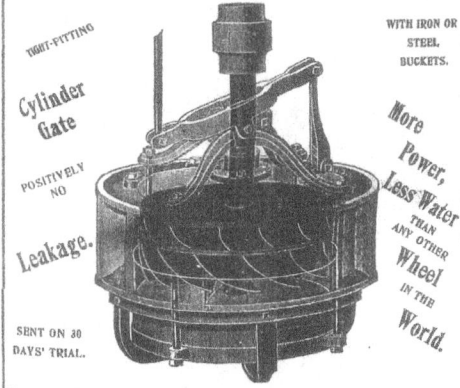

Figure 167. American Miller was the magazine of the milling industry. All kinds of milling equipment and tools were advertised as were testimonials from millers and mill owners. There was competition among turbine manufacturers as turbines began replacing water-wheels as shown in this 1906 issue.

Hedges Paper Mill

The Hedges Paper Mill was located on First Street (which turns into Oak) and is shown on an early map as being located where the Hyundai Ideal Electric Company is now. The Paper Mill was no doubt steam powered; as steam and hot water were required during paper making, and the mill was too far above the Rocky Fork to make water power possible. As far as records go, this was the only paper mill in Richland County. The Hedges Paper Company was in a large 50 x 100 foot building and made paper from straw.

Graham wrote in his *History of Richland County* that Mr. Hade purchased the old paper mill in 1871 for $20,000. In 1873, the Mansfield Paper Company was organized and incorporated by H. Colby, J. H. Red, E. Hade, H. L. Reed, and J. Hade with $60,000 in capitol. They took possession of the mill, but it did not survive the panic of 1873. After the panic, it was again in the possession of Mr. Hade. Attempts were made to revive the business, and for a time it ran "with fair prospects of success."[39]

In 1880, an article in the *Bellville Star* announced: "The paper mills (Mansfield) are running on full time. The mills are managed by eastern capitalist."[40]

A second announcement, appearing just over two and a half years later, is not quite as enthusiastic. In February 1883, "Jacob Madden who was scalded in the bleach tank at the Mansfield Paper Mill has sued the proprietor for $1,000 damages."[41]

Leyman–Robinson–Richland City Mills

These mills were on Toby Run, east of Springmill Street and north of Sixth Street, located in an area behind the old Hartman Sprang building that is now occupied by a golf business. The mills went through a series of owners.

According to historian Graham, the first sawmill propelled by water in Mansfield was erected in 1820 by John Wright, an Irishman, on the opposite side of the stream from the planing mill of McVay and Allison.[42]

Afterwards, Henry Layman built the first water-powered gristmill in Mansfield. Later, the mill was owned and improved by John R. Robinson. For many years he did custom work for Mansfield and vicinity. About 1866 or 1867, John Damp took possession and added steam power with a thirty-five horse-power engine. The Richland City Mills, while in his possession, were destroyed by fire about 1868."[43]

Robinson was a good businessman and did well. The mill must have been profitable, and with other profitable interests, he built Mansfield's "Oak Hill Cottage" in 1847. In 1850 he was among the principal investors in expanding the newly formed Sandusky, Mansfield & Newark Railroad south from Mansfield through Mt. Vernon to Newark. From his mill experience, Robinson realized that the railroad would be a huge asset to the many mills in various parts of Richland County as a means of turning surplus grain into flour or meal and shipping it by rail to Sandusky for lake transportation to the east. Robinson was appointed Superintendent of the railroad in 1850. A station, engine turn table, and roundhouse were located on the west side of Walnut Street half way between Fifth and Sixth streets where Robinson could no doubt see his railroad interests from Oak Hill.[44]

The Commissioners of Richland County gave notice through *The Mansfield Herald* to builders that they would "on the 29th day of June, 1857 sell to the lowest bidder, the building of a stone Arch of the Millrace on the East Diamond Street in the City of Mansfield, near the residence of Wm. S. Higgins."[45]

Garber noted in his file on Leymand-Robinson-Richland City Mill that the bridge arch was across the trailrace, now Main Street, one block to the right, or east, of the flour mill of H. & J. S. Love. Diamond Street then ran east and west, not north and south.

John Damp's Grist Mill

An announcement in *The Mansfield Herald* in June 1868 revealed that when John Damp became the superintendent of the flouring mill located on Walnut Street, he made a number of improvements. Before he installed a steam engine, the mill had no propelling power and a limited water supply. He attached a turbine waterwheel to the water works, abolished some of the former mill gearing, and installed modern and improved gearing that he claimed gave the machinery double the speed and power. The article stated: "If you want good work done in the line of flour, just call on Mr. Damp, and you will not regret. We speak from the card, having never received a pound of poor flour from Mr. John Damp's Mill."[46]

At that time Walnut Street did not end at Sixth but continued on north following the railroad tracks out of town along what is now North Main. The mill was later expanded or relocated. The 1853 Mansfield map shows Toby's Run passing under the south end of the expanded mill building indicating where the turbine was located. The mill building was located at the bridge on North Main near Longview. How long the mill was in operation is unknown but it was gone by 1880.

Mansfield Woolen Mill

Although the Mansfield Woolen Mill located at the foot of Mulberry Street was steam powered, it was an interesting addition to the manufacturing variety in Mansfield in the late 1800s. According to Graham in his *History of Richland County*, the original building was built for a tannery. In 1870 Mr. Gledhill purchased the building, enlarged it, and converted it into a woolen mill. The building was enlarged even more to 30 x 40 feet and was four stories high. It was sold in 1873 to an incorporated company with J. H. Reed as president and James G. Hedges as

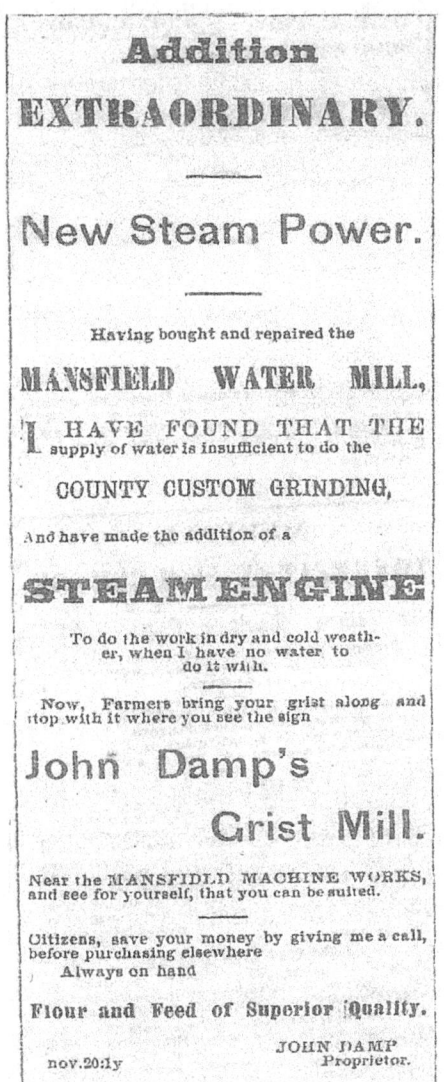

Figure 168. Ad appearing in The Mansfield Herald in 1867. John Damp gristmill on Walnut Street in Mansfield was forced to add a steam engine to supplement water power in 1867. Water power was cheap but adding a steam engine increased the costs by having to buy fuel and to hire an engine operator.[47]

JOHN DAMP'S MILL STILL FURTHER IMPROVED.—This Flouring Mill, situated on Walnut St., in this city, has been most decidedly improved since it has been under the superintendence of Mr. Damp. When he first took charge of it, it was but an ordinary affair, having no propelling power but water, and of that only a limited quantity. Now it has a first rate Steam Engine with all the modern improvements. Lately Mr. Damp has attached a Turbine Water wheel to the water-works, besides, having abolished some of the former mill geering, and put in place some of the most modern and improved geering—giving to the machinery at once double the speed and power it had before. If you want good work done, in the line of Flour, just call on Mr. Damp, and you will not regret. We speak from the card, having never received a pound of poor flour from Mr. John Damps Mill.

Figure 169. Article appearing in The Mansfield Journal in 1868.[48]

Superintendent and Treasurer. Although they added new and improved machinery, following the panic of 1873 times were so hard and unprofitable that the doors closed for several years. In 1876, John Wood, who previously held a large interest in the mill, purchased the entire concern. In 1879, in company with Mr. John Gilliland, the spindles were again started. Twenty to thirty hands were employed. With the fifty horse-power engine and first class machinery, they successfully manufactured cashmeres, flannels, and yarn for a short time.

By 1881, the Mansfield Woolen Mills were in dire straits, with liabilities of $11,000.00 and assets of only $7,500.00. On June 9, 1881, the Sheriff closed the mills, and on December 1, 1881, the machinery was sold to an Indiana firm.[50]

"Union is Strength."
Union Woolen Factory.

THE subscribers having formed a co-partnership, intend carrying on, and are now ready to receive wool to manufacture into

Cloths, Satinets, Tweeds, Kerseymeres, Flannels and Blankets,

on shares, or by the yard, to suit customers, on as reasonable terms as at any establishment in the country. Our Machinery and Fittings are all new, and experienceus workmen, old, so that we cannot fail to give general satisfaction. Also,

Wool Carding, Spinning & Cloth Dressing.

We wish to have it distinctly understood that we want to have the wool for carding and spinning washed clean, and we will do your wool-picking without any charge.

The Union Woolen Factory is at the old Mill Stand of David Smith, on the Rockey Fork, 2 miles above Lucas, Monroe township. Wool Carding 4 cents; Carding and Spinning 12½ cts. per pound.
GLEDHILL & CRAFTS.
Monroe, July 3, 1850.—3m.

Figure 170. 1852 Article in the Shield and Banner.[49]

Cash for Wool
At the Union Woolen Factory.

THE subscribers take this method of informing their numerous customers and the public generally that they are prepared to pay cash for any amount of wool, or for manufacture on shares or by the yard into cloths, cattinets, Kerseymeres, plain or crossbarred flanns's or blankets at as low terms as any establishment in the county. Also that we have a large stock of goods that we wish to exchange for wool. Persons wishing to exchange and get their cloths at once will do well to give us a call. We are prepared to do any amount of carding, spinning, or cloth dressing as usual. Union Woolen Factory is on the Rocky Fork of Mohican, 4 miles below Mr. Campbell's Mill and seven miles east of Mansfield.

All kinds of produce taken in payment for work —cash not excepted.
GLEDHILL & CRAFTS.
Monroe tp., May 12, 1852.   2m.

Figure 171. 1850 Article in the Shield and Banner.[51]

Hedges Oil or Flax Mill

The Hedges Oil or Flax Mill was located in the west part of Mansfield on the south side of Route 430, a short distance down and over the hill from the former Peoples Hospital; now the Sheriff's Department. The stream coming down from Liberty Park fed the Painter's Mills before the stream entered the Rocky Fork.

Garber concluded that the *1830 Sherman Map* showed a gristmill at that location. The exact locations were more probable than accurate. The mill may have been converted and may have been the early water-powered mill that Hedges sold to John U. Tanner in 1834. In 1843, the property was sold to Tanner who was still listed as owner in 1856. How long the oil mill was in operation or whether the transactions were more for the land than the business is unknown. The 1856 map indicated James Riatt still owned the land, but no actual mill history has been found. A 2014 visit to the site revealed nothing.

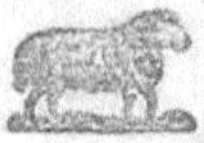
WOOL WANTED.
AT THE
Union Woolen Factory,
On the Rocky Fork, 4 miles below Mr. Campbell's Mill.

IN exchange for cash at the highest market price—or Cloths, Sattinets, Flannels and Blankets. Manufacturing done on shares or by the yard, as usual. Carding and Spinning by the pound. Fulling and Cloth dressing done on short notice, and in a workman like manner.

We also take in Wool at the following places, viz: at Wm. Hartupees, Springfield tp., by Peter Wertz, Spring-mill, and Sturges, Grimes & Co., Mansfield. Good work insured on all clean wool.

WALTER GLEDHILL.

May 25th, 1853.—6w.

Figure 172. 1853 Article in the Shield and Banner.[52]

Union Woolen Factory!

WOOL WANTED in exchange for Cloths, Cassimeres, Tweeds, Satinets, Plain or Barred Flanels, Blankets, Stocking Yarn, &c. Also, Manufacturing on shares, or by the yard as usual. Wool Carding and Spinning by the pound. All work done in a manner that cannot be surpassed; and for the accommodation of patrons, have the usual arrangements with Sturges, Grimes & Co., Mansfield, Mr. Hartupel, Springfield tp., and Mr. Geo. Owings, (Miller,) at the Spring Mill, to have Wool left with them, and I will attend and deliver yarn there every two weeks throughout the season.—Wool for Carding and Spinning is expected to be washed clean.

WALTER GLEDHILL.

Monroe tp., May 14, 1856-tf.

Figure 173. 1856 Article in the Shield and Banner.[54]

GLEDHILL.S UNION WOOLLEN FACTORY.

Wool Carding, Spinning and Manu facturing.

THE subscriber, grateful for past favors, takes pleasure in making known to his customers and all others interested, that he is again ready to CARD ROLLS, Card and Spin, or to Manufacture Wool into any kind of goods wanted, on shares or by the yard to suit customers. For the accommodation of Patrons, I have the usual arrangement with
Messrs. Sturges & Co., Merch'ts, Mansfield.
" Rupert & Pifer, " Ganges.
Mr. J. Kinninger, " Haysville.
" Wm. Hartupee, " Springfield tp.
To have Wool left with them and I will take the wool and return the Rolls or yarn every two weeks throughout the season. I have on hand a large stock of

Plain and Fancy Cassimeres,

Plain and Barred Flannels, Satinetts and Blankets to exchange for Wool on fair terms.

WALTER GLEDHILL.

Lucas, June 3. 1857—3m.

Figure 174. 1857 Article in The Mansfield Herald.[53]

Mills South of Mansfield in Washington Township

The Bentley Mill

The Bentley Mill was located along Mansfield–Washington Road, just south

Figure 175. Water still flows from the spring that years ago supplied the Bentley Grist and Saw Mills. It is not known whether the pond is original size but the mills could have been on the hillside or in the valley below.

of Hull Road, in northern Washington Township. Today on the way up the hill, a beautiful ranch style home attached to an old spring house is on the east side of the road, with a pond in front. This spring-fed pond may well have been for Bentley's Mill just below. At an earlier time the volume of water was no doubt sufficient to power a sawmill and gristmill. No remains of the mill foundations can be seen, but a small amount of water still flows from the spring.

Graham wrote that shortly after Wright erected his mill in 1820, Robert Bentley Sr. built a sawmill and afterwards a gristmill on his farm. The farm was about two miles south of Mansfield, and he obtained water from a spring on his farm. After many years of use, the Bentley mill eventually decayed.[55]

Graham provides additional information on the Bentley family who settled in Ohio in 1815. He wrote:

> With his family, he camped about a week upon the south-west quarter of section 10, while he was building his cabin. He brought with him two yoke of oxen, two horses ahead of them, two cows, two calves, and a fine mare which Mrs. Bentley rode with her child Mary. Mr. Bentley was appointed Associate Judge of the Court of Common Pleas in 1821, and served seven years. In 1828 he was elected to the State Senate, and reelected again in 1830, serving in that capacity for four years. In 1839 he removed to Mansfield, where he resided until his death in 1862. He was for some time connected with military service, was a Major General of Militia, and a prominent military man in his day."[56]

Garber was unable to trace the ownership linage; nor did his notes indicate just how long the Bentley Mill operated.

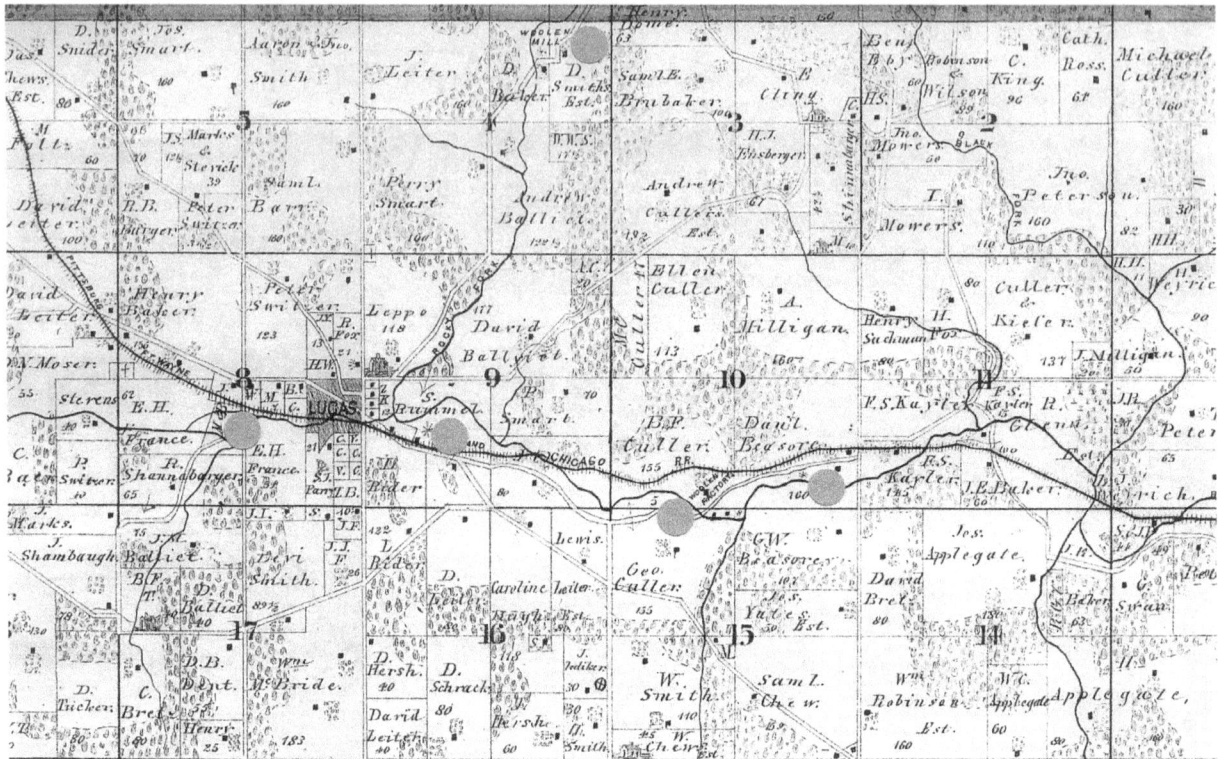

Figure 176. Map of Lucas area. A portion of the 1873 Monroe Township map showing the course of the Rocky Fork (center) and the mills (the gray circles) in the Lucas area and downstream before it joins the Black Fork (right) which flows from the north.

The Culler Woolen Mill

A February 1878 article in the *Bellville Messenger* specified that John Culler built a woolen mill a mile and a half east of Lucas about 1848, but that it never did a great deal of business. The mill was built near Jacob Culler's sawmill that was built in 1832 below the old Zuby Mill.[57]

The Culler Woolen Mill was located southeast of Lucas, just off the Lucas–Perrysville Road on Kaylor Road, a short distance after crossing the bridge over the Rocky Fork. The mill dam was thought to have been just above the bridge and the mill, on the south side of the road between the road and the Rocky Fork, but some distance downstream. Floods have erased most traces of the headrace, and modern homes now make up the spot on most maps named "Culler."

Garber interviewed O. D. Culler in July 1949, when Culler was 83 years of age, and Culler remembered many details of the Culler woolen mill operation. Culler, a successful businessman and volunteer community leader, was respected in the community. Culler described the mill building as 2 ½ stories high and 40 x 60 on the first floor. The dam was 4 to 4 ½ feet high. There was an eleven-foot fall of water at the wheel, originally an overshot wheel that was 8 feet wide and 10 feet in diameter. O. D. and his brother installed a 22-inch Leffel Turbine while it was still a woolen factory. The factory was well equipped with one picker, a breaker, carding machines located on the second floor, a twister that made two- or three-ply yarns, a blanket-sized loom, 3 other looms, and in the basement where the fulling and dying operations were done, a fulling machine with 2

Figure 177. Culler Woolen Mill is the large building in the center foreground. The original of this photo was loaned by O. D. Culler, July 11, 1949. This is an enlargement of a portion of that photo showing the valley, including the Culler property.

Figure 178. Jane Kaylor and her mother Lillian Manner were photographed in front of the Culler Woolen Mill holding shuttles they used to pass yarn back and forth between the looms. Skill and concentration were required to maintain the pattern in the cloth being woven.

hammers. The spinner took the full length of the mill on the first floor, occupying one side. The looms were on the opposite side. The woolen mill manufactured flannel, broadcloth, blankets, jeans, wool batts, and yarn, etc.

Brothers George and Frank Fry and George Ferguson worked the carding machines. Andy Baxter and a man named Coldwater, both Englishmen, worked on the spinners. Four or five girls worked the looms, and one man worked in the office and store.

By the middle of the 1880s, the financial condition of the mill was failing, and it was closed. Later it was converted to a gristmill. After the woolen mill was discontinued, one pair of 20-inch buhrs was installed in a portable Nordyke & Marmon mill for use in farm grinding. Corn mill, buckwheat flour, etc., was ground for customers, but not regular flour.

A sawmill also operated in connection with the mill, both when the waterwheel was used and when the turbine was installed. Enoch France was thought to have had overall charge of the factory, or he may have been an early owner. Henry Mowers, George W., and John W. Culler were owners or partners. Mowers dropped out and the Culler brothers ran it thereafter.

O. D. told Garber the story of an injury that he sustained about 1876 when he was a small boy of 10 or 11. Frank and George Fry worked on the breakers. One day Frank bribed him to bring him a fine apple from the orchard on the Culler farm. O. D. concealed the apple under his shirt and

Figure 179. Mrs. Joan Culler Walsh of Butler, Ohio, a descendant of the Culler family, holds one of the shuttles that was handed down through the family from the old Culler Woolen Mill. The shuttle was passed back and forth in the looms. Harley, her twenty-some-year-old pet parrot is looking over her shoulder.

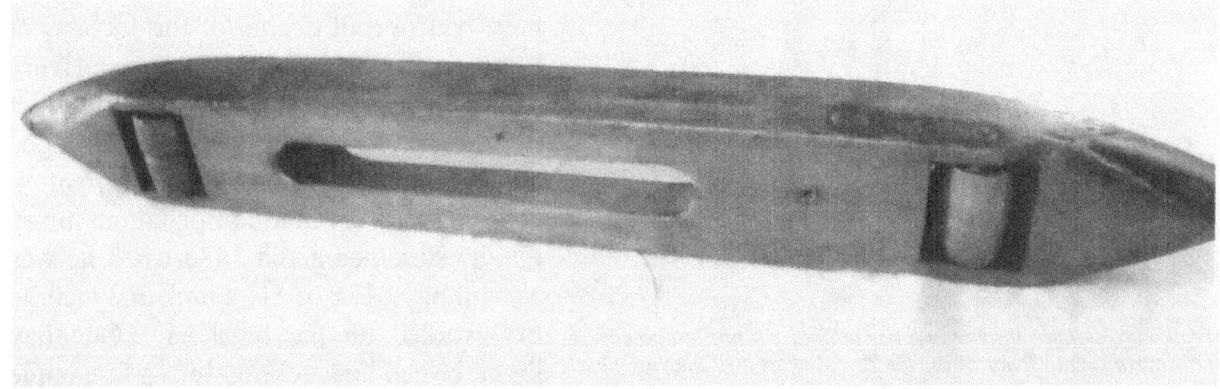

Figure 180. The handmade shuttles were of a special design and must have seemed a bit heavy after a few hours on the job. The days were long with no coffee breaks.

succeeded in getting by the supervisors and to the breakers where Frank was working. Culler walked the two or three feet between the machines down to Fry who took the apple. As Culler dropped his hand after passing the apple to Frank, the revolving and projecting equipment on the breaker caught his hand and cut the fingers to the bone. O. D. insisted that his injury happened because he disobeyed instructions to keep away from the machinery.

O. D. noted that from Lucas for a distance of about 1½ miles, there had been three gristmills and one sawmill run by water power, all on connecting lands. They were the Rummel Mill, Lucas Mill, Dorman Mill, Culler Mill, and Beasore's sawmill.[58]

Jacob Culler was an early settler, and in 1832 he owned 500 acres of land where the mills stood. No trace of the mills is evident but one interesting artifact is a shuttle from the Culler mill owned by Mrs. Joan Walsh, a descendant of the Culler family. She has the shuttle and a photograph of two early employees. The area in the valley where the mill once stood is a beautiful, scenic area.

Daniel Beasore's Saw Mill

The Daniel Beasore Saw Mill was located about quarter of a mile downstream from the Culler Mills and was built between the Rocky Fork and the present road. The mill was just east of Route 603. Evidently it was constructed sometime before 1845 and was still running in the early 1880s until diminished water levels in the Rocky Fork hampered its operation. Little else has been found on the history of the Beasore family or the mill.

The LaRue–Baker Grist Mill

The LaRue-Baker Grist Mill was located east of Lucas, along the east side of Hanley Road, between the bridge and the railroad tracks. Graham indicates in his *History of Richland County* that LaRue built the third mill in the township in 1830 on Rocky Fork, about one mile west of Lucas.[59] Both the 1856 and 1873 Atlas maps show the mill on the west side of Hanley; however, Garber's notes and a visit to the site indicate the mill was to the east, near the bridge, due to the fall of the land. No trace remains, and according to the early maps, the stream has been altered over the years.

George Rummel, when interviewed by Garber at his home in Lucas in July 1949, said that Meanor Matthews operated the three-story mill located one-half mile west of Lucas. Water from springs west of the mill was channeled into a millrace that ran into a small pond of perhaps half an acre. A large waterwheel, similar to one at Wolf Mill, was fed by a flume that channeled water under the road. Hiram Baker owned the mill after Matthews.[60]

When Garber interviewed Mrs. Lewis Chandler, daughter of Hiram Baker, in September 1949 at her home in Bucyrus, Ohio, she said that her father operated the mill for many years, but he never actually owned it. Meanor Matthews, a brother-in-law, was the owner. Mrs. Chandler was sometimes the one who locked up the mill at night. Because she was always afraid of the shadows and the lonesomeness there, she hated the mill.

Before Matthews owned the mill, a man named Goudy may have ran the mill. He moved from there to the Beam Campbell mill. When Chandler married in 1895, the 3½-story mill was running. It had a bolting system for making flour, but flour was never made there. They did only custom work. Three of Matthew's men were millers, and two of them married Hiram Baker's sisters.[61] The mill was torn down before 1900.

John Tucker, a retired school teacher with an excellent memory, was 86 years of age when Garber interviewed him in July 1951. On a drive with Garber, Tucker pointed out the locations of various mills and other points of historical interest, information that Garber considered very accurate.

Tucker confirmed that the mill had a large millpond and that a flume ran under the road to feed the water to the mill. He described the mill as about 40 x 50 feet with a Comb roof, rather than a gambrel or hip, and as three stories above the basement with two run of buhrs. He said that water power was its only source of power with an overshot wheel that was about 12 feet in diameter and 5 feet wide. He recalled that Meanor Matthews was the last to operate the mill as a flour mill and that Baker ran it as a feed mill for several years until about 1900.[62]

The Ahlefeldt-Rummel Mill

The Ahlefeldt-Rummel Mill, the second gristmill in Monroe Township, was built in 1830 by Richard Oldfield almost half of a mile east of Lucas on the Rocky Fork. Later Abraham Marks and still later Silas Rummel owned it. A sawmill was attached to the mill, one considered among the best in the township.[63]

Figure 181. The Ahlefeldt Mill. In this photograph taken about 1885, the gristmill is the 3-story building in the background, and the sawmill is the low building to the right. Silas Rummel is at the left of the door of the miller's house with Oliver Rickerson, a miller who was the operator of the mill at the time. Otis Rummel is in the top door of the mill, George L. Rummel is in the second-story door, and in the ground-floor door are the operators of the sawmill, Corwin Rummel on the left, and John First on the right.

Silas Rummel learned the millwright's trade as a young man and followed it for twenty years. In 1863 he purchased and ran the old Campbell Mill on the Rocky Fork for five years. After selling it, he purchased the Oldfield Mill in Lucas and ran it until 1902.[64]

George Rummel and Mary (Rummel) Brenstunl described the mill in a 1949 interview with Garber as about 40 x 60 feet with one 48-inch run and two 42-inch runs of buhrs. A cider press was located there as well. The sawmill was originally an up-and-down mill, but later changed to a circular sawmill. All were connected to water power. A 15-foot head of water was at one time reduced to 9 feet by flooding in the tailrace with silt. All one summer and fall Rummel and two sons worked to clean out the tailrace and return the head of water to 13 feet.

The waterwheel for the gristmill and the one for the sawmill were later changed to turbines. One turbine was a 42-inch Leffel and the other a 48-inch one made in Urbana.

The mill capacity was 50 barrels of flour a day. The output was largely packed in barrels and shipped. "Golden Eagle" was the best brand of flour manufactured. Silas Rummel sold the mill about 1900 to Charles Fike, L. Sheets, and Ira Ernsberger. Later L. Sheets bought out the others, and eventually turned it over to his son-in-law who was operating it when it burned.[65]

John Vail told Garber in a 1947 interview that he purchased the old Rummel (Oldfield) Mill in 1903. Earlier, he had eliminated the millstones and converted the mill to a roller system; but

Figure 182. Steam engines or tractors powering portable manufactured circular sawmills were the death knell to many remaining water-powered sawmills. This undated photo (compliments of Shelby Historical Society) was taken near Plymouth.

because of vibrations, they shook the whole building. Vail reconditioned, repaired, and modernized the mill by installing a Plansifter System. When the rollers were removed, Fike, Sheets, and Ernsberger were hired for the installation of the Plansifter System. Vail ran the sawmill and cider press in conjunction with the mill. Shortly after the mill was overhauled someone attempted to set it on fire twice. On both occasions Vail successfully put out the fire. Unfortunately, as a result of a third attempt by the arsonist in 1906, the mill burned down.[66]

Washington Township

The Stewart–Wickert Grist and Saw Mills

The Stewart-Wickert Grist and Saw Mills were located near a jog on present day Sites Road, about a half mile east of State Route 39. Nothing remains of the mill as it was stripped, the millstones dumped into the forebay or basement, the building moved, and the site erased by a bulldozer. Bentley Run, emptying into the Rocky Fork, was the spring-fed stream in the valley powering the mill.

John Stewart was a remarkable man. Born in Pennsylvania in 1787, he came to Richland County in 1815 and settled in northeastern Washington Township. A man of some education, in 1816 he was the township's first Justice of the Peace, a post he held for 22 years. That same year he was appointed to the vacant post of county surveyor, and he held that post for 18 years. In 1820 he began an 8-year stint as County Auditor. Records suggest these overlapping posts were acceptable or perhaps no one else was interested or had the ability to fill them.

He cleared land for a farm, built a sawmill, and in 1823 added a gristmill. A few years later the gristmill burned to the ground. A second mill built on the same foundation outlasted all other mills in the township. A 14-foot waterwheel with a 3-foot face powered 40-inch millstones and associated machinery.

The mills prospered. In September 1827 Stewart placed an ad in the *Mansfield Gazette*:

Wheat Wanted

The subscriber will pay after the first day of next month for wheat delivered to his mill three miles south of Mansfield 31 ¼ cents in cash or 37 ¼ in salt or dry goods. He has on hand a quantity of poplar or walnut boards he will exchange for wheat.

John Stewart.

Records indicate that in 1836 Stewart shipped over 300 barrels of flour to the east via Lake Erie. One customer wanted a number of barrels marked "Buffalo" indicating their destination. Running the mill was a family affair as Stewart's wife gave him 10 children, 7 girls and 3 boys. When two of his sons grew to adulthood, they ran the mill under a signed contract that specified one third for them, two thirds for their father.

Later miller George Wickert and son ran the mill for many years. They were the last to make flour in what was known as the Stewart–Wickert Mill. About 1909-1910, a Russian named Paul Satko was the last to operate the ancient mill. He made corn meal and did custom feed grinding.

The mill went through two more owners until 1916, when partners Reed Carpenter and Peter Ross purchased the mill building and moved it nearly a quarter mile east to the Hartman farm for use as a barn. Moving the strongly built mill constructed of massive timbers must have been a chore. Unfortunately the mill-turned-barn later burned.

A good citizen, Stewart and his father signed the incorporation papers for the First Associate Reform Church of Mansfield. An offshoot of the Presbyterian Church, a later merger brought the two factions together to form the United Presbyterian Church of North America. Stewart paid the pastor's salary, and his mill cut some of the lumber for their first church building.

Stewart, the respected mill owner, office holder, and educated man, died in 1866 at the age of 78. His wife, mother of his 10 children, died in 1883 at 96. Surprisingly, she signed documents with a rather crude "X" indicating she could neither read nor write.

The Rocky Fork – Where Did The Water Go?

With a population of about 5,000 in 1850, the arrival of three railroads turned Mansfield into a mid-west boom town. By 1880 the census population had almost doubled to 9,839, and ten years later to 13,473. The increase in water usage by industry, home, and drinking was more than the city wells could supply. Some wells became contaminated by industrial waste and sewage. The solution was to divert water to the Mansfield Water Works from two large springs near the old reformatory that were good-flowing springs, with one rated at 400 gallons a minute. Both springs are now down to a trickle, one feeding the pond at the old reformatory, and the Laird spring is located just to the south. As the city diverted water into the Mansfield Water Works, tension grew between the city and the mill owners. The following appeared in an 1880 issue of *The Richland Star:* The mill owners on the Rocky Fork are getting their Dutch up over the fact that the inhabitants of Mansfield are drinking up so much of the stream that their mills lay idle a good part of the time for lack of water to run them. Therefore they ask the law to make Mansfield pay $4,500 in damages. It will be quite an interesting suit, and awakens the inquiry as to where a man can legally get a drink, and water to wash his face.[67]

The lawsuit continued to heat up, and nearly a year later the following article appeared in *The Richland Star*:

To Whom Does The Water Belong?

There are now five cases pending in the Common Pleas Court against the City of Mansfield, for directing water out of its regular course, and using it to the detriment of certain parties who own mills on the stream below the city.

The fact is apparent that men have been damaged, and it does seem just that men should have what water is necessary to supply their needs without paying for it. This is an interesting case and the Mansfield Herald informs us that the trial is to take place in the September term of Court. The parties asking damage are Henry L. Goudy, damages claimed $2,000; Silas Rummel, $1,400; Jeremiah Dorem and Mariah Dorem, $400; Mowers & Co., $1,000; George Mowers, $450.[68]

"The "missing water case" would drag on for quite some time. Would the court house drinking fountain dry up or would the Rocky Fork mill wheels cease to turn? The six lawyers involved were no doubt rubbing their hands together thinking of their bank accounts.

In February 1882 the following information appeared in *The Bellville Star*:

Jeremiah and Maria Dorem, owners of the grist mill situated about one mile east of Lucas, have filed a petition with the County Clerk in which they claim damages to the amount of $400 against the city of Mansfield, on account of diverting the water of the springs known as John's and Laird's springs from the natural channels. They claim that previous to the time the water was diverted, that the mill would grind 60 bushels of wheat a day and now it will grind 40 bushels.[69]

In December 1882, just before Christmas, the *The Bellville Star* announced that "The case of Goudy et al, mill owners, against the City of Mansfield for diverting water from its regular channel and causing damage as they claim, has been on trial four days, and will probably last a week longer."[70]

A final verdict was not reached until March 1884 when "after two weeks trial decided on Saturday by the jury rendering for the defendant. Goudy had asked for a second trial and lost more than the Rocky Fork water as it was reported that the attorney's fees and court costs were more than the $2,000 damages he claimed at that time."[71]

The water continues to flow at the court house drinking fountain.

The Union Woolen Factory

The Union Woolen Factory was located north of Lucas along the Rocky Fork and present day Smart Road (Township Road 356), very near the northern border of Monroe Township. The 1840 County map shows Smith's Mill at that location. In 1856 the mill property was listed as a woolen mill owned by D. Smith. The mill was on the east side of the stream. Little has been found on the early years or the Smiths. The mill later passed to a Mr. Gledhill.

John Tucker, a life-time resident of Lucas, remembered the Gledhill mill and told Garber in a 1951 interview (when Tucker was 86 years of age), that Gledhill operated it until it was shut down for good. About 1885 Gledhill removed the machinery from the mill and transferred it to Galion where it was installed in a mill. Tucker described the Union Woolen Mill as 2 ½ stories above the basement, about 40 x 50 feet, and said that it always operated with water power.

According to Tucker, Gledhill and Smith were related, Mrs. Gledhill being a Smith. Smith bought the 80 acres where the mill stood and used it as a barn. Tucker used to work for him, recalling that he put hay in the old building many times. About 1895 Smith sold the mill building and it was torn down. Material from the mill was used to build a house that stands at the foot of Sand Hill near Lucas.[72]

The Balliett Grist and Saw Mills

The Balliett Grist and Saw Mills were located on the Rocky Fork north of Lucas on present day Smart Road (Township Road 356). Pinpointing a location is difficult, but the mills would no doubt have been between the river and the road.

In February 1948, Garber interviewed Mrs. Hunt, mother of Richard Hunt and the great, great granddaughter of Steven Balliett, who owned and operated the mill. Mrs. Hunt told Garber that Stephen Balliett owned and operated the mill known as the Balliett Mill until it burned down in 1878. The mill was large, about three stories tall, and both it and the sawmill associated with it used water power. After the gristmill burned, Stephen Balliett continued to operate the sawmill for some time. A pond of considerable size was used with the operation of this mill.[73]

The Balliett Grist and Saw Mill met its end on February 17, 1879. The story that appeared in *The Ohio Liberal* two days later read:

> The bright light which illuminated the eastern sky about half past ten o'clock Monday night was caused by the burning of Balliett's Mill, lately run by John Brubaker, about two and a half miles from the city. There was an insurance of about $450 on the property. The fire is supposed to have originated from the stove in the mill.[74]

Garber spent a good portion of his free time over nearly a half a century interviewing and collecting material on his favorite hobby—water-powered mills. By his careful calculation and research, there were 190 water-powered mills of all types in Richland County in 1840. Of that number, 82 were gristmills. By 1860 when Richland County had been reduced in size by the creation of newer counties, there were still 34 gristmills, more than any other county in Ohio.

When Garber passed away in 1984 his lifetime collection, started when he was a youngster, filled eight 3-ring notebooks. It is unfortunate that he did not write his own book on Richland County mills. The three who put this book together using his collection will always wonder whether he would have approved of the effort or how much of his insight we have missed.

D. W. Garber

D. W. Garber - Author and Historian

Dwight Wesley Garber was born on April 26, 1896, in Butler, Ohio, to Jacob Silas Garber and Maria Swank Garber. His great grandfather, Daniel Garber, served with the 102nd Ohio Volunteer Infantry during the Civil War. Daniel's son, Jacob, was an avid collector of Lincoln memorabilia, and it was he who instilled in his children a love of history and family genealogy. Garber, from the time he started school, was a collector. He began collecting books before the age of ten, and he never lost that love of collecting or his love of history. He instilled in his only child Constance (Connie) a love of history, and she graduated with a Bachelor's degree in history in the summer of 1940.

Connie started collecting books after her two sons were in college. She took over her oldest son's bedroom, converted it into a small library, and began to collect in earnest. The youngest son, Michael, inherited the family love of history. He received his Bachelor's degree in history in 1971, and after he retired, he continued on to complete a Master's degree in history. By the time he was twenty-five, he was as addicted to the hunt for that special book as his mother. When they went "booking" together, one would always say with a smile, "We would not be doing this, were it not for granddad" as they headed for the next bookstore.

Garber loved the local history of Richland County, Ohio. His ancestors were pioneers in the Mansfield-Butler area where he grew up. He was proud of his ancestry, and he traced his immediate branch back to Michael Garber, his great-great-great grandfather. His parents were poor, but almost anyone in Butler was in much the same situation. In recalling his childhood, he once wrote, "As the last of three brothers I usually inherited well worn garments to wear and it was not unusual for them to have patches on patches." Underneath the shirt and a pair of pants was nothing but the bare skin of a small boy. Shoes came off in the spring and remained off except for church and Sunday school until winter arrived.

His grandparents, Pennsylvania Germans, lived on a farm a half mile from the village and took care of him during the warmer months of spring, summer, and fall. His Granny loved having him around and talking to him. She baked the most wonderful melt-in-your-mouth cookies just for him, large sugar cookies with a face outlined with raisons. The cookie jar was never empty, and he was never scolded for taking any. Before she went to bed at night, she folded her dress and clothes on a chair, placing her stockings crossed in an "X" on top as a sign that she would live to see another day. His grandfather chewed "Sweet Cub Fine Cut" tobacco. Once, when Garber was 7 or 8, his grandfather ran out of tobacco and sent him into town with two dimes to get a ten-cent package. He got to keep one shining little dime.

Times were tough in Butler when Garber was a boy, but changed for the better in 1902 when the Post Office started rural mail delivery and his father Jacob got a mail route out of Butler, providing a steady income for the family. With his route, he became one of the most well known people in Worthington Township. He also led singing schools, a popular form of entertainment, and he was an active member of the Methodist Church where his wife Maria was in the women's group. He was also a long time member of the Odd Fellows lodge.

As a youngster Garber spent hours playing in and around the Myers-Kanaga-Plank water-powered gristmill just west of Butler next to his grandparent's farm. The genial old miller permitted him free access to the mill, and he explored it from top to bottom. He fondly recalled how he and his friends walked across the Clear Fork on stilts and climbed the hillside above the mill where they stole a few apples from an orchard known as the Appleseed orchard, planted from seedlings from Johnny Appleseed. In later years in a letter he recalled wistfully, "The pleasant hum of activity could be plainly heard at my grandparent's home. I often sat along the bank back of the mill where the sluice discharged the overflow from the millrace into the creek and fished and visited with "Daddy" Cushman, a warm-hearted old man who found the deep water back of the mill an excellent place to enjoy his favorite pastime. I thus absorbed the atmosphere of an old time gristmill from close association." At every opportunity over the years, he visited, explored, purchased, or was given old mill records, trade publications, and manuals, etc. He also conducted personal interviews and collected information from published and documentary sources relating to mills.

In the fall of 1913 Garber quit school and went to the Naval Recruiting Station in Detroit, Michigan, with a friend and joined the Navy. He was only seventeen at the time, requiring his parents to telegraph permission for him to join. He chose the Navy training course for pharmacy at the Naval Station Great Lakes (NAVSTA Great Lakes) and graduated on August 6, 1917, with a rank of Pharmacist 2nd Class. Later he met Vera Swalberg there during World War I where she was working as a Navy Yeomanette, a naval term for a female secretary. He worked on base and later on a training ship. During the disastrous flu epidemic during 1917 that took so many lives, he and others that he worked with would take a dying sailor's hand and help him sign the insurance form so his family would receive the $5,000 benefit.

Garber's next assignment was to Pearl Harbor, Hawaii. When the war ended in 1918, Vera was let go along with hundreds of thousands of other service personnel. Garber sent for her, and she arrived by ship on May 18, 1919. They were married in Honolulu the next day at the First Methodist Church. Connie was born there a year later. She often boasted in jest that she was a first citizen of Hawaii. She accompanied her parents to Samoa when the Navy first sent them there. Samoa was still a very primitive island. About 1926, her parents were faced with a heart-wrenching decision, for it was time for Connie to begin schooling. They made the difficult decision to take her back to live with her grandparents in Butler where she started first grade. Vera always regretted missing that time with her daughter.

While stationed in Hawaii and Samoa from 1919 to 1926, Garber studied botany. During his six-year association with the Bishop Museum, he provided a very fine collection of over one thousand specimens and copious field notes that were included in the monographs on Samoan flora published by the museum. He also provided a collection of botanical specimens to the Osborn Botanical Laboratory at Yale University. In addition, he produced four volumes of transcripts of interviews conducted with natives in Samoa while he served in the Public Health Department of the Island Government. He held sick call every day of the week and even delivered a few babies, including one pair of twins.

From 1927-1929 Garber served as secretary to the fleet surgeon. His duties took him back to the Great Lakes Naval Hospital in Illinois, followed by time aboard the USS Arkansas and the USS Wyoming, then to the Naval Hospital in Portsmouth, New Hampshire. In 1929 he began a four-year tour of duty at naval bases in the Panama Canal Zone, followed from 1933 to 1936 by recruiting duty in Birmingham, Alabama. Then he was placed on the inactive list until World II.

In 1936 he was appointed to a Civil Service position at the U.S. Narcotic Farm at Lexington, Kentucky, as an assistant to the Senior Custodial officer. The institution was less than one year old at the time. He organized, wrote, and compiled all of the orders and routine governing the custodial staff. During the following years he served the 1100-1200 prisoners and narcotic inmates, and also organized, classified, and published a manual on the key and lock system of the institution which consisted of more than 5,000 keys.

Recalled to active duty on March 3, 1942, during World War II, he was assigned to recruiting duty in Chicago for a year, and Cincinnati for 3 months before he was transferred to the U.S. Navy Auxiliary Air Station, Harvey Point, NC. In 1943 he was promoted to Chief Pharmacist, Lieutenant Junior Grade. On the last day of 1944 he retired from the Navy after 25 years of active service.

After returning home in 1945, he was drafted by the Commonwealth of Kentucky as the Chief of Registration and Research. With two secretaries and over one hundred clerks and training officers in his department, he was responsible for drawing up and publishing all memoranda, orders, and monthly training activities. His reports were submitted to all colleges and universities in the Commonwealth as a guide for GIs who were being released by the hundreds of thousands for possible enrollment under the GI Bill. His duties included battles with hot-headed congressmen who were sure their constituents were being neglected. He "burned them up with factual information which refuted their complaints." When he could occasionally get away, he returned to Ohio for a few days and a visit to an old mill, where he bought old newspaper files if he could find them, did extensive research, and made prolific notes.

His position with the Commonwealth of Kentucky lasted only until he discovered that he could not work for another government agency and collect his Navy pension at the same time. He retired and sometime in 1945 he and Vera moved to Florida. After a time in that sunny climate they became dissatisfied. Late in 1945 or early 1946, they returned to Ohio where they moved into a two-story house with a big front porch in Bellville, Ohio. Once settled in their new home, Garber turned his attention to the history of Ohio watermills, especially those located in Richland County. From that point on Vera became a "mill widow" as she sometimes went along on mill trips with him, where she sat in the car reading a book while he searched a mill stream or clamored around inside an old mill while interviewing some old-timer. His interest started with the mills he knew best on the Clear Fork and expanded to a wide area in all directions. His typewritten notes were more than dull statistics. They included interesting history, events, people, and sometimes even genealogical information on mill families. The pictures he took or located are a treasure because many of these old mills had vanished, were being torn down, or were in ruins.

On his trips to a library or to conduct an interview he was always well dressed in a jacket and tie and a jaunty hat. His neat appearance opened doors for him. All of his writing was done on a small portable typewriter. He wore out two of them after the war, and as his early records copied from newspapers and other sources were typed word for word, it may well be he took it with him in the days before Xerox machines and microfilm.

Occasionally he would walk to the town square and sit for a while with the old-timers on the park benches. His stories about his interesting experiences in the Navy and on the islands were popular with his cronies, most who had never been far from Bellville. But when word got back to him that a few thought he was just making up stories, he was furious at being thought a liar. He never went back.

On May 6, 1956, his first of 176 "Tales of the Mohican Country" was published in *The Mansfield News Journal* and ran until September 7, 1964. The first story was about the Winchester Woolen Mill south of Butler. Few people realize the work involved in producing almost weekly articles along with a picture or illustration. Before the actual writing began, he traveled to libraries and other sites to do research, often conducting extensive correspondence to seek out and confirm facts and information. Garber gained a good readership following and widespread recognition for this series. By1964 after 176 articles in *The Mansfield News Journal* he was tiring and developing other interests. He began writing for the *Columbus Dispatch Sunday Magazine* section and working on other projects that were important to him; including a young man by the name of Robert Carter.

During the preparations for the 1964 sesquicentennial celebrations in nearby Lexington, Ohio, Garber met Robert Carter, a young electrician who was a like-minded history buff. A warm friendship developed that eventually extended to include their families. Vera and Carter's wife Jackie and their 4 small children often kept each other company while the two men were off exploring a mill or delving into a research project.

In 1965 Garber published a small pamphlet titled *Abraham Lincoln's First Endorsement* supporting the story of Lincoln's endorsement for President in Mansfield in 1858. A monument was erected in the Mansfield square in 1925 to commemorate that historic event, but over the years there had been doubters. Garber carefully researched the subject and came to the conclusion that it did occur and documented his findings. His personal interest came from his father who had a long time interest in Lincoln and a very large collection of Lincoln memorabilia. His father died while he was in the service, and the family divided and scattered the collection while he was away, much to his dismay. Garber's limited edition Lincoln pamphlet is now a rare collector's item.

In 1967 he published another 20-page booklet titled *The Holmes County Rebellion*. The story of the resistance against the Civil War, the draft, and dissatisfaction with the government led to Union troops being called to put down the insurrection. Garber's interviews and research uncovered a new history of the event.

Garber's long association with the Ohio Historical Society led to the publication of *Waterwheels and Millstones: The History of Mills and Milling in Ohio*. The society printed an edition of 2,500 copies, and it has become the bible of milling for mill hobbyists throughout the state. A great deal of state-wide travel and several years of research were required. His knowledge of mills gained considerable interest. The book, long out of print, was published in 1970, the same year that he and Vera moved to California.

Connie taught school and lived in Stockton, California, where her husband, Arthur Cullen, was the Director of Covell College, part of the College of the Pacific (later to become a University). When their son-in-law died in January 1970, they moved to Stockton to be near her, leaving behind another phase of life. They both missed Ohio, but felt their place was near their daughter.

Before long in California, Garber came to the attention of the Jedediah Strong Smith Society. Smith was a fur trader and mountain man who was the first to cross the mountains into California.

Although several books had been published about Smith's exploits from St. Louis and adventures over the western mountains, it was Garber who discovered that as a young man Smith had lived in the Perrysville, Ohio, area with his parents. That unknown part of Smith's life was brought to light in four articles Garber wrote for the *Pacific Historian*, a publication of the University of the Pacific in Stockton. The four were later reprinted in one small hard cover book, another collector's item.

Garber hired a young Navy wife, Theresa Flaherty, to serve as his amanuensis, not only to type his manuscripts, but also to help with his extensive correspondence. Both the Garbers missed the young Carter family back in Ohio, and were delighted to meet Flaherty's two small children of about the same ages as the Carter's youngest. In addition, the Navy connection led to the development of a warm friendship and allowed Garber to share his own early Navy experiences.

One sizable manuscript that Garber and Flaherty worked on was of Johnny Appleseed, one of Garber's major interests during his years in Ohio. Over the years Garber researched every avenue and resource, gathering any bit of information he could find on the pioneer nurseryman. Perrysville's prolific writer Rosella Rice and her family had known Appleseed when she was a youngster. For over 30 years he tracked down every article she wrote for several magazines, hoping she had recorded something more on Johnny. Little was found but he never gave up. After a couple of rewrites the finished Appleseed manuscript was submitted to the Ohio Historical Society; however, it was kindly rejected with numerous comments to Garber about changes. Basically what he authored was a very scholarly study of Appleseed. What they wanted was a reader-friendly book they could sell in the gift shop. Disappointed, the manuscript was laid aside.

When Flaherty's husband Gerry returned home in 1972, the family moved to Guam for a year, then to New Orleans for another year, before being assigned to the USS Coral Sea, an aircraft carrier homeported in Alameda, California, close enough to resume their relationship with Garber. Vera had passed away on June 17, 1973, leaving Garber despondent and grief-stricken. The Flahertys' return encouraged him to focus once again on his work.

He persuaded Flaherty to organize his collection of James Ball Naylor material, and with his guidance, to write a biography of this Ohio Legend who was a writer, poet, and politician, among other things. They conducted research at the Huntington Library in San Marino, California, and discovered Naylor's youngest daughter living in the San Francisco Bay area. Garber's unique talent in conducting interviews and gleaning the essence from volumes of research material served as a priceless example for Flaherty. His uncanny ability to ask just the right questions encouraged people to open up, and he listened carefully.

When Gerry returned from a Westpac deployment, he arranged for Garber to visit the USS Coral Sea in port, and Garber was delighted. Its number 2 boiler had been taken off a battleship that Garber had served on. With the boilers shut down, a chief warrant officer from the Engineering Department took him down into the bowels of the ship where he was able to really look around. It was a highlight of his later years.

Garber was mentor to both Carter and Flaherty, but he did not live to see the fruits of his efforts. He died on October 29, 1983, and was buried next to Vera in La Grange, Oregon, where she had grown up and still had family.

Garber had maintained his close ties to the Carters in Ohio, engaging Carter as an occasional Ohio researcher. With material that he donated, Garber's prodding and his teaching eventually paid off. Carter self-published four books, *The History of the Sandusky, Mansfield & Newark*

Railroad, in 2002; *Tom Lyons The Indian That Died Thirteen Times,* in 2003; *The History of Lexington, Ohio,* in 2007; and *The Mansfield Riots of 1900,* in 2009.

Flaherty continued working on the Naylor biography even when Navy orders took her family to the East Coast. A completed manuscript was submitted to several publishers, but was rejected each time. She was deeply distressed at letting Garber down. With his typical wry sense of humor, he let it be known that it was her choice whether it would be a minor distraction or an overwhelming obstacle.

It became a major distraction for more than thirty years, but in 2007 Flaherty tackled the project once more. The result was *The Final Test – A biography of James Ball Naylor*, published in 2011. It was followed by her Tribute Series to Naylor, consisting of four additional books thus far: *Vintage Verse,* in 2011, mostly unpublished poetry written by Naylor; *Ralph Marlow,* in 2011, a reprint of Naylor's 1901 best seller, with additional material including a forward and afterword by Flaherty and numerous contemporary reviews of the book and period photographs; *A Literary Playground – Short Stories* by Naylor, in 2012; and *The Misadventures of Marjory,* in 2014, a reprint of Naylor's last novel.

Garber's library went to his daughter Connie, and after she passed away, to her son Michael, an avid book collector like his mother. Although Cullen never lived in Ohio, he had met the Carters; and he knew of his grandfather's friendship with them, of Carter's interest in mills, and knew that Carter accompanied him on several "mill trips." Part of Garber's mill collection had been donated to the Ohio Historical Society shortly after he moved to California.

What stayed with the family were the eight 3-ring notebooks of Garber's lifetime mill collection; specifically all of his notes on watermills in Richland County. On a trip to visit friends, the Carters stopped at the Cullen home, and Robert and Michael agreed that a book focusing on the Richland County watermills would be fun to do. They agreed to assemble and publish this wonderful historical collection rather than leave the somewhat fragile pages lying somewhere on a dusty shelf unused or misused.

In 2003, Flaherty reconnected with the Carters on an RVing trip to Ohio. The two couples became good friends. The following year, the Flahertys met the Cullens, and the circle of friendship of the three couples, brought together because of Dwight Wesley Garber, was completed. *Water-Powered Mills of Richland County* is the result of their combined efforts.

NOTES

Section 1

Water-Powered Mills on the Clear Fork of the Mohican River

1. Garber notebook No. 2, Logan-Barr Mills, tab 7. Pages are not numbered. There are 8 notebooks. All subsequent quotations from D.W. Garber will be cited by Notebook Number, Mill, and Tab Number if available. Garber's notebooks were numbered and labeled but the mills were entered as they were studied and not necessarily in alphabetical order. As the mills changed ownerships, Garber often placed the relevant material under the new owner's name, which would change the notebook cited. The original notebooks are in the possession of Garber's grandson, Michael Cullen, who gave access and unrestricted permission to Carter, for their use.

2. Ibid.

3. *Morrow County Sentinel*, vol. LI, April 20, 1899. County death records have Samuel Barr's death April 11, 1899. The Morrow County history books, written during the temperance period, somehow managed to tip-toe over the eyebrow lowering story of Bungtown, the Logan-Barr distillery, and the mills. Today only two original houses remain, and Bungtown is all but forgotten.

4. *Ohio Register,* vol. I, no. 7, June 5, 1816.

5. Garber, Dwight Wesley. "Tales of the Mohican." comp. by Mary Jane Henney. (Mansfield, OH: Richland County Genealogical Society, 2003), 72-73. Number 55 in a series of newspaper articles by Garber in the *Mansfield News Journal* between May 6, 1956 and September 27, 1964.

6. This photograph of John Garrison was given to Garber by Norman Fink of Fredricktown, Ohio. This same photograph also appears in the *Cenennial Program for Fredrickton* and also in the *Knox County Citizen*, vol. XXIX, no. 4, August 10, 1950.

7. Ibid.

8. Garber notebook no. 3, Garretson Mills, tab 15. Ms. Dickson stated that the mill had a distillery that made enough whiskey "to pay for the property."

9. Carter drove out to the site in 2013 where both the headrace and the location of the mill could be seen. The exact sequence of ownership of the Garrison-Woods-Field-Otto Mill is not clear. Garber, in a series of interviews between 1949 and 1950, raised questions as to that sequence. In October 1949, he interviewed Charley Scott, then 84 years old, who remembered that the Otto Mill was a 3 ½ story building with two sets of buhrs and a waterwheel, but never a turbine. Scott believed that the mill had been torn down some "30 years ago" [c 1919] and that Otto was the last to operate it. Mrs. Bell Stevens, from Ontario, Ohio, interviewed on January 27, 1950, concurred that the mill was 3 ½ stories and that it still operated in 1899. Mr. James Wheeler, from

Millsborough, stated on January 27, 1950, that the dam for the "Fields-Otto mill was about 4-5 feet high. Garber noted in 1950 that the millrace could be seen where it crossed the Lexington-Ontario Road and from there, followed to the millsite.

10. Graham, A. A. *History of Richland County, Ohio: (Including the Original Boundaries) It's Past and Present*, (Mansfield, Ohio, A. A. Graham & Co., Publishers, 1880), 578. In the gubernatorial election in 1843, candidate Leicester King received only four votes from Springfield Township – Andrew Wood, Sr. Mathew Mitchell, Henry Crabbs and Joseph Roe. Although the Wood and Mitchell families were competitors in the milling business, they were united in their opposition to slavery.

11. Perrin, W. H. and Battle, J. H. *History of Morrow County and Ohio*. (Chicago: O. L. Baskin & Co. 1880), p. 506.

12. *Mansfield Gazette*, vol. 2, no. 29, November 18, 1824.

13. *Mansfield Gazette*, vol. 3, no. 17, November 23, 1825.

14. Garber notebook no. 1, Mitchell-Baird Mill, tab 5. Typed note to Garber from Carter with information on the Mitchell Mill. Not dated.

15. Ibid. Garber speculated that the dam would have resulted in a very large pond, one that might have extended beyond today's Highway 314.

16. Graham. *History of Richland County*, Ohio, 597. Ichabod Clark had offered the use of the shed house of his distillery to the first meetings of a new Presbyterian Church being established in the area. This new Troy congregation would later build a log church and establish a cemetery on part of Clark's donated land. The cemetery is still there, at the end of the Clear Fork Lake dam.

17. *Richland County Audit Records*. Additional research necessary to pin-point specific names and time.

18. Andreas, A. T., *Atlas Map of Richland County, Ohio*, Chicago, ILL, 1873, p. 65.

19. *Richland Shield & Banner*, vol. LXV no. 44, March 7, 1883.

20. Additional research might reveal more details on John Williams but identifying the "unnamed man" who succeeded Williams may be more of a challenge.

21. Garber notebook no. 3, Conger-Williams Mill, tab 5.

22. Graham, *History of Richland County*, p. 593.

23. Carter, Robert A. *Tales of the Old-Timers: The History of Lexington*. (Ashland, Ohio, Privately Printed, 2007), pp. 6-13.

24. Roeliff Brinkerhoff, *A Pioneer History of Richland County*. Ed., Mary Jane Henney, (Mansfield: Richland County Chapter, Ohio Genealogical Society, 1993), p. 39; Carter, Tales of the Old-Timers, p. 11.

25. Carter located the site of the sawmill run by Watson's son Michael in the summer of 2013. The headrace for this mill is still seen between the millsite and the big yellow barn.

26. Garber, D.W. *Waterwheels and Millstones: A History of Ohio Gristmills and Milling*. (Columbus: The Ohio Historical Society, 1970), 134. "Carding mill: Machines used to clean, separate, and process wool. Fulling mill. A mill which scoured, cleaned, and softened the fabric after it was dyed, and prior to it being napped and smoothed under pressure."

27. Garber notebook no. 2, Watson Mills, tab 2.

28. Ibid. The comments referred to in this section are from interviews by Garber. Those interviewed included Harry Palm (September 20, 1949), Morris Graham (September 7, 1949),

Lewis Dickson (September 27, 1949), Harry Smith (September 6, 1949) and James Hiskey.

29. *The Richland Star*, vol. II, no. 23, March 6, 1879.

30. The term "nigger-head," is a word that today is considered racist and offensive, and rightly so; but to millwrights it referred to granite boulders that rolled into Ohio during the ice age from Canada. Usually black, a dark gray, or occasionally a pinkish color, they were usually rounded off and ranged in size from that of a football to very large boulders. Because they were so hard and locally available, they were a cheaper source of millstones than those that had to be purchased at high costs from the east coast. A good millwright could slowly make his own, using a hammer and chisel very carefully – a process that could take as long as one to two months.

31. Email sent to the editor January 28, 2014. Bob and his sons returned to the site and with great difficulty managed to load the millstone into the truck and take it to Carter's home where it occupied a place of honor among six other millstones. When they relocated, they attempted to move the stone. Unfortunately, the band on the French buhr broke, and the stone fell apart.

32. Garber notebook no. 3, Mercer-Griebling Mills, tab 20.

33. Garber notebook no. 1, Lexington Mills, tab 2. Because the McLain Mill was build on the site of the Watson-Hahn Mill that had been destroyed by fire, Garber decided to have McLain's Mill separate. The term "Nigger Clock" and "Nigger Buhrs" are inappropriate, but were common terms used in the period covered. No offense on the part of the authors is intended.

34. Ibid.

35. Existing records are not clear. If Garrison had built the mill, then Mercer bought it as part of the land purchase from Garrett; if not, then it was Mercer who built the mill.

36. Garber notebook no. 2, Mercer-Griebling Mills, tab 20.

37. Griebling, Louis G. *The History of the Griebling – Mercer Mill: The Griebling Family; Tales of the Old Timers* [Typed Manuscript, 1983,] pp. 1-3. Unpublished manuscript. A copy was given to Carter by Clarence Griebling in March 1983; Garber notebook no. 2, Mercer-Griebling Mills. Between October 1949 and January 1950 Garber received two letters from Louis G. Griebling. He also interviewed him in Lexington on September 27, 1949.

38. Ibid. Letter from Louis G. Griebling dated October 14, 1949,

39. Graham, *History of Richland County,* p. 601.

40. A corn cracker mill essentially is a gristmill built specifically for grinding corn. The grooves in the millstones of a corn mills are deeper and there are not as many as there are in the typical millstone used to grind wheat for flour. The terms, corn cracker mill and gristmill, were often used simultaneously.

41. Personal notes of Carter of a conversation with Garber. Date not noted.

42. Baughman, A.J. *History of Richland County*, p. 339. "In the list of interesting localities in Troy Township. King's Corners had an important place. In the years that are past, Squire Jacob King was an influential and prominent resident of that locality and the 'Corners' were named in his honor."

43. Garber notebook no. 1, Strausbaugh Mills, tab 9. Interview with Harry Palm, December 4, 1946.

44. Ibid. Interview with James Hiskey August 19, 1949.

45. Ibid. Interview with Harry Palm September 20, 1949.

46. Garber notebook no. 2, Strausbaugh Mill, tab 8. Excerpt from a letter loaned to Garber, addressed to Mr. George O. Neal from the James Leffel & Company confirming that a 48-inch Leffel Standard, Left Hand turbine was "furnished to Mr. John Strausbaugh in 1866." Location of the original letter is not now known.

47. The location of the original Boy Scout letter is not known but Carter has a copy of Garber's response containing the comments cited.

48. Garber notebook no. 2, Marshall Mills and Phelps Mills, tab 27.

49. Ibid.

50. Ibid.

51. Ibid.

52. Ibid. See also *The Bellville Star* for October 13, 1881, December 21, 1882, August 24, 1884 and February 15, 1885.

53. Because of its location in Richland County, Garber spent much time in researching the Stump Mill, and the notes used in this section are found in his notebook. Reference is also made to the *Bellville Dollar Weekly,* vol. 1, no. 1, Friday, March 1, 1872; vol. 1, no. 7, April 12, 1872; vol. 1, no. 35, October 25, 1872; vol. 11, no. 10, 1873; vol. 11, no. 25, August 22, 1873, vol. 1, no. 31, September 27, 1872, and vol. II, no. 28, September 12, 1873. In addition, see *The Bellville Star* vol. IX, no. 20, February 11, 1886; vol. IX, no. 13, December 24, 1885; vol. 8, no. 30, April 23, 1885; vol. IX, no. 18, January 28, 1886; vol. IX, no. 44, July 29, 1886; vol. X, no. 9, November 25, 1886; vol. XI, no. 17, January 19, 1888; vol. XI, no. 28, April 5, 1888; vol. XI, no. 55, 1888; vol. XI, no. 35, 1888 and vol XII, no. 7, November 15, 1888. These newspaper citations provide the reader with a timeline of ownership.

54. Ibid.

55. Ibid.

56. Graham. *History of Richland County*, p. 814.

57. Garber notebook no. 3, Zent-Fitting-Bowers-Shaler Garber Mill, tab 12. Ownership of the land on which the mill was located is convoluted to say the least.

58. Ibid. See the page with the heading "Jacob Zent Sr." The genealogy is confusing. Additional research into the family tree could verify or correct the idea that John Zent Sr. had a son also named John Zent Sr. This is unlikely, and it is possible that Garber made a mistake. The task of correcting our errors is left to those who follow us.

59. Ibid. Garber did considerable research in the old county records. He found the Deed Records at the Recorder's Office, Richland County, Ohio, essential in tracing the ownership of the property on which the mills were located. See *Deed County Records* (identified in all subsequent entries as DCR). All entries that follow refer to the property located at northwest ¼, section 9, Township 19. See DCR, vol. 13, 212 1835-1835; Jesse Holly to John Hiskey; vol. 29, 208; John Hiskey to F. M. Fitting 1845-1845, with water privileges; vol. 35, 332; F. M. Fitting to David Bowers, 1852-1852; vol 35, 332, 48 4/160 acres; David Bowers to Abjah I. Beach 1864-1864, vol. 54, 333; Abjah I. Beach to Isaac Bowers, 1864-1864, vol. 51, 339; Isaac Bowers to Solomon Shafer, vol. 53, 228, 1866-1866; Solomon Shafer to Henry Ramer, vol. 63, 631, 1871-1872; Henry Ramer to Michael Stuff, vol. 63, 629, 1872-1872; Michael Stuff, vol. 82, 457, 1882-1882; Mary H. Shafer to Helen Shafer, vol. 82, 457. Additional research in the deed records will also identify

some of the quitclaims that went to Jacob Zent Jr. and resulted in his gaining control of the land and the mill in 1835.

60. Ibid.

61. *The Bellville Star*, vol. V, no. 24, Mar. 16, 1882 and vol. VI, no. 7, Nov. 26, 1882.

62. Garber notebook no. 1, Zent-Fitting-Bowers-Shaler-Garber Mill, tab 12. The name clipper is a derivative of the word "clip" which can mean, "to move or run rapidly."

63. Ibid. vol. XI, no. 16, January 12, 1888. There is some confusion as to who was who in the Shaler family. *The Bellville Star* on June 19, 1884, introduced another Shaler, stating the Frank Shaler had called on the paper. *The Bellville Star* also reported that Frank Shaler was proprietor and that the name had been changed from Regulator Mills to Shaler's Mills.

64. Ibid. vol. XII, no. 21, February 21, 1889.

65. *The Bellville Independent*, vol VI, no. 35, January 3, 1895. Advertisement in which the Cockley Milling Company announced the opening of their New Elevator effective January 1, 1895. Three days later, on January 4, 1895, the Garber mill burned to the ground. See also Garber notebook no. 3, Garber Mill, tab 13.

66. Garber notebook no. 3, Bellville Planing Mill, tab 4. Transcribed copy of an article, "Bellville Past and Present. The Planing Mills," *The Richland Star*, vol. I, no. 50, September 12, 1878.

67. Graham, *History of Richland County*, 1880, pp. 805-806.

68. *The Richland Star*, vol. IV, no. 21, February 17, 1881.

69. Garber, *Waterwheels and Millstones*, p. 136. "Muley mill: An up-and-down sawmill was a successor to the sash mill. It ran faster and with greater efficiency, thus providing a larger production."

70. Garber notebook no. 3, Bellville Mills, tab 4. Between 1838 and 1859, ownership of the mill property exchanged hands several times. The last owner of the mill, George O. Neal, gave Garber access to an abstract covering the mill property from the date of the original grant until c. 1908 which is cited here. The location of the original abstract is not known.

71. *The Western Sentinel*, vol. 3, no.17, March 28, 1832.

72. Graham, *History of Richland County*, p. 430. See also Baughman, *History of Richland County,* pp. 19-8, vol. 1, p. 380.

73. Garber notebook no. 3, Bellville Mills, tab 4. See Endnote 70.

74. *The Bellville Weekly*, vol III, no. 26, September 11, 1874.

75. *The Bellville Star*, vol. X, no. 25, March 17, 1887.

76. Ibid, vol. X, no. 45, August 4, 1887.

77.*The Bellville Independent*, vol. III, no. 3, May 1, 1890.

78. Garber notebook no. 3, Bellville Mills, tab 4. Information cited from the land abstract covering the mill property from the date of the original grant until c. 1908 loaned to Garber by George O. Neal January 30, 1947. See endnote 72 as well.

79. Ibid.

80. Ibid.

81. Ibid. The comments pertaining to this first bag of flour is found in Garber's notes. Cullen recalls his grandfather telling him that story many times over the years. It was a story that he was quite proud of and one that he enjoyed telling.

82. Ibid.

83. Ibid. A copy of the newspaper article and dated Thursday February 28, 1952, is present.

84. Baughman, *History of Richland County*, p. 380.

85. Garber notebook no. 2, LeFever Carding Mill, tab 25.

86. Baughman, *History of Richland County*, vol. 1, pp. 380, 449. Baughman used the name "Mr. Cornell," first name not known.

87. Ibid., p. 449.

88. Garber notebook no. 3, Greenwood Mills, tab 19.

89. Ibid. Garber interview with Anna E. Aungst on September 20, 1951.

90. Mershon, Peggy. *Mansfield News Journal,* December 2013. It is hard to imagine the conditions endured by our ancestors 200 years ago. Today we lose power for few days and the world is coming to an end, and even worse if it is freezing outside.

91. Ibid.

92. Ibid. Letter from Roy Leedy to Maria (Swank) Garber regarding the swindle by the Switzer brothers.

93. Ibid.

94. Baskin, O.L. & Co., *History of Morrow County and Ohio*, Chicago, IL 1880. p. 834.

95. Garber notebook no. 2, Shauck Mill, tab 11. Ralph Lowe told Garber in an interview on March 25, 1951, that "The sawmill at Shauck's was near the gristmill and received water before it did. The sawmill was powered by a large undershot wheel about seven feet high with deep buckets. A pair of white oxen was kept at the saw mill for working the logs onto the skids and into the mill and for other essential work."

96. Ibid.

97. Graham, *History of Richland County*, p. 551. See also: Andreas, A. T. *Atlas Map of Richland County, Ohio,* Chicago, IL, 1873, p. 68. *Map of Perry Township* shows the land and millsite owned by J. J. Eby.

98. Graham, *History of Richland County*, pp. 551, 862.

99. Baughman, A. J., *A Centennial Biographical History of Richland County*, Chicago: The Lewis Publishing Co., 1901, pp. 295-296.

100. Graham, *History of Richland County*, p. 551.

101. Ibid. See also: Perrins, W. H. and J. H. Battle (historians) *History of Morrow County, Ohio*, O.L. Baskin & C., Historical Publishers, Chicago, 1880, 800. Hanawalt was also spelled Haniwalt. The tax records for 1839, 1844, 1862, 1869, 1880 and 1881 all spelled the name Haniwalt and the local county histories spelled the name Hanawalt. We elected to use Hanawalt.

102. Graham, *History of Richland County*, p. 560.

103. Garber, *Tales of the Mohican*, "A Mill Was Often The Center of Pioneer Town," pp. 57-58.

104. Garber notebook no. 1, Hanawalt Mill, tab 21, "History of the Baughman Family"

105. Ibid.

106. Information pertaining to Jacob Myers and his family came from primary sources and included many of Myers' personal papers; especially those pertaining to his milling background and his involvement with the Mormon Church. No study of Jacob Myers is possible without access to copious notes and binders put together by Garber and referred to when discussing the Myers Mill. These notes and binders were used by Cullen in writing his graduate paper at the University of West Florida, Pensacola, FL, and his paper was subsequently used in preparing the

history of the Myers-Kanaga-Plank Mill.

107. *Messenger and Advocate*, November 1836, p. 414.

108. Myers presided as an Elder in the Washington branch in 1833, but was not made an Elder until June 6, 1835. See Joseph Smith Jr., History of the Church of Jesus Christ of Latter-Day Saints, Period 1. *History of Joseph Smith the Prophet by Himself*, 2nd edi., vol. 2 (Salt Lake City: Published by the Church, 1951, reprint, Salt Lake City: The Deseret Book Co., 1967, 228.) The question is raised, would he have been recognized as an Elder without having first been baptized (he was baptized sometime in 1834)? These were very early in the evolution of the Church, and it may have been quite reasonable for someone like Myers to serve as the Elder prior to actual promotion to that position.

109. Brennerman, O. E., *The Story of Perry Township*. (Lexington: Snyder's Print Shop, 1953.) p. 2. The accuracy of Brennerman on his claim that there was a wagon train of 50 wagons is questionable. No confirmation on this wagon train has been located. Jacob Myers' experiences with the Mormon Church is outside the scope of this book but is very much an interesting story in and of itself. Myers built a number of mills for the Mormons on his travels west. It was he who built Haun's Mill at Shoal Creek, Mo. - the site of the infamous Haun's Mill Massacre, where seventeen Mormons, including children were killed by Missourians at the mill or who died within a few days following the attack. Two of Myers sons, Jacob Myers Jr. and George were at the mill at the time of the attack and both were wounded. Jacob's leg wound never healed and his leg was amputated and buried in the Bassett Cemetery near Haun's Mill. Myers and his family would move to Illinois and then on to Iowa where he lost his wife Sarah in 1861. Sometime after Sarah's death, Jacob Myers simply ran out of steam, and he returned to Ohio where his daughter Delilah and husband Lewis Leedy welcomed him. He spent the remainder of his life living with them ands died there in 1867. He is interred in the Brethren (Dunkard) Church (known also as Owl Creek Church) near Ankenytown, Knox County, Ohio, next to his daughter Delilah.

110. Unless cited otherwise, the information used in describing the history of the Myers-Kanaga-Plank Mills came from notes written by Garber, from the paper written by his grandson, and from notes provided by Carter.

111. This was a story often told. Carter, Cullen, and his mother Connie often heard this story told with a devilish look on Garber's face and with a twinkle in his eye.

112. Carter and Cullen hope that someone who reads this will have additional information on both the Butler Axe Handle Company and the Richland Handle Company and will share it so that corrections can be included in any update that might be done in the future.

113. *The Richland Star*, vol. III, no. 52, September 23, 1880.

114. Many of the main gears or "bull wheels" had replaceable wooden teeth that would sheer or break off to prevent destruction of the whole gear assembly but often the damage was so severe that the mill would be shut down for months while a new gear was ordered, delivered, and installed.

115. *The Bellville Star*. vol. 8, no. 31, May 7, 1885.

116. Ibid. vol., 8, no. 35. May 28, 1885.

117. Garber notebook no. 2.

118. *The American Miller*, January 1, 1909, p. 66.

119. *The Democrat*, Thursday, December 9, 1915.

120. Garber notebook no. 2. Garber's letter to Hal McCune.

121. Original letter in the possession of Carter. Although it is not clear in Garber's notes, he probably meant the flood of 1904 rather than 1913. In 1913, he was aboard a Navy ship off the coast of Vera Cruz, Mexico, and newspaper accounts indicate that considerable damage was done to covered bridges during the 1904 flood.

122. *The Messenger*, November 4, 1897. Lists by name many of the first settlers in Worthington Township.

123. Garber notebook no. 2.

124. Ibid. Original note to Christian Wise from Noble Calhoun regarding payment for surveying the town.

125. Garber, *Tales of the Mohican*, p. 1.

126. Baughman, *History of Richland County*, 1908, p. 46.

127. Garber notebook no. 2, Winchester Mills, tab 22.

128. Ibid. See also Garber, *Tales of the Mohican*, p. 1.

129. Baughman, *History of Richland County*, 1908, vol. 1, pp. 468-469.

130. *The Mansfield Herald*, vol. XVIII, no 29, June 20, 1868.

131. *The Bellville Dollar Weekly*, vol.2, no.16, June 20; no. 1, June 20, 1873.

132. Garber notebook No. 2. See *The Bellville Star*, vol. VI, no 39, June 28, 1883.

133. *The Bellville Star*, vol II, no. 28, April 10, 1884 and vol. VII, no. 33, May 15, 1884.

134. *The Bellville Star,* vol. VII, no 24, March 13, 1884.

135. *The Bellville Star*, vol. VIII, no. 27, April 2, 1885. "Independence News Item. We noticed in the *Mansfield Democrat* that Esq. Calhoon has some notion of converting the Alexander factory near his place into a skating rink. We would advise him to move it to Independence, so as to accommodate our dudes." Also Garber notebook no. 2, Winchester's Mills.

136. *The Bellville Star*, vol. VII, no 24, March 13, 1884

137. *The Bellville Star*, vol. VII, no. 36, June 5, 1884.

138. Interview with Floyd Norris, August 1947.

139. Garber notebook no. 2, Winchester Mill, tab 22, "Winchester. Interview with Homer Calhoun and Mrs. Cora Stull, June 14, 1949.

140. Ibid. Transcribed notes of the interview with Mrs. Cora Stull.

141. Ibid.

142. Ibid. Interviews with Mrs. Floyd (Calhoun) Noris, March 25, 1948.

143. Ibid. Interview with Homer Calhoun and Mrs. Wilbur Floyd Dall, May 18, 1955.

144. The painting by Mrs. Griffin is now in Cullen's possession, and she has given him permission to use these paintings as he sees fit.

145. *Richland Jeffersonian*, vol. VI, no 51, October 16, 1844. "Sheriff's Sale By virtue of a vendi exponsas execution to me directed by the Court of Common Pleas or Richland county, Ohio, I will offer at public sale at the residence of Noah Watts, in Worthington Township, in said county on the 30th day of October, 1844, ... the following property to wit: one buggy wagon, one two horse wagon, two single carding machines, one yoke of oxen, and one lot of walnut lumber 2000 feet more or less, taken on execution of the property of Noah Watts, to satisfy an execution in favor of Samuel Graber. Wm. Kerr, Sheriff. Sheriff's Office, Mansfield, Oct. 16, 1844."

146. *The Mansfield Gazette*, vol. 1, no. 26, December 25, 1823

147. Ibid., May 27, 1824.

148. Ibid., September 9, 1824.

149. *The Brinkerhoff Scrapbook* is located in the Ohio Historical Society in Columbus, Ohio.

150. Graham, *History of Richland County*, Ohio, p. 633.

151. Garber notebook no. 3, Herring Mills, tab 22. Notes taken by Garber in an interview with E. E (Ebb) Lime on 23 March 1957. Lime was 16 years old when he moved to Butler. He was born in 1876 and was 82 years old when he met with Garber.

152. Ibid.

153. Ibid., Alexander Saw Mill.

154. Garber notebook no. 2, Daniel Teeter Saw Mill.

155. Ibid. Garber notebook no. 1, Henry Foults Saw Mill.

156. Garber notebook no. 3, Samuel Graber Carding Mill, tab 16.

157. Garber notebook no. 2, Rocky Point Mill, tab 17. Interview with Mrs. Charley H. Lee, July 17, 1961.

158. Ibid. Interview with Charles Lee, July 17, 1961. Charley believed his father's stories but since his father was only 9 years old at the time, it is more likely that it was his grandfather, Ebenezer who took the early morning or late evening drives to unknown locations.

159. Ibid., Rinehart Family.

160. Ibid.

161. *The Richland Star*, vol. 1, no. 20, September 12, 1878.

162. Ibid., vol. IV, no. 18, January 27, 1881.

163. Ibid., vol. VIII, no.10, December 4, 1884.

164. Garber purchased these French buhr millstones from the Van Zile Mill in 1938 for $10.00. The segments or panel of very hard French buhr are held in place by a steel band heated to expand and then dropped into place. The millstones are an example of the millwright's artisanship.

165. Garber notebook no. 2, Clear Fork Mills, Rocky Point Mill. Interview with Jesse Van Zile, August 1938.

166. Ibid.

167. Graham. *History of Richland County*, p. 845.

168. Ibid.

169. Garber notebook no. 2, Manner Mill, tab 26. A copy of this letter was given to Garber by Guy Keister on March 1, 1950. It was found among the George C. and J.A. Keister papers by Guy Keistser and provides proof that Manner was not a millwright but a contractor who built mills and repaired them.

170. Ibid.

171. Ibid.

172. Ibid.

173. Ibid. 1827 was the year that Jacob Manner and his father came to Ohio and acquired the Peter Kenney Mill, later the Darling Mill property. Garber was given permission to collect whatever he found; and the toll dish that he found in the dirt, he noted could be an associated item from both the Kenney Mill as well as the Manner Mill at Newville.

174. Ibid., The Schrack Grist Mill, Saw Mill and Oil Mill, tab 13.

175. Ibid., Interview with Mrs. McGrew on December 7, 1946.

176. Ibid.

177. Ibid. Louis Bromfield and his wife Mary are both buried in this cemetery as well.

178. Ibid.

179. Willis, James A., *The Big Book of Ghost Stories*, Mechanisburg: PA: Stackpole Books, pp. 109-119.

180. *Mansfield News Journal*. September 12, 1948. See also, Mitchell, Brett J., *Triple Murder the Crimes Committed by Celia Rose,* HistoricalPreservation.org Press, 2006.

181. Willis, *The Big Book of Ghost Stories*, pp. 109-119.

182. Garber Notebook No. 2, Schrack Mills, tab 13.

183. Bromfield, Louis, *Pleasant Valley.* Harper & Brothers, NY, 1945.

184. Daniel Teeter had another sawmill located on Possum Run and previously discussed on page 65.

185. Butler Museum, Butler, Ohio. Author unknown. Garber had two brothers who worked at the factory at one time and a sister who worked in the office for a brief period before she left for college.

186. Graham, *History of Richland County*, 1880, p. 661.

187. Knapp, H. S., *A History of the Pioneer Times of Ashland County* [Ohio], from the Earliest to the Present Date. J. B. Lippincott & Co., Philadelphia, 1863, p. 363.

188. Hill, George W., *History of Ashland County, Ohio*, np., 1880, pp. 281-283.

189. Garber notebook no. 2, Thomas McMahan Grist and Saw Mills, tab 28. Interview with Dr. Robert C. Paul, June 7, 1950.

190. Ibid.

191. Ibid.

192. Ibid. Interview with Harry Cannon of Loudenville in September 1949.

193. Ibid.

Section 2

Water-Powered Mills on the Black Fork of the Mohican River

1. Information pertaining to the Runyon Saw Mill is from one of several copies of the *Richland County Auditor's Records* owned by Carter and additional research that he has done. Additional records will be cited: Carter, *Richland County Auditor's Records* and other sources.

2. Ibid.

3. Ibid.

4. Ibid.

5. Ibid.

6. Ibid.

7. Ibid.

8. Garber notebook no.4, Abbott Mill, tab 2, Garber interview with H. Dale Kuhn, September 19, 1951.

9. Ibid.

10. Graham, *History of Richland County*, 1880, p. 422.

11. Garber notebook no. 5, Kerr Mill, tab 29, Garber interview with J.C. (Chalmers) Dunlap, Februrary 26, 1952.

12. Ibid. Richland Run was a feeder stream flowing north into the Black Fork in Cass Township.

13. Carter, *Richland County Auditor's Records* and other sources.

14. Graham, *History of Richland County*, p. 571.

15. Garber notebook no. 5, Kerr Mill, tab 29, Sharon Township. Garber interview with Mr. & Mrs. John Kerr, September 27, 1952.

16. Ibid.

17. Ibid.

18. Ibid.

19. Graham, *History of Richland County,* 1880, p. 571.

20. Garber notebook no. 4, Coltman Mills, tab 21, Sharon Township.

21. Graham, *History of Richland County*, 1880, p. 571.

22. *The Shelby Daily Globe*, article about the Gamble Mill, August 28, 1951.

23. Garber notebook no. 4, Gamble Mill, tab 15.

24. Part of this information comes from Carter's personal collection.

25. *The Daily Globe*, Centennial Edition, no. 35, August 2, 1934.

26. http://www.rootsweb.ancestry.com/~ohscogs/industries-CenterMills-CityMills.html.

27. Ibid. This is an outstanding website. Virtually all reference to the Heath Mills up to this point is taken from this website. The Shelby Chapter of the *Ohio Genealogical Society* helped very much to clear the confusion of the Garber notes.

28. Garber notebook no. 5, Heath Mills, tab 26. Garber interview with Mrs. S. D. Inscho, August 28, 1951.

29. Ibid.

30. Ibid. Garber interview with Robert Sheffler, November 10, 1951.

31. Garber notebook no. 4, Gamble Mill, tab 15, Garber interview with H. Dale Kuhn, August 28, 1951.

32. Graham, *History of Richland County*, 1880, p. 420.

33. Baughman, A. J. *History of Richland County Ohio from 1808 to 1908.* Chicago: S. J. Clarke Publishing, Co., p. 456.

34. Graham, *History of Richland County,* 1880, p. 571.

35. Garber notebook no. 4, Duncan Mill, tab 27. Garber interview with Robert Sheffler, September 19, 1951.

36. Ibid. Garber notebook no. 4, Gamble Mill, tab 15, Kuhn interview.

37. Baughman, *History of Richland County Ohio*. Chapter 12. See Article in the *Mansfield News*, February 28, 1903. Also available at: http:/www.rootsweb.ancestry.com/~ohrichla/Hist-Plymouth1903.htm.

38. Garber notebook no. 4, Gamble Mill, tab 15. Kuhn interview.

39. Graham, History of Richland County, 1880, p. 557.

40. Garber notebook no. 4, Guykendall Grist Mill, tab 23.

41. Graham, *History of Richland County,* 1880, p. 397.

42. Ibid., p. 557.

43. Garber notebook no. 4, Ganges Grist and Saw Mill, tab 29. Garber interviews with Ray Weaver, November 20, 1963; George W. Armstrong, November 24, 1951; and Arthur W. Cox, February 23, 1952;

44. Ibid.

45. Graham, *History of Richland County,* 1880, p. 397.

46. McCord, William B., ed., *History of Columbiana County, Ohio, and Representative Citizens*. Chicago: Biographical Publishing Com., 1905, p. 112.

47. Graham, *History of Richland County,* 1880, pp. 394-395.

48. Garber notebook no. 4, tab 29, Armstrong interview.

49. Baughman, A. J., *A Centennial Biographical History of Richland County, Ohio*: The Lewis Publishing Co., 1901, pp. 196-197.

50. Graham, *History of Richland County*, 1880.

51. Ibid., pp. 582-583.

52. Graham, *History of Richland County*, 1880, p. 417.

53. Ibid., p. 415

54. Newspaper clipping from unidentified source found in Garber's notes.

55. *Richland County Deed Records*, volume 5, p. 480.

56. Graham, *History of Richland County*.

57. Ibid.

58. Graham, *History of Richland County*,1880, p. 913.

59. Garber notebook no. 5, Osbun Mill, tab 34. Garber interview with Hugh Osbun, current owner of the Osbun farm, on February 5, 1950.

60. Ibid.

61. Baughman, *History of Richland County*, 1908, p. 360.

62. Ibid. See also article in the *Butler Enterprise* for April 6, 1900.

63. Garber notebook no. 4, Charles-Linn Mills, tab 19. Garber interview with Tracy Pittenger on June 18, 1951. See also: Dwight Wesley Garber, "Tales of the Mohican." *Mansfield: News Journal*, pp. 37-38.

64. Ibid.

65. Ibid.

66. Ibid.

67. David Linn Diary – loaned to Garber by Mrs. Charles Dorman on March 23, 1951; and Garber's *Mansfield News Journal* article.

68. Garber notebook no. 4, Mrs. Charles (Norma Tingley Linn) Dorman interview, March 12, 1951.

69. Garber notebook no. 4, Harvey Imhoff interview, June 18, 1951.

70. *Western Sentinel*, vol. 2, no. 27. June 8, 1931.

71. Graham, *History of Richland County*, 1880, p. 613.

72. Ibid.

73. Ibid.

74. Ibid.

75. Garber notebook no. 4, Tracy Pittinger interview, date not noted.

76. Garber notebook no. 4, Dickson & Taggart Carding Mill, tab 25.

77. Ibid.

78. Baughman, *History of Richland County*, vol. 1. 1908, p. 360.

79. Graham, *History of Richland County*, 1880, p. 611.

80. Ibid., p. 623. The relationship between the Montgomerys is not clear but presumably they were related.

81. *Mansfield Gazette & Richland Farmer,* vol. VII, no. 43, July 7, 1830.

82. Baughman, *History of Ashland County*, Ohio, Chicago: S. J. Clarke Publishing Co., 1909, 411.

83. Garber notebook no. 5, Montgomery Mill, tab 33. Garber interview with Lona L. Swineford and her sister Abigail on December 29, 1959.

84. Ibid.

85. Cites his notes only.

86. *Mansfield Gazette and Richland Farmer*, vol. V, no. 36, May 28, 1828.

87. *Mansfield Gazette* article, May 19, 1830.

88. *Mansfield Gazette*, vol. VIII. no. 27, March 16, 1831.

89. Graham, *History of Richland County*, 1880, p. 610.

90. Baughman, Article in the *Mansfield News*, December 2, 1898.

91. Sherman, John. *Recollections of Forth Years in the House, Senate, and Cabinet*, London and New York: The Werner Company, 1895.

92. Ibid.

93. *Ohio Liberal Scrapbook*, Ohio State Museum Library.

94. Baughman, *History of Ashland County*, pp. 835-837.

95. Baughman, *The Butler Enterprise*, Friday, October 31, 1902.

96. Baughman, *History of Ashland County*, 1909, pp. 710-11. All information pertaining to the Staman family history has been taken and paraphrased or copied from Baughman's book.

97. Knapp, *A History of the Pioneer and Modern Times of Ashland County, From The Earliest to the Present Date*. Philadelphia: Chicago: J. B. Lippincott & Co., 1863.

98. Graham, *History of Richland County,* 1880, p. 534.

99. Garber notebook no. 5, Hershey-Staman Mill, tab 38. Garber interview with Jay Middleton on March 8, 1948.

100. Ibid.

101. As indicated Garber had a very good relationship with Guy A. Kister. They both shared a deep love for the history of water mills. Mr. Kister was more than willing to share information about his family and their experience as millwrights and millers and it was he who provided Garber with the letter cited here.

102. Baughman, "A Trip to Staman's Mill," *The Butler Enterprise*, July 18, 1902.

103. This is another case where the correct spelling of the name "Gongawan" is uncertain – at least in Garber or Carter's notes on water-powered mills or distilleries. Again family and mill histories have been taken and paraphrased or copied from Graham's book. See also Garber notebook no. 5, Yeaman Mills, tab 50.

104. Ibid, *History of Richland County, Ohio*, 1880, p. 829. Again family and mill histories have been taken and paraphrased or copied from Graham's book. 105. Ibid.

106. Ibid.

107. Garber notebook no. 5, Yeaman Mills, tab 50, Garber interview with Mrs. John D. Harlan, July 6, 1949.

108. Andreas, A.T., *Atlas of Richland County, Ohio*, Chicago: Self Published, 1973, p. 37.

109. Garber's notes are of interest of course. This is unfortunately one of those rare occasions where he neither cited his sources nor the dates the notes were taken.

110. Aby, Franklin Stanton. *The Swiss Eby Family: Pioneer Millwrights and Millers of Lancaster County, Pennsylvania, United States of America.* Chicago: F. S. Aby, 1924, pp. 13-14.

111. Garber notebook no. 5, Lewis Grist Mill, tab 31. Garber interview with John Vail, March 3, 1948.

112. Ibid.

113. Hill, George William. *History of Ashland County, Ohio, with Illustrations and Biographical Sketches*, Ashland, OH, Williams Bros., 1880, 75.

114. Baughman, *History of Ashland County*, pp. 863-64.

115. Caldwell, J. A., *Atlas of Ashland County, Ohio*, 1874, p. 7. See: Baughman, *History of Ashland County*, pp. 863-64.

116. Baughman, *History of Ashland County*, pp. 863-64.

117. Ibid.

118. Garber notebook no. 4, Charles Mill, tab 18. Garber interview with C.M. Switzer on Mrch 9, 1948.

119. Ibid. According to Garber's notes, Switzer gave him his ledger of accounts while he operated the mill but no ledger has been located in Garber's collection and may have been disposed of by Garber. Much of his mill collection was given to the Ohio Historical Society, his personal notes excluded.

120. Ibid. Garber interview with Earnest W. Stafford, May 5, 1959.

121. Ibid. The information given to Garber was incorrect. The mill was located at the corner of First and Bond streets in Lucas, far above any possible water power. Electricity came to Lucas in 1920 which may have been the motive for moving it.

122. "Landmark Destroyed," *The Mansfield News Journal,* July 31, 1957.

123. Baughman, A.J., *Mansfield News Journal*, December 1898.

124. Caldwell, J. A., *Atlas of Ashland County, Ohio*, 1874, p. 94.

125. Baughman, *History of Ashland County*, p. 144.

126. Graham, *History of Richland County*, p. 658.

127. *Records of Township Trustees of Green Township, 1819 – 1832.* See listing for 1827.

128. Knapp, *A History of the Pioneer and Modern Times of Ashland County*, pp. 304-305,

129. Ibid., pp. 335-336.

130. *Ohio Shield and Democrat*, vol. 1, no. 35, September 7, 1837.

131. Garber notenbook no. 4, Greentown Mills, tab 31. Garber interview with Weldon Fightner, June 14, 1949.

132. *The Richland Star,* December 30, 1850, vol. 4, no.14, Dec. 30 1860.

133. Garber notebook no. 4, Grentown Mills, tab 31. Garber interview with Gar Beachler, June 14, 1949.

134. Ibid., Fightner interview.

135. Ibid. Garber interview with O. D. Culler, July 11, 1949.

136. Ibid. Garber interview with John K. Cowan, May 25, 1950.

137. Baughman, *History of Ashland County*, page number not cited.

138. Graham, *History of Richland County*, p. 658.

139. *1874 Ashland County Atlas*, p. 94.

140. Garber notebook no. 5, Karnahan-Jennings Mill, tab 28. Garber interview with Edna and Miss Lena Jennings. Date not recorded.

141. Ibid. Garber interview with William Simms, June 9, 1950.

142. Garber notebook no. 5, Honey Creek Mills, tab 27, Garber interview with C. E. Weirich, July 1, 1952.

143. Ibid. Garber interview with Mr. and Mrs. Simms, June 1, 1950.

144. Jennings, Warren, *The Ohio Gazetteer and Travelers Guide* containing a description of the several towns and counties with their water-courses, roads, improvements, mineral production, etc. Together With An Appendix or General Register. Columbus: Isaac N. Whiting, 1841, Revised edition, 286. This book is also available on line at: https://archive.org/stream/ohiogazetteertra00jenk#page/n7/mode/2up.

145. Garber notebook no. 5, Taylor Mill, tab 45. Garber interview of John K. Cowan, May 23, 1950.

146. *Richland Jeffersonian,* December 28, 1843.

147. Frary, I. T., *Early Homes of Ohi.*, Richmond, Virginia: Garrett & Massie, 1936.

148. Knapp, *History of Ashland County*, p. 305.

149. Hill, *History of Ashland County*, p. 76.

150. Simpson, Helen August. *Early Records of Simpson Families in Scotland, North Ireland, and Eastern United States: With A History of the Families of Hout, Stringer, Potts, and Dawson.* Philadelphia, PA, J. B. Lippincott, 1927, pp. 332-39.

151. Duff, William A., Letter to Mary Eddy, copied by Garber on July 3, 1956 and is a transcription of material furnished by Mary Eddy.

152. Ibid.

153. Ibid.

154. Ibid.

155. Because of the information provided in the Duff Letter, it is unfortunate that the *Ashland Times* for the year 1875 is missing in the Ashland County Genealogical Societies extensive microfilm newspaper files.

156. Hill, *History of Ashland County*, pp. 332-29.

157. Garber, D. W., "Tales of the Mohican: Farmers Blew Up the Mill Dam," Mansfield, OH: Richland Genealogical Society, 2003, 220. Originally these were individual articles written by Mr. Garber and printed in the *Mansfield News Journal*. The articles were compiled by Mary Jane Henney and Tales of the Mohican was reprinted with permission of the *Mansfield News Journal*.

158. Ibid.

159. Ibid.

160. Ibid.

161. Garber notebook no. 5, Loudenville Mill, tab 44. Garber interview with H. J. Bebout, March 13, 1952.

Section 3

Water-Powered Mills on the Rocky Fork of the Mohican River

1. Graham, *History of Richland County, Ohio (Including the Original Boundaries) Its Past and Present.* Mansfield: A. J. Graham & Co., 1880, p. 590.

2. Baughman. *History of Richland County Ohio from 1808 to 1908.* Chicago: S. J. Clarke Publishing, Co., 1908, p. 34. See also The Mansfield News, August 23, 1902 for additional information.

3. Ellis, Franklin. *History of Fayette County, Pennsylvania with biographical sketches of many of its pioneers and prominent men*, Philadelphia: L. H. Everts & Co., 1882, pp. 94-96. See Graham and Baughman histories of Richland County for additonal information on the Crawford Expedition of 1782.

4. Ibid.

5. Ibid., pp. 103-104. See also: Van Tassel, Charles Sumner. *Story of the Maumee Valley Toledo and the Sandusky Region.* Chicago: The S. J. Clarke Publishing Co., 1929, vol. 1, pp. 79-292.

6. *The Richland Shield & Banner*, vol. XVI, no. 6, July 9, 1856.

7. Garber notebook no. 7, Spring Mill and Welch-Wentz Mills, tab 27.

8. *Mansfield News Journal*, December 23, 1946. Garber transcribed the article but did not include the volume and number.

9. Garber notebook no. 7, Spring Mill and Welch-Wentz Mills, tab 27.

10. Baughman, *History of Richland County, Ohio*, p. 331.

11. Ibid., p. 332.

12. Hand drawn map by Garber copied from the Recorders Office, Deed Records, Vol 26, p. 455.

13. At this point in his notes, Garber clouds the story with the following: "Andrew painter, who had a carding and fulling mill east of Mansfield had a son Jacob, but it is not believed that he is the Jacob Bender or Painter of the Laird & Bender firm." See Garber notebook no 6, Laird & Bender Mill, tab 24.

14. Ibid. It is assumed that the sale Garber described was associated with the Laird-Bender sale; but Garber's source is again not stated.

15. Garber notebook no. 7, William Tingley Woolen Mill, tab 35. Garber interview with Mrs. Charles Dorman (Norma Tingley Linn) on March 12, 1951.

16. See *Deed Records, Richland County*, vol. 41, pp. 23-24. See also Land Record 1, Virginia Military, 379.

17. *Mansfield Gazette and Richland Farmer*, May 14, 1828, vol. V, no. 35.

18. *Mansfield Gazette and Richland Farmer*, May 13, 1829, vol. VI, no. 35.

19. Garber notebook no. 7, William Tingley Woolen Mill, Carr and Ferson Carding Mill, Tingley and Ferson Carding Mill, and the Ferson and Baird Mill, tabs 35-36.

20. *Mansfield Gazette*, vol. 4, no. 9, October 19, 1826.

21. Ibid. See also Garber notebook no. 7, Ferson and Baird Mill, tab 38.

22. Ibid.

23. Garber notebook no. 7, Thomas Baird "Fulling and Dying" and Ferson & Baird Mill, tab 38.

24. Ibid.

25. Graham, *History of Richland County, Ohio (Including the Original Boundaries) Its Past and Present.* Mansfield: A. J. Graham & Co., 1880, pp. 233-236.

26. *Mansfield Saving Bank & Trust Company Almanac*, 1928, pp. 43-44.

27. Baughman, *History of Richland County,* 1908, Vol, 2, p. 330.

28. Garber notebook no. 6, Newman-Beam-Rogers-Campbell Grist Mill, tab 15; *Bellville Star,* March 6, 1884.

29. Ibid. Other individuals who owned the mill during the last few years of its existence included Riley Amsbaugh and H L. Goudy; Garber interview with Mrs. Hunt, February 27, 1948.

30. *Mansfield News Journal*, March 16, 1952. Volume and Number are not cited.

31. Garber notebook no. 6, Andrew Painter's Carding Mill, tab 8. Garber interview with Henry Painter, Mansfield, Ohio, February 9, 1950. Henry Painter made the comment to Garber that Jacob, Henry, and Michael were millers or weavers and variously operated the mill following the death of Andrew. This statement is in conflict with his statement that Andrew Painter lived to see his mill closed c. 1900. This could be resolved with additional study on the family genealogy.

32. Ibid.

33. *The Mansfield Gazette*, vol. 2, no.1, July 1, 1824

34. Ibid., vol. 4, no. 41, June 14, 1827.

35. *The Western Sentinel*, vol. 2, no. 24, May 13, 1831.

36. Ibid., vol. 3, no. 38, August 24, 1831.

37. Baughman, *History of Richland County*, vol. 1, p. 331.

38. Graham, *History of Richland County*, 1880, p. 498.

39. Graham, *History of Richland County*.

40. *Bellville Star*, vol. 3, no. 42, July 25, 1880.

41. Ibid., vol. 6, no. 42, February 18, 1883.

42. Graham, *History of Richland County*, p. 498.

43. Ibid.

44. Ibid.

45. *The Mansfield Herald*, vol. 7, no. 27, June 10, 1857. Garber notebook no. 6, Leyman-Robinson Richland City Mill, tab 21. "The bridge arch was across the trail race, and was one block to the right, or east, of the flour mill of H. & J. S. Love. Diamond Street then ran north and south and was incorrectly called east and west. Diamond Street is now Main Street.

46. *The Mansfield Herald*, vol. XVIII, no. 29, June 10, 1868, "John Damp's Mill further improved."

47. *The Mansfield Herald*, vol. XVIII, no. 3, December 11, 1867.

48. Ibid.

49. *Shield and Banner*, vol. XI, no. 51, May 20, 1852.

50. See *The Richland Star*, vol. 4, no. 37, June 9, 1881. See also: *The Bellville Star*, vol. 5, no. 12, December 22, 1881.

51. *Shield and Banner*, vol. A, no 12, August 28, 1850.

52. *Richland Shield and Banner*, vol. XIII, no. 2, June 15, 1853.

53. *The Mansfield Herald*, vol. 7, no. 40, September 9, 1857.

54. *Richland Shield and Banner*, May 14, 1856.

55. Graham, *History of Richland County*, p. 498.

56. Ibid.

57. *Bellville Messenger,* February 11, 1878. Volume and number were not included. Garber questioned if Jacob Culler might have been Joseph Culler.

58. Garber interview with O. D. Culler, July 11, 1949. Garber notebook no. 6, Culler Woolen Mill, tab 16.

59. Graham, *History of Richland County*, p. 545. See also *The Bellville Messenger*, Feb. 11, 1897. "The third mill built in the township (Monroe) was built in 1830 by Mr. LaRue, on the Rocky Fork about a mile west of Lucas."

60. Garber Notebook No. 6, Ahlfeldt-Rummel Mill, tab 25. Garber interview with George Rummel, July 13, 1949.

61. Garber Notebook No. 6, LaRue Mill and Baker Mills, tabs 3-4. Garber interview with Mrs. Lewis Chandler, daughter of Hiram Baker, September 21, 1949.

62. Garber Notebook No. 6, Union Woolen Mill, tab 18, Garber interview with John Tucker, a lifetime resident of Lucas, Ohio, on July 23, 1951. Tucker supplied much of the available information regarding this mill.

63. *Bellville Messenger*, February 11, 1897.

64. Baughman, *History of Richland County*, p. 1041.

65. Garber notebook no. 6, Ahlefeldt-Rummel Mill (Oldfield Mill), tab 25. Garber interview with George Rummel and Mary (Rummel) Brenstunl, July 13, 1947, on the old Rummel property in Lucas, Ohio. I

66. Ibid. Garber interviews with John Vail, on December 4, 1947 and March 8, 1948.

67. *The Richland Star*, vol. 3, no. 47, August 19, 1880.

68. Ibid., vol. 6, no. 43, July 21, 1881.

69. Ibid., vol. 5. no. 21, February 23, 1882.

70. Ibid., vol. 6, no. 12, December 21, 1882.

71. Ibid., March 1884. Volume and number not cited.

72. Garber notebook no. 6, Union Woolen Factory, tab 18. John Tucker interview, July 25, 1951.

73. Garber notebook no. 6, Balliett Mill, tab 1. Garber interview with Mrs. Hunt, great-great granddaughter of Stephen Balliet who owned and operated the Balliett Mill. Interview on February 27, 1948.

74. *The Ohio Liberal*. vol. 6, no. 44, February 19, 1879.

Glossary

Bolting. The process of separating flour from bran or skin of the wheat by using fine mesh silk cloth to serve as a sieve.
Bolting cloth. Silk cloth of fine mesh used for bolting flour.
Bran. The skin of wheat, rye, or oats separated by grinding.
Buhr. Hard rock used in making millstones. Often erroneously spelled bur or burr.

Carding mill. Machines used to clean, separate, and process wool.

Dam. A barrier built across a stream to impound water for use in a mill.
Dress. The pattern for cutting furrows on the face of a millstone.

Flume. A artificial channel used to convey water from a millpond or dam to a mill.
Forebay. A reservoir or extension of a flume or millrace from which water was conveyed to the waterwheel.
French buhr. Millstones shaped from irregular pieces of hard rock obtained from French quarries and without a specific number of segments. Bound together with an iron band and dressed like a solid buhr.
Fulling mill. A mill which scoured, cleaned, and softened the fabric after it was dyed, and prior to its being napped and smoothed under pressure.
Furrow. The grooves on the face of a millstone which provide cutting edges for grinding grain.

Grist. Any quantity of wheat, rye, barley, corn, or any other unground grain carried to a mill by a farmer to be processed.
Gristmill. A mill where a farmer had his meal ground. Constructed with a waterwheel and using millstones.

Head gate. A water gate near a dam or at a millpond to control the flow of water through a race or flume to a mill.
Hopper. A square, funnel-like container, placed upon a hopper rest on top of the hood or cover over the buhrs. From the hopper grain flowed into the shoe and to the eye of the millstones.
Hopper rest. A rectangular frame with four legs placed on the hood and used to support the hopper. Equipped with a shoe and a feeder strap to control the flow of grain.
Hopper shoe. A shovel-shaped receptacle with a strap on the discharge end secured to a movable bar which raised or lowered the shoe to control the flow of grain.

Master wheel. The great cogwheel or bull wheel. The largest gear in the mill, taking power directly from the water-wheel shaft.
Millpond. A reservoir where water is impounded for use in a mill.
Millrace. The channel through which water flows from the milldam to the mill.
Millsite. A desirable location having an abundance of water to operate a mill.
Millwright. A craftsman with an intimate knowledge of mill equipment, its construction, and installation.

Overshot wheel. Water strikes the wheel at the highest point and fills the buckets. The wheel turns forward by weight of the water, which is spilled out after a third of a revolution.

Penstock. A trough or sluice carrying water from the forebay to the waterwheel.
Planing mill. A mill equipped to convert rough lumber into smooth and graded material for use in construction and cabinetwork.

Roller system. The process of grinding wheat into flour with rollers instead of buhrs. The roller system has entirely replaced millstones in the manufacture of flour.
Run. A pair of buhrs, the capstone revolving, the bed immovable.

Sawyer. A workman who sawed planks and boards from logs.
Shoe. A shallow tray beneath the hopper used to control the flow of grain into the eye of the buhr.
Sluice. An artificial channel for water with a head gate to control the flow.
Spring run. A small stream fed by a copious spring with sufficient water to turn a waterwheel.

Tailrace. The channel heading from the mill back to the stream after the water had passed through the waterwheel.
Toll. The amount of grain received by the miller as payment for grinding a grist.
Toll dish. Also toll box or tray; the container used by the miller to measure his toll.

Index

Symbol

1840 Richland County Auditors Records, 138
1856 Richland County Map, 43, 65, 87, 162
1861 Atlas Map, 136
1863 History of Ashland County, 142
1873 Andreas Atlas of Richland County, 66, 95, 162, 167
1874 Ashland County Atlas, 117, 121, 130, 134, 137, 142, 166-167
1880 History of Ashland County, 142
1880 History of Richland County, 86, 142
1883 Tax Records, 172
4th of July, 113

A

A & P Store, 89
Abbott Grist Mill, 85
Abraxes Treatment Center, 85
accident, 36
activity, 33, 106
ad, 178, 188
Adams Road, 106
Adams, Evan, 53
administration, 158
advertise, 6, 22-23, 28, 52, 58, 61-62, 66, 86, 91, 104, 108, 110-111, 113, 131, 138, 143, 147, 154, 161, 164-165, 171, 176
Ahlefeldt-Rummel Mill, 186
Alex W. McConnell Carding & Fulling Mill, 19
Alexander & Zent stone quarry, 30
Alexander and Zent, 58
Alexander Saw Mill, 64
Alexander, Robert, 64-65
Algire Road, 38-39
Almanac, 166
Alta South Road, 13
American Militia, 130
American Miller, 155
Amish, 53
Amsbaugh, Riley, 167
ancestors, 34, 37
Anderson Grist Mill, 97
Anderson, John, 97
Andres Atlas of 1873, 162

Andrew Painter Woolen Mill, 167
Andrew's Run, 63, 75
Andrews, Lavine, 73
Andrews, Lyman, 35
Angust, Anna E., 34
Angust, George, 34
Ankneytown Road, 34
announcement, 23, 25, 29, 49, 66, 155, 164, 170-171
Apple Creek, 43-44
Appleseed, Johnny, 41, 45, 49, 133
apprentice, 101
Archer Saw Mill, 122
architect, 110
Armentrout, Jacob, 49, 62, 165
Armstrong, Andrew, 98, 100-101
Armstrong, Elizabeth, 101
Armstrong, George, 100-101
Armstrong, George W., 98
Armstrong, Lewis, 143
arsonist, 64
article, 9, 32, 56, 107-108, 113-115, 126, 137, 144, 153-155, 165, 167
Ashland County Genealogical Society, 130
Ashland Railroad, 158, 162, 164
Ashland Times, 143
assets, 13
attorney, 68
Augustine, Mr., 116
Ayers Grist Mill, 99
Ayers, George, 98-99
Ayers, Harry, 98-99

B

B & O, 21, 25, 48, 154-155, 158
Backensto, Henry, 101
Baker Saw Mill, 96
Baker, Hiram, 185
Baker, John, 96
Baker, Ray J., 6
Ball, Rev. Mr., 107
Ballet, Steven, 190
Balliett Grist and Saw Mills, 190
Baltimore, 40, 51, 56
Baltimore & Ohio depot, 72

Baptist, 100
barley, 51
barn, 7-8, 15, 22, 37, 40-41, 57-58, 76, 86-89, 99, 101, 109, 135-137
Barr, Samuel, 4
Bartley, Mordecai, 153-154
basement, 45, 50, 53, 71, 89, 101, 105, 135, 147, 167-168
Basore, Henry, 134
Battle of Moorefield, 7
Baughman, A. J., 33, 40-41, 43, 57, 94, 114-115, 117, 122, 127, 133, 153, 158, 166, 170
Baughman, Francis, 40
Baxter, Andy, 183
Beachler, Gar, 132
Beachler, John, 132
Beall, General, 111
Beam, Michael, 166
Bebout, H. J., 146
Bedford Axe Handle Company, 75
Beemiller, Mrs., 4
beeswax, 62, 108, 165
Bell, Jacob, 172
Bell, John, 102
Belleville Flour Mill, 27
Bellville, 21-29, 31-38, 40, 43, 51-52, 58, 62, 94, 167
Bellville Dollar Weekly, 23
Bellville Planing Mill, 26
Bellville Star, 22-23, 25, 29, 32, 38, 51-52, 58, 167
Belmont County, 43-44
Bender & Painter, 158
Bender, Jacob, 158
Benedict, Doctor, 53
Benjamin Staman Grist Mill, 117
Bentley Mill, 180-181
Bentley Run, 188
Bentley, Robert Sr., 181
Berry, Adam, 72
Berry, Guy, 72
Berry, Mark and Barb, 41
Bible, 107
Big Prairie, 76
Big Run, 137, 149
Big Run Mills in Green Township, 137
Birthplace of the Clear Fork River, 3
Bishop, 38, 57
Bishop, Jim, 38
Bistline Road, 95-96
Blackledge, Robert, 155
blacksmith, 4, 46, 57, 71, 98, 114
blockhouse, 55
Blooming Grove Township, 98, 100-101
Blystone, G. P., 53
Booth, John Wilkes, 7

border, 43, 68, 86, 121
bottomland, 11, 45
boundary, 68, 84, 120, 128
Bowers, David, 25
Bowers, Isaac, 25
Bowers, Levi L., 107
Bowman Street Road, 86
Boy Scout Camp, 10, 17
Braden, William, 97
bran, 53
Breitinger, William J., 155
Brenstunl, Mary (Rummel), 187
Brentlinger, E. L., 25
Briner Saw Mill, 86
Briner, John, 86
Briner, John Jr., 87
Briner-Craner Saw Mill, 90
Brinkerhoff Scrapbook, 62
Brodley Saw Mill, 96
Brokaw Road, 74
Bromfield, Louis, 70-71, 74
Brubaker Creek Road, 104, 112
Brubaker Run, 104, 112
Brubaker, Catharine, 166
Brubaker, Jacob, 166
Brubaker, John, 166
Brubaker, Nancy, 114
buhr, 10, 15, 29, 33, 36-37, 61, 89, 95, 99, 101, 121, 135, 137, 149, 155
builder, 26, 62, 82, 87-88, 95, 163
Bull, T. J., 144
Bungtown, 3-4
Burrer family, 99
bushel, 20, 115
businessman, 82, 143
Butler, 23, 31, 47-50, 52-53, 56, 58, 62-63, 70, 74-75, 107, 115, 117, 140
Butler Axe Handle Conpany, 49
Butler-Clear Fork Historical Society, 49, 53, 58, 60, 63, 75
Butler-Newville Road, 56

C

C. & I. Hazlett, 165
cabin, 4, 6, 8, 17, 22, 25, 35, 40, 75, 82, 98, 103, 117-119, 166
Cake, George, 136
Caldwell, 9
Caldwell, Samuel, 9
Caleb Chapel, 144
Calhoun & Company, 57

INDEX

Calhoun Grist Mill, 56
Calhoun, Deroscus L., 58
Calhoun, Droscus L., 58-59
Calhoun, Homer, 59
Calhoun, Noble Sr., 56-57
Calhoun, Thomas, 150
Calhoun, Thomas W., 131
Campbell, John, 166
Canal Commission, 145
Cannon's Corn Meal, 76
Cannon, Harry, 76
Cannon, John, 76
canoe, 142
Cantiwell, G. W., 107
Canton, 25, 166
capacity, 28, 32, 50, 58, 69, 113, 147-148, 167
carding mill, 6, 27, 32-34, 65, 108--109, 137-138, 158
   164-165, 170
cargo, 145, 150
Carlisle, 96, 144
Carlisle, Thomas, 144
carpenter, 16, 36, 39-40, 57, 119, 144
Carr, Solomon M., 164-165
Carr-Ferson (Tingley) Carding Mill, 164
Carter, John, 9, 17
Carter, Robert A., 7, 10, 55, 87
Carter, Samuel, 9-11
Case Company, 29
Cass Township, 96-97
Cedar Fork, 37, 39-41, 43
census, 91, 137
Centennial Exposition, 146
Century, 24, 29, 36, 106, 108, 122, 135, 149, 156
Champaign County, 96
Chandler, Mrs. Lewis, 185
Chapman, John, 133
Charles Lynn Mill, 122
Charles Mill, 106-107, 109, 120-122, 124-127
Charles Mill Lake, 81, 120-122, 127
Charles Mill Lake Conservancy District, 121
Charles, E. H., 122-123
Charles, Elija, 108
Charles, Elijah, 106, 108
Charles, I. Jr., 107
Charles, I. Sr., 107
Charles, J. T, 102
Charles, John, 122-124
Charles, Manuel, 123
Charles-Linn Grist and Saw Mills, 106
Chatlin, Mrs. M. E., 167
Chicago, 26, 154
Christmas, James, 144
cider, 5, 14-15, 34, 36, 69-70, 116, 120, 136, 168
cider press, 5, 14-15, 34, 36, 69, 116, 120, 136, 168
circular saws, 137, 159
Civil War, 6-7, 36, 41, 43, 61, 70, 87, 94, 98, 101, 106,
   113-114, 137, 145
Clapboard town, 116
Clapper and Orewiler, 86
Clark Saw Mill, 171
Clark, Ezekiel, 7
Clark, Ichabod, 7
Clark, Thomas, 113
Clay, John, 104
Clear Fork Sailing Club, 7
Clemens, William, 131
Cleveland, 139, 144
Cline & Urick, 102
Cline Distillery, 103
Cline Grist and Saw Mill, 95
Cline, Joseph, 95
Cline, William, 95
Clingen, Mary, 107
coal, 12, 86
Cockley Mill, 12, 23, 26
Cockley Milling Company, 26
Cockley Road, 9
Cockley, Bill, 11
Cockley, W. W., 23
Coe, James, 76
Coe, Nathaniel McDowell, 142
Colby, H., 177
Coleman, John, 43
Coleman, Sara, 43
collection, 35, 68, 70, 138, 191
Colombiana County, 43
Coltman Cemetery, 88
Coltman Mill, 85, 88
Coltman, Joseph, 86, 88
Columbiana County, 43
Columbus, 13, 29, 39, 136
Columbus & Lake Erie Railroad, 13
column, 72
combination, 9, 11, 16, 25, 77, 116
Common Pleas Court, 189
competition, 26, 29, 32, 48, 92, 118, 123
Con Agra, 149
Condon & Welch, 153
confirmed, 21, 86, 92, 101, 105, 136, 167
Conger, Everton, 7
Conger-Williams Mill, 7
Conine, Ortho, 150
Conine, William, 150
construction, 4, 8-9, 13, 22, 25, 33, 44-45, 57, 61,
   82-83, 85-86, 95, 98, 117, 127, 139-140, 145, 155,
   166
Cook, Jabze, 17
cooper, 50, 57, 71, 147
Copus, James, 122
Corbett's Saw Mill, Grist Mill, & Woolen Factory, 39
Corbett, John, 39
Cotter, Alice A., 114

Cotter, William, 114
Coulson, L. J., 155
Coulter, Judge Thomas, 150
county auditor, 28, 81
county surveyor, 188
courthouse, 136, 153, 170
Cowan, John K., 136
Cox, Arthur W., 98
craft, 29, 48, 74-75, 140
Craft, George, 29, 48
Crain Mill, 24
Crain, C. E. "Ed", 22, 36
Crawford, Colonel William, 154
crossroads, 87, 137
Crown Jewel brand, 51
Culler Woolen Mill, 182-184
Culler, George W., 183
Culler, John W., 183
Culler, O. D., 132, 182
Culver, Calvin, 8
custom, 9, 23, 26, 58, 74, 76, 105, 120, 134

D

Damp, John, 177-178
Daniel Beasore's Saw Mill, 185
Daniel Teeter Saw Mill, 65, 75
Darling Mill, 167
Dauphin County, 24, 101, 111
David Miller Saw and Turning Mill, 16
Davis, Cora, 73
Dayton, 150
Dearborn, 26
Dearborn Hotel, 26
deed, 6, 25, 28, 68, 101, 136, 158, 162
DeHaven, Abraham, 133
Delaware, 12, 39, 100, 130, 154, 165
Delaware County, 39
Delaware Street, 12
depot, 26, 75
Detroit, 8, 58, 100
Dick, Will, 90
Dickson & Taggart Carding Mill, 108
Dickson, James, 5, 120
Dickson, John, 108
Dickson, Lillian R., 120
Dickson, Lola, 5
Dille, Israel, 112-113
divert, 39, 46, 109, 189-190
Dorem, Jeremiah, 189
Dorem, Mariah, 189
Dorman, Mrs. Charles, 162
Douglas, Michael, 170
Douglas, Samuel, 171

Drake, Curtis, 143
dress, 21, 43, 62, 134, 141
Duncan & Stikel, 94
Duncan Mill, 86, 94-95
Duncan, Holland, 94
Duncan, John A., 94
Dunkard Church, 57
Dunlap, J. C. (Chalmers), 86

E

E.P. & E. Sturges Grist Mill, 82
Eagle Woolen Mills, 58
Earick, William, 111-112
Early Homes of Ohio, 139
Ebenezer Lee, 65
Eby Grist Mill, 38
Eby Mill, 38, 121
Eby, Alexander, 121
Eby, Benjamin, 121
Eby, Sarah (Baer), 121
Edsall, Colonel Samuel, 5
Edward Lipset Saw Mill and Oil Mill, 77
Edwinsburgh, 4-5
Eisenbach, Walter, 53
Elizabeth Watson, 9
Elizabeth, Carrie, 29
Emalia Osbun, 104
Endslow, William, 142
English, J. R., 23
enterprise, 32, 44, 52, 72, 107, 115, 117, 145
Erie, 5, 13, 58
Erie Canal, 58
Ernest, Mark, 76
Ernsberg, Ira, 126
Ernsberger, Ira, 187
Evans, Mr., 49
Evans, Ott, 132
Evens, Jo., 107
Evens, Oliver, 44

F

farmland, 14, 74, 76, 162
Farst, A. G., 9
Faust, A. G, 23
Feeder Streams in Perry and Jefferson Townships, 37
Feeder Streams in Troy Township, 13
Ferguson, George, 183
Ferson & Baird Fullig Mill, 165
Ferson, Daniel, 165
Fightner, Weldon, 132

Fike, Charles, 187
Fike, Christian, 111-112
Fike, Cora, 59
Files, John, 58
First Associate Reform Church, 189
First, John, 186
Fitting, F. M., 25
flax, 9, 62, 74, 77, 127-128, 165, 171
Fleming Grist Mill, 113-114
Fleming, David, 114
Fleming, John, 114
Fleming, William, 114
Flemings Ravine, 114
Flood of 1913, 5, 69, 76, 125, 147
flume, 46, 69, 72, 109, 121, 139-140, 153
forebay, 20, 27-29, 31, 47, 76, 188
Franklin Township, 100-104, 113
Frary, L. T., 139
Frederick Shafer Mills, 43
Frederick, Christian, 36
Fredericktown, 8
French buhr, 10, 155
Friends Creek, 104
Friends of the Mill, 139
Fry, Frank, 183
Fry, George, 183
Fry, John, 59
fulling, 6, 9, 19, 27-28, 57, 62, 145, 158, 164-165, 167-168
furrow, 11

G

Galion, 4, 89
Gamble Street, 85
Gamble's Mill, 88
Gamble, John, 88-89
Ganges Five Points, 96
Ganges Grist and Saw Mill, 98
Garber, Benton L., 25-26
Garber, Jacob, 25, 35
Garber, Jacob Silas, 25
Garber, Maria (Swank), 36
Garber, Mary E., 52
Garrett, W., 67
Garrison, John, 4-5, 13
Garrison-Martin-Dickson Mill, 5
Gass Raod, 7
Gates, Jacob, 159, 166
Gatton, John, 46
Gatton Rocks Road, 35
gears, 67-68, 113
General Assembly of Ohio, 144
George Marshall Grist Mill, Saw Mill & Distillery, 21
George Smith Saw Mill, 130
Gevetz farm, 97
Gevetz, Joseph, 97
Gfrer Road, 153
Gfrer, John, 155
Gibson Carding Machine, 101
Gilliland Brothers, 58
Gilliland, Charley, 59
Gilliland, John, 59
Gleckner, Jack, 41
Gledhill, Walter, 154
Godfrey Shawecker, 135
Gold Run, 62
Golden Eagle, 187
Gorman Nature Center, 17
Goudy's Mill, 167
Goudy, H. L., 167
Goudy, Henry L., 189
Gouwger, Joseph, 116
Governor of Ohio, 153
Graham, A. A., 68, 75-76, 86, 88, 90, 93, 105, 108, 110, 113, 116, 119-120, 131, 133, 142, 153, 172, 177-178, 181, 185
Graham, Morris, 8-9
granite, 37, 95, 99, 101
Graves, Sterling, 9
Graves-Watson-Lewis Mill, 9
Gray & Freeman, 144-145
Graybill, 115
Great Chief of the Delaware, 100
Green Township, 68, 128-130, 133, 136-138, 150
Green Township Distilleries, 150
Green Township records, 130
Greentown Indian Village, 130
Greentown Preservation Association, 130
Greentown Spring Mills, 130
Greenwood Mill, 34-37, 48
Greenwood-Crain Grist & Saw Mills, 34
Greer, Mina, 59
Griebling, George Gust, 15
Griebling, Jacob, 14-15
Griebling, John, 14
Griebling, L. B., 16
Griebling, Louis, 69
Griebling, Louis G., 15
Griffin, Jeanie, 60
Gross, Curt, 42
Grove, Joseph, 150
Grubaugh, Jonathan, 150
Guthrie, John, 150
Guthrie, Richard, 131
Guykendall Grist Mill, 97
Guykendall, Ross, 97

H

Hade, E., 177
Hade, J., 177
Haffstodt, Mr., 91
Hahn Mill, 10-12
Hahn, Dr. David "Daddy", 9
Hahn, Reverend Benjamin J., 9
Haislet, Samuel, 91
Half-King, 154
Hanawalt Grist Mill, 40, 42
Hanawalt, John, 40-41
handmade, 53, 68, 70
Hanley, 9, 31
Hanley Milling Company, 31
Hanley, Jerry, 31
Hannon, Thomas, 58
Hardin County, 66
Harlan, 119-121
Harlan, John D., 120
Harlan, Os, 121
Harmon, John, 162
Harmon, Mary, 162
Hartman Sprang building, 177
Harvey Solmon, 75
Haskell, Nathaniel, 145
Hawk, George C., 87
Hawk, Jacob, 87
Hawk, William, 87
Hayesville pike, 67
head gate, 24, 43, 46, 132
Heath Brother's Grist Mill, 90
Heath brothers, 90-91
Heath Mills, 90
Heath's City Mills, 90
Heath, Bert, 91-92
Heath, Roger, 90-92
Hedges Oil or Flax Mill, 180
Hedges Paper Mill, 177
Hedges, General James, 166
Hedges, James G., 179
Heimberger, Clayton, 126
Henry Foults Saw Mill, 65
Henshey, Benjamin, 115-116
Heron Mill, 34
Heron, Samuel, 34
Herring Grist and Saw Mills, 61
Herring Mill, 58, 61, 63-64
Herring, Cyrus, 72
Herring, John Frederick, 57
Herring-Calhoun-Files-Gilliland Mill, 56
Herron Mill, 40
Herron, John Frederick, 40
Hershey, 115-116, 118, 122
Hershey, John, 122
Hershey-Staman Grist Mill, 115

Hershiser Saw Mill, 96
Hesket, Al, 12
Hettinger, Maurice, 60
Higgins, Wm. S., 178
Hiple, Levi, 28
Hiskey, James, 10, 20
historical, 49, 53, 58, 63, 75, 90-94, 117, 130, 154
historical marker, 130
History of Ashland County, 75-76, 115, 122-123, 133, 142
History of Morrow County and Ohio, 6
History of Richland County, 33, 57, 68, 75, 86, 88, 90, 93-94, 102, 105, 108, 110, 113, 116, 119, 130, 133, 142, 153, 158, 166, 170
Holley, James (Jesse), 25
Holmes County, 76
homestead, 70-71, 104, 122, 162
Honey Creek Mill, 134, 136
Honey Creek Road, 34, 133
Honey Valley, 34
hopper, 15, 53, 101, 141
hopper rest, 15
Horsetail Run, 76
Horton, James, 107
Horton, R. D, 107
Howard, I. W., 27
Howard, Johnson, 34
Howard, Otis, 26
Huber, Maria, 122
Hull's surrender, 8
Hunt, Mrs., 167
Hunt, Richard, 167
Hyundai Ideal Electric Company, 177

I

Imhoff, Harvey, 108
improvements, 29, 33, 40, 130, 135
Independence, Ohio, 49
Indian, 8, 34, 37, 43, 55, 82, 100, 103, 117, 119, 130, 144, 154, 166
Inscho, Susan D., 92
intersection, 4, 6, 9, 12, 19-20, 24, 38, 43, 65, 74, 77, 82, 95-96, 101, 121, 133, 153, 166, 169
investment, 28, 66, 68, 82
Irish, William, 138
Isaac Manor (Meanor, Mennor) Grist Mill, Saw Mill & Carding Machine, 137
Isaacs Run, 9
Israel Dille Grist and Saw Mills, 112

J

J. Endslow & Co., 142
Jackson and Beach, 36
Jackson Township, 84-86, 94, 102
Jacob Bell Grist Mill, 172
Jacob Gates Saw Mill, 159
Jacob George Saw Mill, 83
Jacob King Saw Mill, 19
Jacob Staman & Brothers, 116
James Kerr Grist Mill, 86
James McCoy Saw Mill, 159
Jefferson Township, 24, 34, 36, 62
Jennings, Edna, 134
Jennings, Joseph D., 134
Jennings, Lena, 134
Jennings, Warren, 136
Jessie Eyster (Oyster) Grist Mill and Saw Mill, 77
John Buler Saw Mill, 115
John Crooks Saw Mill, 159
John Damp's Grist Mill, 178
John Gongawan Distillery, 118
John Kerr Grist Mill and Saw Mill, 86
John Sherman Map of 1840, 136
John Shield's Saw Mill, 74
John Stafford Grist Mill, 122
John Strausbaugh Mill, 11
John Woodhouse Oil Mill, 127
Johnson Howard sawmill, 34
Joseph Cotterman Grist Mill and Saw Mills, 85
Joseph Rinehart Saw Mill, 137
Joseph Runyon Saw Mill, 81
Journeycake, Charles, 100
Journeycake, Solomon, 100
Jump, Amos, 109
Justice of the Peace, 111

K

Kanaga, Joseph, 48
Karnahan, Robert, xvi, 134
Karnahan, Theresa J., 134
Karnahan-Jennings Mill, 134
Kauffman families, 115, 122-124
Kauffman, Anna (Staman), 123
Kauffman, Christian, 123
Kauffman, Daniel, 122, 124
Kauffman, Fannie, 123
Kaughman, Benny, 20
Kaylor, Jane, xviii
Keifer, Frank, 38
Keith Mills, 158
Keith, Judge H. D., 158

Kelley's Tavern, 162
Kelley, M., 62, 165
Kenney, Judge Peter, 100
Kerr, David, 87
Kerr, James, 86
Kerr, William, 86, 138
Kessler, Samuel, 4
Killbuck River, 154
King, Jacob, 19
King, Squire, 19
Kings Corner, 19
Kingwood Center, 159
Kister, George C., 116-117
Kister, Guy, 68, 116, 134
Knapp Chairs, 94
Knapp, H. S., 75, 94, 115-116, 131, 142
Knox County, 66
Kohler Grist Mill, 114
Kohler, Amos, 114
Kohler, Amos, 114
Kohler, Daniel, 114-115
Koogle Road, 121
Kuhn, H. Dale, 85, 89-90, 93, 95
Kyner, Mr., 11

L

Laird & Bender, 158
Laird & Bender Carding and Fulling Mill, 158
Laird, Jacob, 158
Lake Erie, 5, 13, 58
Lanechart, F. W., 29
Lanehart, William, 29
Langal Mill, 44
Langal, Casper, 43
LaRue-Baker Grist Mill, 185
Larwell, John C., 144
Laughlin, John, 126
Layman, Henry, 177
Leah Ann Hanawalt, 41
Leatherwood Creek, 86
Lee, A. E., 23
Lee, James Albert, 65
Lee, Mr., 106
Lee, Mrs. Charley H., 65
Leedy, Aaron B., 36
Leedy, Daniel, 35-36
Leedy, Jacob, 165
Leedy, Roy, 36
Leedy, Salome, 36
LeFever Saw and Carding Mill, 33
LeFever, Ben, 34
LeFever, John, 33-34
Leffel Standard, 21

Leffell turbine, 12
Leonard, Sally, 9
Leppo Saw Mill, 85
Lewis Grist Mill, 121
Lewis, Charles, 122
Lewis, Samuel, 55
Lewis, William, 9
Lexington, 4-12, 17, 19-21, 23, 26-27, 32, 39, 110, 153, 155, 159-161, 165
Lexington-Ontario Road, 4-5
Lexington-Springmill Road, 9, 153, 159
Leyman-Robinson-Richland City Mills, 177
Liberty Park, 168-169, 171
Liberty Park Lake, 169
Lima State Hospital, 73
Lime, E. E. (Ebb), 63, 69
Lincoln, Abraham, 7
Lindley, Stephen, 170
Linn Mills, 106-108
Linn, Cornelius, 162
Linn, David, 106, 108
Linn, Norma Tingley, 107, 162
linseed, 74, 77, 127-128
Logan, John, 4
Logan-Kessler-Barr Mills, 3-4
Long, William, 4
Longe, Gustave, 94
Longworth, Silas, 122
Loudenville Mills, 144
Loudonville flour, 146
Loudonville Mill & Grain Company, 148
Love, J. S., 178
Lowrie, David, 90-91
Lowrie, David L., 90-91
Lowrie-Heath Mill, 90
Luna Amusement park, 172
Lynn, William, 107

M

Madden, Jacob, 177
Madison Township, 153, 158-159, 165-166
Malabar Farm State Park, 70
management, 29, 41, 52, 95, 147-148, 170
Manner Grist Mill, 68
Manner, Jacob, 57, 68, 70, 116-117
Manner, Lillian, 183
Manner, Marion, 69-70
Mansfield, 4-6, 13, 16, 31, 50, 56, 58, 61-63, 67, 82-83, 89, 94, 101-102, 104, 106-107, 111, 113-114, 116-117, 120, 123, 126-127, 136-137, 145, 153-155, 158-159, 162-171
Mansfield Correctional Institution, 158, 162
Mansfield Gazette, 6, 61-62, 111, 113, 164-165, 170
Mansfield Machine Company, 120
Mansfield News, 114, 153
Mansfield News Journal, 56, 126, 155, 167
Mansfield North Lake Park Mills, 172
Mansfield Paper Company, 177
Mansfield Savings Bank & Trust Company Almanac, 166
Mansfield Woolen Mill, 178-179
Mansfield-Adario Road, 106
map, 3, 16, 22, 34, 43, 49, 62-63, 65, 75, 82-85, 87, 96, 109, 113, 129, 136-137, 146, 158, 162
Marion Avenue, 13, 16-17
Marks, Abraham, 186
Marks, Daniel, 159
marriage, 9, 43, 52, 108, 123, 143
Marshall Mill, 21-22
Marshall Railroad Bridge, 27
Marshall Saw Mill, 34
Marshall's Park, 4
Marshall, Colonel George, 22
Martin's Tavern, 4
Martin, John, 5
Martins Mill, 136
Marvin's Drug Store, 89
Masonic Cemetery, 143
master wheel, 40, 141, 168
Mathew-Mitchell Grist Mill, Saw Mill & Carding Mill, 6
Matson, L. G., 107
Matthews, Meanor, 185
Matthews, W. W., 117
Mauer, W. G., 8
McClain Mill, 11-13
McClain, Charles, 12
McClelland, Hattie, 52-53
McClelland, Val, 53
McClure's mill seat, 94
McClure's Mill Site, 93
McClure, James, 93
McClure, Thomas, 93
McConnell Saw Mill (Orweiler Road Saw Mill), 17
McConnell, Alex W., 19
McConnell, Joseph, 17
McCrary, Thomas, 68
McCune, Hal, 53
McDaniel, Mrs. Dora (Bowers), 42
McGaney & Eunick Carding Machine, 101
McGrew, May, 71
McGuire, B., 136
McKee, Timothy Brian, 11
McMahan, Thomas, 75
McMillen, William, 138
McPeek, John M., 29
McPeek, John S., 29
McVay and Allison, 177

Meanner, Isaac, 133
Meanor, Armstrong, 138
Meanor, John C., 138
Medill, William, 162
Mendenhall's Improved Patent Grist Mill, 160
Menor, Armstrong, 138
Menor, Isaac, 137
Menor, John, 138
Mentzer, John, 167
Menzie, Alexander, 28
Menzie, William, 28
Mercer's Mill, 13
Mercer, Boyd F., 13
Mercer-Griebling Grist and Saw Mills, 13
Mergert, Mr., 74
Mershon, Peggy, 35
Metcalf, Marge, 53
Michael Watson, 9
Middle Park, 175
Middletown, Jay, 116
mill capacity, 69, 147
Mill Run Road, 20, 43
miller, 4, 11, 21, 23, 31-33, 35, 37-38, 43-44, 46, 51-52, 57, 66, 70, 74, 76, 82, 86-87, 91, 99-101, 105, 107, 116, 119, 121, 123, 126, 144-145, 156, 165-167, 176, 185-186, 188
Miller Saw Mill, 49
Miller, Chris, 123
Miller, David, vii, 16
Miller, Elizabeth S., 111
Miller, George, 16
Miller, John, 123
Miller, Martin, 49
millpond, 7, 39, 87, 93, 120, 135-136, 153, 155-157, 162, 164, 168-169
millrace, 22, 42-43, 46, 56, 74, 86, 88, 90, 95, 99, 106, 112, 120, 126, 146, 167, 169
Mills in Hanover Township, 75, 150
Mills on the Clear Fork of the Mohican, 1, 3, 6
Mills South of Mansfield in Washington Township, xii
Millsboro West Road, 5
Millsborough, 4-6
millsite, 18, 24, 26, 29, 43-44, 47, 51, 54, 64, 69, 80, 88, 97, 99, 107, 110, 113, 115-117, 120, 121, 132-135, 142, 163, 167
millstone, 9-11, 15, 61, 89-90, 95, 99, 141
millwright, 6, 8, 10, 16, 22, 31, 41, 43-44, 50-51, 60-61, 67-68, 91, 101, 111, 116-117, 123-124, 134, 138, 168, 187
Mimosa, 147
Missing water case, 189
Mitchell's Mill, 6
Mitchell, Francis, 6
Mitchell, George, 6
Mitchell, James M., 6
Mitchell, Joseph, 6
Mitchell, Nancy, 6
Mitchell, Squire, 6
Mix, T. E., 59
Mock Road, 23, 38
Mohican National Forest, 138
Mohican Park, 138
Mohican State Forest, 75, 77
Mohican Valley Mills, 4
Mohn, John B., 111
Mohn, Leonard, 112
Monroe Township, 68, 128, 154
Montgomery Grist Mill, 110
Montgomery, Abel, 111
Montgomery, Benjamin, 110-111
Montgomery, Jonathan, 111
monument, 44, 118, 139, 168-169
Moody Mill, 27, 30-32
Moody, Reverend John, 28, 32
Mormon, 46-47
Mormon Church, 46-47
Morrow County, 3-4, 6
Morse & Ellis, 31
Mount Zion Road, 166
Mowers & Co., 189
Mowers, George, 189
Mowers, Henry, 183
Mowery, George J., 126
Muskingum Conservancy District, 121
Muskingum River, 154
Muskingum Watershed Conservancy, 122
Musser families, 115
Musser, Jacob, 115
Myers, Jacob, 43-44, 46, 49, 62, 75
Myers, S. L., 53
Myers-Kanaga-Plank Mill, 43, 49, 54

N

Nathan DeHaven Saw Mill, 133
Nathan Tompkin's Saw Mill, 83
National Grange, 41
National Register of Historic Places, 53
Neal, George, 31, 49
Neal, George O., 21, 27, 32-33
Neal, John B., 123
Neely, James, 117
Nelson, Levi, 112
New Hampshire, 35
New Orleans, 57, 145, 150
New York, 57, 89, 114
Newell, Captain, 8
Newman, Andrew, 115-116

Newman, Michael, 166
Newman-Beam-Rogers-Campbell Grist & Saw Mills, 166
Newville, 32, 48, 56-57, 61-67, 69-70, 75, 116, 133
Nicolas Flaherty Saw Mill, 77
Nigger Boy Clock, 12
nigger head, 10, 36, 59, 98-99, 119, 121, 136-137
Noah Watson Tavern, Grist Mill, and Saw Mill, 17
Nordick-Marmon & Company, 25
Nordyke & Marmon, 183
Norris, Floyd, 59
Northern Source of the Clear Fork River, 4
Northumberland County, Pennsylvania, 43
Northwestern Elevator and Milling Company, 147

O

O. Howard & Son, 26
Oak Hill Cottage, 177
Oak Tree Golf Club, 81
Ohio Gazetteer and Travelers Guide, 136
Ohio Liberal, 62
Ohio State Museum Library, 114
Ohio State University, 159
Ohio Volunteer Infantry, 111
old-timers, 7, 69, 94, 195-196
Oldfield, Richard and Elmina (Phelps), 35
Oliver, Allen, 143
Oliver, John, 143
Oliver, Paul, 143
Olney family, 132
Ontario, 4-5, 81
orchard, 41, 45, 49, 99, 171
Orlandus B. Rummel, 52
Osbun Grist and Saw Mills, 104-105
Osbun, Alfred, 105-106
Osbun, Hugh, 105
Osbun, Isaac, 105
Oswalt, Andrew, 113
Oswalt, Levi, 130
overshot wheel, 72, 108-109, 114, 121, 135, 139, 167
Owings, George, 155
oxen, 89, 96, 170

P

Painter, Andrew, 158, 167-169
Painter, Catherine, 169
Painter, Jacob, 158
Painter, Mary, 169
Palm, Charley, 23
Palm, Harry, 20-22

Panama Canal, 75
Parker, David L., 29
Parks, Mr., 116, 175
Parr, Andrew, 72
Parr, Jesse, 131
partnership, 14, 23, 28, 31, 37, 58, 72, 83, 102, 108, 114
Paul, Dr. Robert C., 76
Pennell, Edward, 139
Pennell, Lavern, 139
penstock, 99, 109, 120
Perry Township, 37, 40, 43
Perry Woolen Mill, 39
Perry, Ben, 38
Pervine, G. W., 72
Peterson, Willis (Wilson), 132
Phelps Mill, 22
Phelps, David, 22, 35-37
Phillips, Thomas, 39
Pine Run, 54, 77, 139-140
pioneer, 10, 32-33, 43, 55-56, 81, 89, 100, 121, 127, 162, 166
Piper, John, 62, 75
Pittenger, Tracy, 106
Pittsburg, Fort Wayne, and Chicago Railroad, 154
planing mill, 26, 62, 116, 177
Plank Mill, 23, 43-45, 48-49, 54
Plank, Elam, 47
Plank, Elam A., 48, 123
Plank, Jonathan, 48
Plank, Mary, 47
Plansifter System, 188
Pleasant Hill Dam, 64
Pleasant Hill Lake, 65, 75, 77
Plymouth Street, 9, 11
Plymouth Township, ix, 95
Pollock Carding Mills, 170
Pollock, Clement, 170
Pollock, Robert, 170-171
pond, 7, 15, 83, 86, 109-110, 127, 133, 135-136, 139, 154, 156, 163-164, 169, 171
Possum Run, 63, 65, 67-68
Post Farm, 88
Potts, Harriett, 143
profitable, 32, 58, 65, 95, 118
Purdy, James, 82

Q

Quaker Springs, 133
quarry, 4, 30, 163-164

R

R. McCombs Store, 62
Ralston, John, 104
ravine, 81-82, 114, 117
Records of Township Trustees of Green Township, 131
red beech, 95
Red, J. H., 177
Reed Carpenter, 188
Reed, Daisy, 38
Reed, H. L., 177
Reed, John, 38
reformatory, 159, 162-164
Reinhard, William, 14
relocated, 8, 39-40, 91, 99, 102, 138
reputation, 44, 48, 66, 87, 98, 119, 124
Rerick Atlas of 1896, 67
Revolutionary War, 8, 106
Reynolds, William, 114
Rhur of America, 139
Riatt, James, 180
Rice, Rosella, 150
Richard Oldfield, 186
Richardson, Lee, 38
Richland and Huron Bank, 4, 13
Richland Axe Handle Factory, 75
Richland City Mills, 177
Richland County, 2, 4, 6-10, 12, 14, 16, 18, 20, 22, 24, 26-28, 30, 32-34, 36, 38-46, 48-50, 52, 54, 56-58, 61-62, 64-66, 68, 70, 72, 74-76, 78, 80-82, 84, 86-88, 90, 92-94, 96, 98, 100-102, 104-106, 108, 110-114, 116, 118-124, 126-128, 130, 133-134, 136-140, 142, 144, 146, 148, 150, 152-158, 160, 162-168, 170
Richland Farmer, 111, 164
Richland Grange, 41
Richland Handle Company, 49
Richland Hospital, 167
Richland National Bank, 83
Richland Run, 86
Richland Rural Life Center, 106
Richland Shield & Banner, 7, 154
Richland Star, 9, 26, 49, 66
Rickerson, Oliver, 186
Rider Road, 74
Ridgeway, George, 23
Rinehart, C. B., 66
Rinehart, Gene, 42
Rinehart, I. S., 66
Rinehart, J. B., 66
Robinson, Calvin, 34
Robinson, John R., 177
Robinson, Neil, 167
Rock Road, 4, 82, 87
Rocks, Gatton, 34

Rocky Point Mill (Van Zile Mill), 65
Rogers, George, 89
Rogers, John, 166
Roller Process, 29
roller system, 23, 125, 135
Rose, Celia, 74
Ross County, 49
Ross, David, 74
Ross, John, 104
Ross, Peter, 188
Route 97, 4, 6-7, 21, 23-24, 47, 75
Route 314, 6
Rowland, James, 137
Rowland, Simon, 37
Rowlands, David, 106
Royer, A., 130
Royer, A. J., 133
Royer, Ephraim, 132
Royer, Jack, 135-136
Royer, James, 132
Ruby Road, 6
Ruffler Place, 117
Ruffner cabin, 117-118
Ruffner, Martin, 117, 122
Rummel Mill, 23, 48-52, 54-55, 112, 140
Rummel, Albert, 54
Rummel, Corwin, 186
Rummel, D. J., 52
Rummel, David J., 49, 52, 62
Rummel, George, 185, 187
Rummel, George L., 186
Rummel, O. B., 52-53
Rummel, Otis, 186
Rummel, Silas, 186-187, 189
run (of buhrs), 9. 36-37, 40, 46, 66, 68, 77, 101, 116-117, 131-132, 134, 144, 186-187
Rupp, Gorman, 171
Rutherford, W. B., 29
Rutlege, Thomas, 159
rye, 51, 62, 102, 108, 165, 171

S

S. Clapper & Co., 58
salvaged, 16, 69, 126, 149
Samuel Brallier Saw Mill and Carding Machine, 75
Samuel Graber Carding Mill, 65
Samuel Lattimore Grist Mill, 121
Samuel Lattimore Grist Mill and Saw Mill, 121
Sandstone School, 71-72
Sandusky River, 154
Sandusky, Mansfield & Newark, 154

Sandusky, Mansfield and Newark Railroad, 50
Satko, Paul, 188
sawyer, 119, 166
Schiffles, Benjamin, 101
Schrack Grist Mill and Oil Mill, 70
Schrack, Charles, 70-72, 74
Schrack, David, 70
Schrack, Dell, 74
Schrack, Susan, 71
Seltzer Park, 89-90
settlement, 46, 82, 93-94, 107, 116, 166-167
Seymore Run, 117, 121-122
Seymour Beech Conger, 7
Shafer & Shafer, 23
Shafer Mill, 23
Shafer Saw and Oil Mill, viii, 43
Shafer, A. E, 23
Shafer, Adam, 23
Shaffer, Hoy, 27, 31
Shaler, David, 25
Shaler, Frank L., 25
Shaler, Helen, 26
Shannon Mill, 53
Sharon Township, 84-88, 93
Shatzer, John, 101
Shauck Mills, 37
Shauck, Charles and Arthur, 38
Shauck, Elah, 37
Shauck, Henry, 38
Shauck, John, 37
Sheets, Elza G., 124
Sheets, L., 187
Shelby Carriage Works, 95
Shelby Centre/Center Mill, 91
Shelby Chapter of The Ohio Genealogical Society, 91
Shelby Chronicle, 91
Shelby Flour Mill, 92
Shelby Historical Society, 91-93
Sheriff's Sale, 4, 23, 28, 91, 120, 122, 136-137
Sherman Map of 1830, 112, 136, 162
Sherman, John, 114, 136
Shield & Banner, 7, 154
Shields Run, 62
Ships Run, 100-101
shoe, 141
Shoemaker, John, 59
Shuffler & Barksdale Carriage factory, 86, 94
Shuffler, Robert, 92, 94
Shuler, Paul, 110, 160-161
sick wheat, 107-108
Simmons Run, 62
Simmons, Atho, 54
Simms, Shannon, 134-136
Simms, William, 134
Simon Rowland Saw Mill, 137
Simpson, John, 29, 33

Simpson, John E. (J. E.), 29
Sipe, Daniel, 87
Skinner, Alexander, 144
Slater Run, 62, 74-75
sluice, 51, 160
Smart Mill and Distillery, 171
Smart, James, 171
Smiley, Joe, 114
Smith, Benjamin, 62
Smith, D., 190
Smith, George, 126, 130, 150
Smith, Harry, 12
Smith, Ida, 59
Smith, Jedediah Strong, 150
Smith, Joseph, 5, 47
Smith, Mark J., 139
Snider, John C., 120
Snow Flake, 124
Snyder and Wolf, 98
Solomon Vail, 121
Solomon, A. J., 75
Sowers, Mrs. Charles, 37
Sprague, John, 91
Spring Mills, 130, 153-155, 158
Spring Mills Station, 154
spring run, 97
Springfield Township, 4, 6, 81-82, 153-154
Springmill West Road, 82-83
Staat's Mill, 113
Stafford, Earnest W., 126
Stafford, John, 119, 122
Staley Mill, 96, 102-103
Staman "Ruffner" Saw Mill, 117
Staman families, 115-118, 123
Staman, Barbara (Hershey), 115
Staman, Benjamin, 115-117
Staman, Jacob, 116
Staman, John Kauffman, 115
Staman, Willard G., 116
Stamen, 115-116
State Highway Department, 33, 139, 142
State of Ohio, 32, 130, 139
State Road 13, 34
State Road 97, 20
Steam Corners, 4
steam-powered, 12, 23, 75, 125, 137
Stewart, John, 188
Stewart-Wickert Grist and Saw Mills, 188
Stitzel & Nau, 53
Stitzel, Ed, 53
Stitzel, Jacob A. Sr., 146
Stoffer Road, 34-35
Stoner Mill, 100-101
Stoner's Grist and Saw Mill, 100
Stoner, Jacob, 100-101
Stout, Mills & Temple turbine, 150

Strausbaugh House, 20
Strausbaugh Mills, 20
Strausbaugh, John, 11, 20-21
Strickler, Mr., 66
Stringer Grist Mills, 142
Stringer Mill, 142
Stringer Mystery, 143
Stringer, Elza, 143
Stringer, Mary Dawson, 143
Stringer, Thomas, 142-143
Stringer, Tom, 143-144
Striving Road, 86
Strock, John, 87
Strong and Waring, 28
Stull, Cora, 59
Stump Mill, 23-24
Stump, C., 23
Stump, Israell, 23
Sturges, Eben P., 82
Sturges, Edward, 83
Summit County, 68
Sunshine Biscuits Inc., 148
Swank, Jess, 35
Swearengen, Nicholas, 133
Sweezie, William, 126
Swigart Road, 65
Swineford, Abigail, 111
Swineford, Lona L., 112
Swiss Eby Family, 121
Swiss Mennonites, 115
Switzer, C. M., 123
Switzer, Ed, 25

T

Taggart, Wm., 108
tailrace, 13, 20, 105, 145
Tandy, 120
tannery, 96, 116-117
tavern, 4, 17-19, 62, 76, 98-99, 111, 162
Taylor, A. A., 140, 144-145
Taylor, Augustus A., 142
Teeter, Manuel, 59
The Bellville Independent, 29
The Butler Enterprise, 107, 115, 117
The Mansfield Herald, 58
The Ohio Register, 4
The Rerick Atlas of 1896, 67
The Richland Star, 9, 26, 49, 66
The Rocky Fork - Where Did The Water Go?, 189
The Western Sentinel, 28, 108, 171
Thomas Andrews Saw Mill, 137
Thomas McMahan Grist and Saw Mill, 75
Thomas Parks and Washington and Charles Strong, 28

Three Crosses Methodist Church, 75
Thuma, Roy, 39
thunder-gust mill, 100
toll, 20, 70
timeframe, 119, 136
Tingley & Carr factory, 165
Tingley and Ferson Carding Mill, 165
Tingley, Mary Catherine, 162
Tingley, Thomas, 162
Tingley, William, 162, 165
Tinkey, Jerry, 22-23
Toby's Run, 171-173, 175, 177-178
Toledo, 73, 83, 148
Toledo Junction, 83
Toledo State Hospital, 73
Tressel, L., 120
Tri Fork Press, 32
Troop 131, 10
Troy Township, 3, 6, 8, 13, 16
Trucks, Mr., 98
Trucks-Ayer Mill, 100
trustees, 85, 136, 138
Tube Works Creek, 90
Tube Works Run, 85
Tucker, John, 186, 190
Tucker, John A., 72
turbine, 12, 20-21, 23, 29, 31-32, 52-53, 72, 105, 120-121, 134-136, 143, 149-150

U

Underground Railroad, 6, 65
Union Army, 7
Union Woolen Factory, 154
up-and-down blade, 159
Urick (Eurick-Eurich) Grist Mill, 101
Urick, Christopher, 101
Urie, Mr., 86
Utica, Ohio, 68

V

Vail, H. John, 124
Vail, John, 121, 124, 126
Vail, Melvin, 124
Valley Hall, 72
Van Zile Mill, 65, 67
Van Zile, Orlando, 67-68
Van Zill, Orland, 133
Vanderbilt Road, 20
Vanzile, Jesse, 133

Vanzile, Royer, 134
Velvet Ice Cream Museum, 68
Virginia Military lands, 162

W

Wade, Steven, 37
Wagner, Samuel, 37
Walhonding Canal, 145
Walhonding Railroad, 147
Walker Lake Road, 81
Walker, A. L., 25
Walker, Captain Joseph, 8
Wally Road, 76
Walsh, Mrs. Joan Culler, 184
War of 1812, 4-5, 8, 13, 17, 34, 74, 82, 94, 96, 111, 115, 117, 130, 153, 166
Ward, W. H., 23
Ward, William, 133
Washington Township, 17, 20, 22, 63-64
Washington, George, 106
Water-Powered Mills on the Black Fork, 81
Water-Powered Mills on the Clear Fork, 3
Water-Powered Mills on the Rocky Fork, 153
waterwheel, 14-16, 20, 23, 34, 36, 40, 43, 45, 50-52, 90, 97, 110, 114, 136, 139-141, 153, 159
Waterwheels and Millstones, 36, 90
Watson Lewis Graves Carter Grist and Saw Mill, 10
Watson's Mills, 8
Watson, Amariah, 8-9, 17-18
Watson, Asahal, 9
Watson, Clorisa, 9
Watson, Cynthia, 9
Watson, Noah, 17-18
Watson, Riley, 9
Watson, Theory, 9
Watts Saw Mill and Woolen Factory, 60
Watts, Noah, 61
Watts, Thomas, 61, 65
Wayne County, 44, 68, 76, 116, 134, 142
Wayne, Anthony, 43
Weaver Mill, 98
Weaver, Mary Ann, 123
Weaver, Ray, 99
Weigel, J. H., 52
Weirich Mill, xi, 135
Weirick, C. E., 135
Weirwick, Peter, 40
Welch, A. C., 154
Welch, Joseph, 154
Welch, Margaret Benton, 154
Weller Township, 104, 106, 108, 110-113
Wentz, Peter, 154

Wesson, Earnest J., 131
West Hanover Township, 24
West Virginia Cavalry, 7
Wheat Craft Road, 74-75
whiskey, 18, 98, 102, 126
whisky pickles, 150
Whisler, Jacob, 104
Whitcomb Dam, 25
Whitcomb, Dr. Niles, 28
White, Jake, 112
Whitney Avenue, 89, 94
Wickert, George, 188
widow, 9, 29, 36, 100, 158
Wigton, Elmer E., 69
Wilbur Floyd Dall, 60
Wiler, John, 114, 137
William Downey's Tavern, 62
William Garrett Saw and Grist Mills, 76
William Taylor Grist and Saw Mill, 136
William Thompson Saw Mill, 74
William Tingley Woolen Mill, 162
Williams, Abraham (Isaac), 100
Williams, Charley, 107
Williams, Dallas, 29
Williams, John K., 7
Williams, Judith, 107
Williamson Distillery, 113
Williamson, Deacon, 113
Wills, George, 87
Wilson Road, 60
Wilson Saw Mill, 90
Wilson, Captain D. W., 23
Wilson, Eli, 90
Wilson, Willie, 125
Winbigler, Alfred, 4
Winchester Mill, 56-58
Winchester Mills, 56-57
Wingenund, Chief, 154
Wintergreen Hill, 45
Wise, Christian, 56
Wolf Creek/Pine Run Grist Mill, 54, 139-140
Wolf Grist Mill, 138
Wolf, Isaac, 138
Wolf, Nancy, 89
Wolf, Phoebeann, 9
Wolf, T. G., 119
Wolf, Virginia, 139
Wolf, Warring, 131
Wolfe, Conrad, 112
Wolford, 31
Wood, John, 179
Woodhouse, John, 127-128
Woods-Otto Grist Mill, 4
Worthington Township, 43, 55-56, 61-62, 65
Wrick, Frederick and Elizabeth, 43
Wright, John, 177

Wurts, Abraham, 104
Wurts-Clay Distillery, 104

Y

Yarnall, Daniel, 76
Yeaman Grist and Saw Mills, 119
Yeaman, John Jr., 119
Yeaman, John Sr., 119
York County, Pennsylvania, 37
Young Millwright and Miller's Guide, 44

Z

Zehner, John, 116-117
Zent Mill, 25
Zent, Jacob, 24-25
Zent-Fitting-Bowers-Shaler-Garber Mill, 24, 26
Zigler, Tom, 34
Zimmer family, 119
Zimmerman Powder Mill, 55-57
Zimmerman, Levi, 135
Zimmerman, Peter, 55
Zueyr, Robert, 62